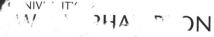

UNIVERSITY OF
WOLVERHAMPTON

LRA END/002

**Walsall Campus Library
& Learning Resources**

Walsall   WS1 3BD

ampton (01902) 323275

WP 2095949 4

Selected titles in the Cassell Education series:

G. Allen and I. Martin (eds): *Education and Community: The Politics of Practice*
G. Antonouris and J. Wilson: *Equal Opportunities in Schools: New Dimensions in Topic Work*
D. E. Bland: *Managing Higher Education*
L. Burton (ed.): *Gender and Mathematics*
L. B. Curzon: *Teaching in Further Education* (4th ed.)
P. Daunt: *Meeting Disability: A European Response*
J. Freeman: *Gifted Children Growing Up*
L. Hall (ed.): *Tracing the Tradition: An Anthology of Poetry by Women*
J. Lynch: *Education for Citizenship in a Multicultural Society*
A. Pollard and S. Tann: *Reflective Teaching in the Primary School* (2nd ed.)
A. Pollard: *The Social World of the Primary School*
A. Pollard *et al.: Changing English Primary Schools?*
R. Ritchie (ed.): *Profiling in Primary Schools: A Handbook for Teachers*
A. Rogers: *Adults Learning for Development*
B. Spiecker and R. Straughan (eds): *Freedom and Indoctrination in Education: International Perspectives*
W. Tulasiewicz and C.-Y. To: *World Religions and Educational Practice*
J. Wilson: *A New Introduction to Moral Education*

Selected titles from other Cassell series:

J. French: *The Education of Girls*
G. Klein: *Education Towards Race Equality*
L. Measor and P. J. Sikes: *Gender and Schools*
A. Osler (ed.): *Development Education*
K. Riley: *Quality and Equality: Promoting Opportunities in Schools*
R. Todd: *Education in a Multicultural Society*
M. Wallace and A. McMahon: *Planning for Change in Turbulent Times: The Case of Multi-racial Primary Schools*
J. Webb: *Multi-faith Topics in the Primary School*

Improving Gender and Ethnic Relations

Strategies for Schools and Further Education

Edited by

Basil R. Singh

UNIVERSITY OF WOLVERHAMPTON
LIBRARY

Acc No.
2095949

CLASS

CONTROL
0304328693

370.
1934
IMP

DATE
27 JUN 1997

SITE
WL

CASSELL

Cassell
Villiers House
41/47 Strand
London WC2N 5JE

387 Park Avenue South
New York
NY 10016–8810

© Basil Singh and the contributors 1994

All rights reserved. No part of this publication may be reproduced or transmitted in any form
or by any means, electronic or mechanical including photocopying, recording or any information
storage retrieval system, without prior permission in writing from the publishers.

First published 1994

British Library Cataloguing-in-Publication Data
A catalogue record for this book is available from the British Library.

ISBN 0-304-32869-3 (hardback)
    0-304-32871-5 (paperback)

UNIVERSITY OF WOLVERHAMPTON
LIBRARY

CLASS

Acc No.
2059949

Typeset by Colset Private Limited, Singapore

Printed and bound in Great Britain by Redwood Books, Trowbridge, Wilts.

Contents

Notes on Contributors   vii

Introduction: Improving Social Relationships through Teaching Methods   1
Basil R. Singh

1   Can Monolingual Teachers Teach Language Awareness Successfully to the Benefit of All Children?   19
Wendy F. Reeds

2   Personal and Social Education: A Vehicle for Prejudice Reduction   42
Lynn Powell

3   Experiencing Temporary Disadvantage through Drama as a Means of Prejudice Reduction   60
Carol Bianchi-Cooke

4   Using Curriculum Material and Teaching Methods to Reduce Prejudice and Maintain Academic Standards in an A Level Human Geography Course   76
Anna Schlesinger

5   The Effects of Cross-ethnic Tutoring on Interracial Relationships and Academic Achievements   99
Cecilia J. Datta

6   An Investigation into Prejudice Reduction among Young People in Youth Clubs   118
Peter Davies and Neil Hufton

7   Women in Science: Access, Experience and Progression   136
Viv Shelley and Pat Whaley

Name Index   164

Subject Index   166

Notes on Contributors

Carol Bianchi-Cooke (Cert. Ed., B.Ed., RSA, MA) has been a lecturer in charge of the performing arts for many years at a college of further education in north-east England. She is a writer and performer who also runs drama workshops. She has an interest in multicultural education.

Cecilia J. Datta (Dip. Ed., Dip. R.S.A., B A , M.Ed.) has taught in inner-city schools in Glasgow and London. She was manager of an environmental education project in Tyne and Wear. She has specialized in teaching English as a second language in a multicultural comprehensive school. Her research interests are in the area of co-operative learning/peer tutoring.

Peter Davies (Cert. Ed., M.Ed.) has been an Assistant Youth and Community Officer for many years with an LEA in north-east England. His responsibilities include multicultural education, health education and mainstream sport, with additional responsibilities for staff development in general and staff training in particular.

Neil Hufton (BA, Dip. Ed., MA) has been in teacher education since 1967. Educated at Cambridge and Nottingham Universities, he taught in schools and then lectured in the Sociology of Education at Loughborough College and at Teesside Polytechnic. He headed the Polytechnic's Department of Education for nine years before moving to his present post, with responsibilities for INSET, at the University of Sunderland. His main research interest is in the nature and acquisition of practical knowledge of teaching.

Lynn Powell (BA Hons, M.Ed.) has been teaching for 22 years in comprehensive schools, including 17 years as head of modern languages in a large comprehensive in north-east England. Her main academic interests outside modern languages are language awareness, personal and social education, experiential learning (including residentials) and equal opportunities.

Wendy F. Reeds (Dip. RSA, M.Ed.) has taught in primary schools for many years in north-east England. In the past few years she has been teaching English as a second language (E2L) to primary school children from ethnic minority backgrounds. She now runs a language unit for children with language disability.

Anna Schlesinger (Cert. Ed., M.Ed.) has for many years been a lecturer in geography at a college of further education. During the past four years she has been a member of the College Equal Opportunities Working Party and head of its Committee for Racial Equality. Her other interests are creative writing and travelling.

Viv Shelley (Ph.D., C.Chem., MRSC) is a lecturer in science at the University of Durham and a tutor with the Open University, and has previously worked at the University of Northumbria. She is co-ordinator for the Women into Science and Technology course at the Department of Adult and Continuing Education at the University of Durham. Her personal research interests are in chemistry and in adult education, particularly access to science.

Basil R. Singh (B.Sc., BA, (Phil.) MA, (Reader in Education) Ph.D. (Lon.)) was educated at London University. He taught in schools in London for many years before taking up an appointment at Sunderland Polytechnic (now the University of Sunderland) in 1974, as lecturer in education. He has lectured in a range of subjects including the philosophy of education, child development and equality issues. His main academic and research interests are in co-operative learning, prejudice reduction and human rights.

Pat Whaley (BA) is a historian working in the Research Department of the School of Education at the University of Sunderland, where her doctoral research is on mature women entrants to teaching. She has a long-standing interest in adult and continuing education, access and equal opportunities, which has developed through her work with the Open University.

Introduction: Improving Social Relationships through Teaching Methods

Basil R. Singh

> If you want people to live by social justice, there is only one way to do it, and this is to initiate them into the practice of social justice.
>
> (Hirst, 1990, p. 51)

The methods described below are means by which social scientists have attempted to create a 'practice' – a social learning environment – in which students would have a chance to develop a sense of social justice, a sense of harmony and a sense of mutual respect.

The schools and social institutions in general reflect the power and status order in society which make it difficult to bring about educational changes within schools. Consequently, merely putting pupils of different races, classes or sexes to work together in the classroom will not reduce prejudice based on race, class or sex; nor will it change the status order of the respective groups. But if schools are willing to make the commitment to particular value goals, there is ample evidence to show that they can bring about desired changes. The evidence cited in this introductory chapter shows quite clearly that teaching methods could help to *reduce* bias or prejudice based on race, class and sex, and reduce conflicts and status differentials between pupils.

As far back as 1954, Gordon Allport suggested that race relations would improve if black and white students interacted under conditions of mutual interdependence and equal status in a normative climate supporting interracial co-operation. Since then a growing body of research has shown that students of different races who work together in co-operative learning groups are more likely to name one another as friends than similar students in traditional classrooms. The formats of specific co-operative techniques have varied, but positive effects on race relations have been found consistently to have beneficial effects on other outcomes of education, such as student achievement and self-esteem (Sharan, 1980; Slavin, 1980).

One type of social contact which has received considerable emphasis is that involving co-operation in the achievement of joint goals (Deutsch, 1949). Research has shown that co-operative activity often results in greater respect and liking among the persons involved, even when these persons are from different racial groups (Cook, 1978).

According to Cook (1978), mere contact is not sufficient to promote intergroup harmony. A number of contingencies that would qualify the nature of the contact to make it more positively oriented would include: (1) co-operative activity towards a common goal; (2) equal status contact; (3) opportunity to disconfirm stereotypes; (4) normative support from authority figures; and (5) high acquaintance potential.

THE IMPORTANCE OF NORMATIVE SUPPORT BY AUTHORITY FIGURES

Normative support by authority figures is seen as a necessary condition to obtain positive inter-ethnic contact effects. Some evidence suggests that teachers' attitudes towards interracial contacts have a significant impact on the quality of students' interaction (Epstein, 1985).

Weigel and Howes (1985) also point out that those students who have the most negative attitudes towards interracial contact are the ones most susceptible to the influence of an authority figure – the very person who can prescribe or proscribe certain behaviours within the class. Teachers have the opportunity to reinforce desired behaviours. Even 4-year-olds will demonstrate greater sharing when reinforced (Fischer, 1963). Experimental studies have shown that a powerful influence on children's perception of others is the behaviour exhibited by adults (Bryan and Walbeck, 1970).

IN PURSUIT OF COMMON GOALS

The adverse effects of competition were clearly demonstrated by Sherif *et al.* (1961) in their classic 'Robber's Cave' experiment. In this field study, the investigators used a variety of strategies to encourage out-group competition between teams of boys at a summer camp. In an earlier study by Sherif and Sherif (1953) the investigators observed that contact is likely to produce favourable attitude changes between members of socially distant groups only when the contact involves

> joint participation as members of an in-group whose norms favour such participation. . . .
> In situations in which in-group members meet with members of an out-group held at considerable distance on very limited scale . . . there is little likelihood of change in attitude of in-group members.
>
> (Sherif and Sherif, 1953, pp. 221–2)

It would seem from the Sherif and Sherif experiment that a mere contact situation is not sufficient to reduce antagonism between rival groups. What is required are superordinate goals to force groups to co-operate across group lines. According to Sherif and Sherif, only such superordinate goals can make the contact effective and thereby help to reduce prejudice and group tension. After their later work Sherif and his colleagues (1961) theorized that

> only when erstwhile rivals come into contact in the pursuit of vital purpose that grips all participants can contact situations furnish opportunity for creative moves toward reducing intergroup hostility. The participants must feel a common steadfast pull in the same direction, if not toward the same actions . . .
>
> (pp. 146–7)

They added that

> Without some interdependence among the parties in contact, face to face situations produce lowered thresholds for the verdict of 'what else would you expect from such a . . .?' . . . Contact is an effective medium for change when groups are directed toward superordinate goals overriding their separate concerns.
>
> (Sherif *et al.*, 1961)

In his later work, Sherif (1966) reported that, when previously antagonistic groups were brought into contact, the occasion was utilized only to further group conflicts even when the activities in the contact situations were satisfying in themselves for the group members. It was only in situations which provided superordinate goals of high appeal to both groups that they co-operated across group lines.

PEER PRESSURE, IN-GROUP BIAS AND NORMS OF EQUALITY

According to Allen and Wilder (1975), subjects who express in-group preference also expect others to exhibit the same bias. Although in-group favouritism is an important determinant of in-group bias, research by Stephan and Stephan (1985) has shown that when norms of equality and fairness are invoked they can act as a counter to bias.

CO-OPERATIVE LEARNING AND SELF-ESTEEM

According to Johnson and Johnson, 'The relationship between cooperative experiences and interpersonal attraction may be partially caused by the higher self-esteem of collaborators' (1992, p. 182). Their explanation is that 'the better one is known, liked and supported, the higher one's self-esteem tends to be. The higher one's self-esteem, the higher one's acceptance of and liking for others and the lower one's prejudices against others.' Thus, 'cooperation promotes higher self-esteem and more healthy procedures for deriving self-esteem than do competitive and individualistic experiences' (p. 182).

The study by Johnson *et al.* (1983) shows that co-operative learning techniques promote higher levels of self-esteem and healthier processes for deriving conclusions about one's self-worth. The available research evidence seems to show that an interdependent co-operative environment can change the self-defeating attributions that affect so many students and negate self-fulfilling prophecies made by students who are considered by themselves and others as failures (see Slavin, 1985).

CO-OPERATIVE LEARNING AND HIGH ACQUAINTANCE POTENTIAL

There is some evidence to show that co-operative learning techniques have the potential for fostering positive relationships among heterogeneous ethnic groups. They do this by creating a high degree of acquaintance potential: that is, a situation which provides the opportunity for members of the contact situation to come to know each other as individuals serves to foster positive inter-ethnic relationships. A situation with a high degree of acquaintance potential could help members to discover the uniqueness of individual members, i.e. to gain knowledge of the personal attributes of the others. According to Marks *et al.* (1981), people tend to respond more positively to individuals than to groups. The work of Brigham and Malpas (1985) shows that a series of individual-level contacts may be less stressful and anxiety provoking than contact among multiple members of groups. Perhaps, as Brigham and Malpas point out, individuating members helps to differentiate the group and simultaneously allows the individual to maintain his or her unique identity.

CO-OPERATIVE LEARNING AND GENERALIZING FRIENDSHIP

Slavin (1985) has demonstrated in his studies that friendship comes to extend beyond one's immediate team-mates and category boundaries. Other studies carried out by Johnson and Johnson (1981, 1982) and Warring *et al.* (1985) show that individuals who participated in co-operative learning groups had more interactions in school outside of lesson times as well as more out-of-school interactions than individuals who participated in individualistic learning situations. There is also some evidence (Sharan and Shachar, 1988) which shows that pupils from both lower and middle classes benefit considerably in academic terms from co-operative learning groups when compared with whole-class teaching groups.

CO-OPERATIVE LEARNING AND DISCIPLINE PROBLEMS

Research by Aronson (1978) and Blaney *et al.* (1977) shows that co-operative learning methods have produced consistently positive results even in schools characterized by a great deal of tension, discipline problems and interracial skirmishes. Children in these inquiries expressed a greater liking for school and experienced significantly greater increase in self-esteem than children in the control classrooms.

PEER-TUTORING AND ACADEMIC GAINS

In a recent review of 'peer-tutoring', Sharpley and Sharpley (1981) examined 82 peer-tutor programmes, according to the characteristics of the participants, the characteristics of the tutoring process and the adequacy of research designs. They conclude that recent work supports the claim that both tutors and tutee show attainment gains and sometimes improve in social behaviour and attitudes to each other. The Sharpley and Sharpley review indicates that children who themselves have learning and behaviour problems can benefit from acting as tutors, that the socio-economic status of the participants makes no significant difference, and that one-to-one tuition can be more effective than small-group tuition. The works of Gredler (1985), Topping (1987) and Fitz-Gibbon (1983) show that cross-age peer-tutoring on a one-to-one basis results in academic gains for both tutor and tutee as well as closer social relationships.

CO-OPERATIVE LEARNING AND EQUAL-STATUS CONTACT

Although Allport (1954) predicted that positive interactions would result if co-operative, equal-status conditions were achieved, Elizabeth Cohen (1972), working with expectation theory, predicted that in such an environment biased expectations of both majority and minority group members may lead to sustained white dominance and subordinate status for minority group members.

In accordance with this theory, Cohen and Sharan (1980) argue that 'if we bring together students of different racial or ethnic status, domination of the task group by high status members will only confirm stereotypes of superiority held by both groups for the high status members and stereotypes of inferiority held for low status members' (p. 365). Consequently, 'If beliefs about general incompetence of low status persons are confirmed by interaction, the goals of the educators can be defeated rather than enhanced by intergroup interaction' (p. 365).

Cohen and Roper (1972) attempted to reverse this trend by their expectation training experiment, where the low-status participants became teachers of the high-status participants on a new and challenging task prior to any opportunities for the mixed-status group to interact and make evaluations of each other. In this experiment, the tendency of whites to dominate the group interaction was greatly weakened when whites became students of specially trained, competent black peers. Accordingly, the Cohen and Roper study showed that treated groups exhibited patterns which could be called equal-status interaction, i.e. neither whites nor blacks were systematically found in top-rank positions (see Cohen and Sharan, 1980, p. 365).

According to Cohen and Sharan (1980), high-status members are expected to be more competent on new tasks, they will have their contributions evaluated more highly, and they will become more influential. The reverse will be true for low-status members. In accordance with expectation states theory, it could be predicted that, where there is a state of diffuse status characteristics, in a social setting where actors believe it is better to possess one state rather than another, then certain groups could be expected to behave in certain stereotypical ways (e.g. blacks might be perceived as athletic and musical, and women as sensitive and intuitive). The source of these expectations, according to Cohen and Sharan, is the belief system in the culture. However, these beliefs are not necessarily consciously held and are susceptible to change with time, place and learning. Cohen (1982) proposes that, if equal status is to be promoted, then the status characteristic derived from the culture must be altered prior to the contact setting for members of both the high- and the low-status group. Otherwise the patterns of interaction will serve to reinforce existing expectancy.

It would seem from the works cited in this review that co-operative learning methods and peer-tutoring techniques develop students' positive attitudes towards self and others especially when students work towards common goals or objectives. These techniques help to reduce stress, bias or prejudice, promote inter-ethnic harmony, and enhance self-esteem, motivation and learning. They also promote a better liking for school. Thus the merits of co-operative learning techniques and co-operative environments in reducing prejudice and improving academic performance are supported by a substantial body of evidence gleaned from carefully conducted social-psychological experiments. However, I am not suggesting that these methods constitute the solution to race, gender or other social problems; I am suggesting that there are positive results when children spend at least a portion of their time in the pursuit of common goals and in working co-operatively together. These effects are in accordance with predictions made by social scientists working in these areas.

ON RESEARCH METHODS

According to Robert Burgess (1984), in the past few years 'the shape, substance and style of educational research and evaluation have undergone considerable change'. He adds that 'No longer are researchers who work within this field preoccupied with quantitative methods based upon statistical sampling, measurement and experiment, for much research now uses qualitative as well as quantitative methods' (p. vii).

The contributions to this book are no exceptions to the trend depicted by Burgess. Most of them are first-person accounts that address major value or social issues, and they utilize mainly qualitative (with some quantitative) methods in a variety of educational settings in order to investigate those issues.

TEACHERS AS RESEARCHERS

In recent years there has been considerable discussion about the role of the teacher in educational research (see Nixon, 1981). Many of the accounts in this book focus on qualitative methods that can be used by teachers engaged in 'action research' projects. Much attention has been directed towards approaches that teachers can use in carrying out classroom-based research. What follows in the first six chapters are attempts by teachers to develop and implement research strategies in a variety of formal and informal educational settings. It is hoped that these chapters will provide the reader with some insights into the processes involved in carrying out these kinds of inquiry.

ACTION RESEARCH

According to Louis Cohen and Lawrence Manion (1989), there are many differing definitions of action research. They point out that 'usage varies with time, place and setting' (p. 217). However, a conventional definition of action research offered by Cohen and Manion is that it is a 'small-scale intervention in the functioning of the real world and a close examination of the effects of such interventions' (p. 217).

If we accept the 'conventional definition' proposed by Cohen and Manion, then it would seem that the investigations reported in this book exemplify action research as a method of inquiry. Most of the investigations are 'situational': that is, they are concerned with diagnosing problems in specific contexts and attempting to resolve them in that context. Most of the inquiries are 'collaborative': that is, they involve practitioners working together on projects. And most are 'participatory' in that team members themselves were involved either directly or indirectly in implementing the investigations. Most of the work was 'self-evaluative': in other words, modifications were continuously made within the ongoing situation. The ultimate objective was to improve practice in terms of some value or social perspective (Cohen and Manion, 1989, p. 217).

This book is concerned with qualitative methods and deals not with any particular method, but with a variety of activities which were used to collect qualitative data (Burgess, 1985, p. 7). The objective was to study individuals in their natural settings, to see the way in which they attributed meanings in social situations and responded to certain interventions.

All the methods employed in these investigations are characterized by their flexibility. The researchers were able to formulate and reformulate their ideas throughout the collection and analysis of data. The data were collected not in order to support or refute any *particular* hypothesis, but to clarify certain ideas, categories or concepts.

Most of the investigations relied heavily on observations, interviews, questionnaires and discussions for the collection of empirical data. Over the period of time in which the investigations were undertaken, information collected was shared, discussed and recorded in various ways. This sequence of events formed the basis of reviews of progress (Cohen and Manion, 1989, p. 225). The methods adopted for the various inquiries did not aspire to be rigorously scientific or truly experimental. For example, there was no real control over independent variables, and findings were generally restricted to the environment in which the investigations were carried out.

The teachers who have contributed to this book do not pretend to conduct complex experiments with sophisticated statistical techniques for testing evidence and measuring results. But this is not to imply that they did not adopt some techniques of investigation, or that they did not think systematically and critically about what they did. Indeed, all the investigations reveal careful and systematic observations guided by wide reading and inspired by a vision to change students' negative perceptions about others and thereby to improve education for the benefit of everyone.

No attempt was made to disguise the aims of the various studies, and little precaution was taken not to influence students' responses. The investigators were therefore not 'neutral' in their value commitments to their research. They saw no need to pretend to be neutral about issues they felt to be important to themselves in particular and to social justice in general.

Problems of random allocation and selection of control groups, which are clearly relevant to researchers in the quantitative tradition, were not considered vital to these investigations which relied heavily on qualitative data. Action research, as adopted in these studies, threw up its own problems which are discussed in these chapters. The attraction of the techniques adopted was that they enabled the practitioners to work towards socially desirable changes and to expand their own knowledge and understanding of issues to which they are committed.

It is apparent from these studies that investigators were concerned to improve *their own practice* by means of *their own practical actions* and by means of *their own reflections* upon the effects of those actions (Elliott, 1983). Indeed, enhancing their own understanding in order to effect some change was seen as more important than the ability to generalize. Many of the contributors saw action research as a means of professional development within their own institutions.

If teachers are self-motivated to undertake their own classroom-based inquiries, in order to reduce bias, prejudice or to change the stereotypical views of students, as these teachers were, then as Elliott (1980) puts it, they 'need not only understand what it is they're doing in their classrooms, but how their actions are influenced by institutional, social and political structures' (p. 321). The contributors to this volume are quite aware of the social and political forces operating upon educational institutions. Some indications of this awareness are contained in the literature review preceding each chapter and in the brief descriptions of the context of the institutions in which the inquiries were carried out.

ON VALIDITY

As I have indicated, various methods were employed to investigate particular issues to which the teachers were committed. Validity was inferred from agreement between the data sets and invalidity from disagreements (see Brewer and Hunter, 1989). Validity was therefore appraised through a process of constant checking for accuracy and incompatibility. Among the procedures for checking and cross-checking were, of course, human judgement and intuitive reasoning.

ON TRIANGULATION

Although the idea of 'triangulation', or the use of more than one method to provide cross-checking or to offer mutual validation, has provided the guiding principle in these inquiries, Graham McFee (1992) has argued recently and in criticism of 'triangulation' that 'one cannot be sure that the different methods address one and the same issue' (p. 215). McFee does not think that 'triangulation within a method' where 'data are built up from inputs of various perspectives . . . provide[s] the sort of mutual support integral to the method of triangulation' (p. 215).

Nevertheless a casual glance at the research literature indicates that researchers utilize a variety of approaches in the course of finding out about the social world (Burgess, 1985, p. 2). Burgess has quoted McCall and Simmons (1969) to emphasize the point that it is misleading to regard any approach as embodying a single method. Participant observation, for instance,

> refers to a characteristic blend or combination of methods and techniques. . . . [It] involves some amount of genuinely social interaction in the field with the objects of the study, some direct observation of relevant events, some formal and a great deal of informal interviewing, some systematic counting . . . and open-mindedness in the direction the study takes.
>
> (McCall and Simmons, 1969, p. 1; quoted in Burgess, 1985, p. 3)

Other researchers seem to agree with McCall and Simmons. Davies *et al.* (1985), for instance, warn us that we must not forget 'that observation, interviews, questionnaires, documentary analysis, and so on, are neither inherently qualitative nor quantitative. All quantification involves judgement as to qualities and all qualitative statements invoke hierarchy, number and amount to give shape to meaning' (p. 290). Thus, according to Davies and his colleagues, a research method 'should not be "all or nothing issues" (for example, to measure or not, to observe or not), but rather about how much and when' (p. 290).

Following Davies *et al.* (1985) and McCall and Simmons (1969), most of the contributions to this volume employed a number of techniques. The aim was to provide some means of cross-checking the outcomes of one approach in terms of the outcomes of another. The idea was to bring two or more viewpoints – those of the teachers, the students and the observers – to bear on a particular issue and into some relationship with each other, so that they could be compared and contrasted (Elliott, 1991, p. 82).

The teachers are fully aware that the use of a variety of instruments for the investigation of certain issues and for providing cross-checks on their findings does not constitute a statistical validation. They have tried to communicate their inquiries as clearly as possibly without trivializing the complexity of the social and political processes influencing institutional life. Many of the contributors believe that practical action at the level of the school, college or youth club could be used as a means by which to challenge sexist or racist beliefs and perceptions. The approaches adopted were seen as potentially emancipatory, in that they could liberate teachers and students from a system of education which denies some individuals their dignity (Weiner, 1989, p. 45).

The inquiries undertaken for this book were not motivated by a desire to test the research findings of others, but were responses to 'dilemmas, anxieties and aspirations acknowledged by teachers in their own schools and classrooms, youth clubs or educational institutions' (Rudduck, 1985, p. 125).

DIFFICULTIES INHERENT IN DOING ACTION RESEARCH

Action research intervention is very difficult for anyone, let alone the teacher-researcher. According to Finemann (1991),

> It requires the ability to attend and respond in situ to the here-and-now issues. It also requires perseverance and stamina to squirrel away all manner of observations and records of 'what is going on' to be retrieved later and pored over. The gradual sifting and collating of qualitative data is maddening.
>
> (p. 15)

It is because of the difficulties inherent in doing any kind of research that teachers, who are extremely busy people, need to be encouraged and complimented for undertaking any kind of investigation into their own work. Although the contributors to this book found the inquiries at times 'maddening' and had to persevere in the midst of frustration, they have themselves said how much they benefited from actually doing the work.

Among other things, the studies encouraged a systematic approach to the collection of information and a respect for evidence. Perhaps out of this kind of work will emerge people with experience who will be able to undertake further research, including research of the more traditional, experimental and statistical kind. Granting this, one could argue that the academic community must encourage teachers to do their own research which will provide the conceptual, analytical and technical skills that professional teachers require if they are to improve their teaching.

There should also be more space in learned journals for teachers to make their works public. There is a great deal of talent among teachers in schools and colleges. The academic community can do a great deal to develop this talent by enhancing teachers' professional status and personal development for the benefit of all children. One way to prevent this talent from developing is for the academic community to insist, especially at the outset, on an over-rigorous methodological, statistical and experimental approach to research, especially of the traditional kind.

The kinds of inquiry undertaken here should not only help teachers to become competent critics and interpreters of their own practice, but also provide them with some grounding in research skills (Rudduck, 1985). They are ways of getting teachers into the mysterious work of research, which according to Rudduck

> offers a way of marking out a path of professional development [and] ... a way of structuring a familiar situation that allow the teacher to explore it in depth, to gain new insights, to set new goals and to achieve new levels of competence and confidence. In this way the teacher has a sense of professional progress that he or she is making.
>
> (p. 124)

According to Jean Rudduck (1989), reflective research is certainly a way of helping teachers to sharpen their perceptions of the everyday realities of their work; it helps them to identify worthwhile problems to work on, and through their inquiry to extend their own understanding, insight and command of the situations in which they work. It also helps teachers to recognize contradictions of purpose and value and to monitor the effects of strategies designed to achieve the purposes they have in mind (Rudduck, 1989, p. 67). Rudduck sees the practitioner-researcher and reflective classroom-focused research as ways of building personal excitement, confidence and insight – and these, she argues, are important foundations for career-long personal and professional development (p. 68).

AIMS OF THE BOOK

To a large extent the aims of the book are inherent in the above discussion about what its contributors were intending to do. One of the aims is to give the reader some understanding of how practising teachers could carry out small-scale, school- or institution-based investigations for changing stereotypes, reducing bias or prejudice (broadly defined) and fostering social relationships among students of different sexes, ethnicity and social backgrounds. The other aims are to provide some insight into attempts to foster positive self-image and respect for others, and to provide some understanding about collaborative group inquiry. Most of the contributions focus on strategies and tactics for collecting data and on the use of a range of qualitative methods. Chapter 7, which is evolved from a research project, is concerned with access and the role of women in scientific and technical courses in higher education.

Thus the book, which is derived from small-scale inquiries carried out by teachers and youth workers in their own institutions, aims to give the reader an understanding of how these studies were negotiated, implemented and accomplished. The book describes some of the problems that the teacher-researchers faced, as well as the necessity for subtlety, diplomacy, perseverance and rigour that characterizes any such investigation. Problems of gaining access to other colleagues' classrooms, of negotiating with colleagues and then training them to help carry out investigations and conduct interviews, are made explicit. The book therefore has a great deal to offer teachers and other practitioners, especially at a time of growing interest in effective schooling, in the idea of teachers as researchers, in action research and in collaborative investigations.

The book will also be of interest to those who plan to carry out and write up a small-scale investigation in a limited time, under demanding circumstances, and will provide guidance on how to do it and the pitfalls to avoid. The chapters give warnings about personal difficulties and institutional constraints which have to be overcome in attempting to initiate inquiries into prejudice reduction and how to foster better social relationships in schools, colleges and youth clubs.

There is no simple solution to the problem of bias or prejudice relating to sex, race, class or culture at the school, youth club and college levels in a society exhibiting prejudice and bias throughout its institutions. Yet, as Cohen argues, 'if society is willing to make the commitment to particular value goals, there is nothing ... that says that schools cannot alter in such a way as to become more supportive of desired social change' (1975, p. 299).

It is not the purpose of these chapters to discuss ways and means of changing a whole school or institution; but rather to concentrate on certain teaching methods, strategies and processes that have been successfully tested and which could be used without much adjustment or increased resources to foster social relationships, reduce prejudice and advance the achievement of all students, irrespective of their social class, sex or race. The contributors seek to draw the reader's attention to some of the evidence of existing research as well as to the evidence of their own investigations.

The book will be of interest to teachers who are attempting to implement the intention of the Education Reform Act 1988, which requires the governing body and headteacher of every maintained school to provide a curriculum that 'promotes the spiritual, moral, cultural, mental and physical development of pupils at school and of society'. In its cross-curricular elements No. 2, the National Curriculum Council stresses that these dimensions arc 'concerned with the intentional promotion of pupils' personal and social development through the curriculum as a whole ... [and] include all aspects of equal opportunities and education for life in a multicultural society'.

The hope is that other teachers wishing to develop their own skills as teacher-researchers, or their ability to become reflective practitioners, will find this book instructive. They will learn how their colleagues tackled their own problems and the benefits they derived from such inquiries, but more importantly they should learn about ways of improving their own practice for the benefit of students. It is also hoped that the content of this volume will prompt further discussion in this area and may encourage teachers to undertake research.

SUMMARY OF CONTENTS

Wendy Reeds has always believed that monolingual teachers can teach an awareness of languages successfully to the benefit of all children in a multilingual school. In Chapter 1 she investigates the effects of the teaching of language awareness to monolingual *and* bilingual pupils by monolingual teachers in an inner-city primary school. Her aim was to inquire whether language awareness could help to raise the self-esteem of bilingual children and to reduce prejudice among all pupils. In carrying out this investigation, she had to collaborate with a team of (English as a second) language teachers and the other teachers of the school, in planning, implementing and evaluating the project.

Action research was chosen as the most appropriate method of investigation in this study, and it involved qualitative techniques for the gathering of data and the interpretation of results. All the people involved in this study were teachers, who were learning to do research by practising in their own classrooms. They were not academic researchers with a knowledge of advanced statistics or research procedures. They were concerned to solve certain problems within their own classrooms or school. The methods used were collaborative and participatory, aiming to bring about change without threatening anyone.

The results indicate: (1) a clear increase in interest in learning community languages and a decline in learning French; (2) a rise in the number of children offering to share their knowledge of language with others; (3) a rise in the self-esteem and confidence of ethnic minority pupils. Although the investigation shows that monolingual teachers can teach language awareness successfully to all children, it appears from the study that this process does not increase the self-esteem of monolingual children. Consequently, Reeds suggests that teachers should bear this in mind when doing this kind of work, and should try to counteract this negative tendency.

The chapter discusses the problems encountered in setting up the project and in implementing and assessing its results. It offers advice to teachers who would like to do similar work, and indicates the pitfalls to avoid when, for example, devising (and implementing) a questionnaire for young pupils.

In Chapter 2, Lynn Powell looks at how a module on personal and social education (PSE) could help to reduce racial prejudice in a group of 14-year-old pupils in an almost all-white urban comprehensive school. The module comprised active learning techniques, and both cognitive and affective strategies were involved. Much of the intervention was focused on pupils' acquisition of 'principles' and on their ability to transfer the learning acquired to other contexts. The results indicate that this type of intervention, employing the chosen methodology, could be successful in reducing racial prejudice in some pupils of this age range and social background. It was her belief in the potential of PSE to change pupils' attitudes for the benefit of everyone that led Lynn Powell to embark on this study.

Since the aim of the study was to improve practice, action research was chosen as the most appropriate method. As a teacher without much statistical background or experience in experimental research design, Powell found action research a suitable method for her work; it allowed her to review and modify her study during the teaching–learning process.

The main conclusion of this study is that, in a PSE module of this type, one should avoid direct teaching against racism, but should try instead to teach the principles: for example, teaching about stereotyping in general in a range of contexts other than that of (merely) oppressed groups. Although the results did not meet with all of her expectations, Powell found that one of the exciting parts of the whole inquiry was collaborating with colleagues and pupils: 'the whole project [was] a rewarding experience in terms of my own personal and professional development – worth under-taking for this reason alone'.

Coming from a background of the performing arts, Carol Bianchi-Cooke (Chapter 3) was interested in the use of drama as a method of reducing prejudice. With this in mind she devised a programme for lecturers at a college of further education to investigate whether or to what extent the experiencing of temporary disadvantage could result in prejudice reduction.

In order to carry out the investigation, workshops were organized in accordance with the ideas of Augusto Boal's Forum Theatre. The main assumption underlying the work is that effective learning takes place through a combination of thought and personal experience, i.e. a fusion of personality and intellect. Drama was therefore chosen as a medium through which emotion could be used to aid understanding, and hopefully both could result in changes in negative perceptions of others.

Cooke was guided by the ideas of Augusto Boal (1979) and Paulo Freire (1972) in setting up the investigation. Boal, for instance, sees the theatre as a medium of education and as a service to the oppressed, who can use the theatre to express themselves by using language and extending their linguistic competence.

Cooke discusses the difficulties of implementing such a study and, more impor-tantly, the problems of evaluating it. Problems of evaluation arise because, as she puts it, 'the aims and objectives ... may be modified in response to audience parti-cipation, ability and interest'. She sees the prescriptive model as inadequate in evaluating the effects of experiencing temporary disadvantage, and for this reason she adopts a less prescriptive but more descriptive approach to evaluating the inquiry.

The work shows quite clearly how such methods can be used to raise consciousness of issues relating to disadvantage, especially when participants come to experience and think about such feelings themselves. Hopefully, through meaningful experience, participants may come to change their perception in a positive way.

As a lecturer in geography at a college of further education, Anna Schlesinger has always been interested in the teaching of geography so as to change the negative perceptions that students have of others. In her investigation (Chapter 4) she sought to discover whether a particular combination of curriculum material and various teaching approaches could help to change the perceptions of students working for their A level, in a 'mainly white' tertiary college. Her aim was to counter bias and stereotypes, and to encourage a global perspective and change of attitude among students.

A number of mainly qualitative action research methods were used for the purpose of this study. Like most contributors to this book, Schlesinger does not attempt to engage in elaborate statistical techniques for gathering the data or interpreting the results. Raw scores are presented in the form of percentages for whole groups, and evaluation is from descriptive accounts taken from field notes and interviews with students and staff. As the reader will be aware, there are obvious difficulties in presenting results in this way, especially when they do not show individual differences or changes in individual responses.

Nevertheless the method used in this inquiry closely follows that of the simple action research model used in the Further Education Unit (FEU) Project (1988), with its stages of 'plan, act, observe, reflect' and allowing for revision after reflection. It has the same aim as the FEU: to improve classroom practice through action research.

A method of triangulation is attempted to cross-check the findings from the various techniques employed.

The study indicates: (1) that concentrating too much on the *causes* and *problems* of developing countries could help to reinforce negative images of those countries; and (2) that while some students were unhappy with the collaborative and peer-tutoring methods of instruction and wanted to return to the didactic form (because they were anxious about their impending examinations), others, especially in the collaborative group, reported that the method helped them to understand the issues and that they thereby gained from it.

Valuable advice is offered to teachers who wish to undertake similar work in their classrooms. Although Schlesinger has been disappointed by the overall results, she has experienced important personal benefits such as gaining confidence in and insight into the teaching of her own subject and collaborating with colleagues.

Cecilia Datta has considerable experience in working with bilingual students from ethnic minority groups. In Chapter 5, she describes her study relating to cross-ethnic tutoring carried out in an inner-city comprehensive school. Her main aim was to initiate a period of cross-ethnic tutoring as a means of collaborative and co-operative learning between monolingual and bilingual pupils. Her other intention was to foster positive inter-ethnic relationships between these groups. Students were paired off – one bilingual student with one monolingual student – across curriculum areas and into control and experimental groupings. The results show that, while friendship between monolingual and bilingual students improved among students in the experimental group, there was considerably less improvement in friendship and more hostility among students in the control group.

Like most of the studies in this book this investigation relied heavily on qualitative data derived from interviews and observations. No attempt has been made to engage with sophisticated statistical techniques for gathering the data. Raw scores are presented in the form of percentages for individual pupils. However, a great deal of care has been taken in pairing off and dividing students, in assessing their course work and in interviewing them. Much effort has been expended in getting the co-operation of teachers to assist in this inquiry, and consequently much experience has been gained in collaborating with colleagues. The study offers some guidance and advice to teachers who may want to undertake similar work in their own institutions.

Trying to carry out an investigation with young people in an informal setting, where attendance is on a voluntary basis, is challenging to anyone. In Chapter 6, Peter Davies and Neil Hufton report such an investigation, carried out in seven (all-white) youth centres in a northern Local Education Authority (LEA). One of the investigators worked with that LEA as a Youth Service Officer for many years. The inquiry was carried out in collaboration with a number of colleagues who had to be trained in order to implement the strategies decided upon. It was intended that each centre leader would work with a group of about eight young people, using a questionnaire and a board game at the beginning and end of a chosen set of activities. They were expected to ascertain elements of change in pre-post test of attitudes. Workshops and role-plays were adopted and implemented during the intervention. The core of interest in the inquiry was prejudice reduction in the everyday context of youth centre activity.

The approach can best be described as a collaborative, qualitative piece of action research which relied heavily on field notes, discussions, observations and questionnaires. Because attendance at the centres was on a voluntary basis, it was difficult to administer quantitative tests to measure attitude change on a pre- and post-treatment basis, especially in view of the fluidity of the component members of each of the groups. Members of each group never remained the same for long enough to allow such an experimental approach to take place. However, the results are sufficiently reliable to indicate important issues for future research.

The perceived goal was to find workable procedures for the reduction of bias or prejudice through practicable youth centre activities. This required not only close collaboration among the various leaders, and but also trust among the youths who were there on a voluntary basis. Many youth leaders were enthusiastic about the investigation because they saw it as a means of professional development and as a way of enhancing their own prestige.

The results indicate a general positive change of perception towards ethnic minorities. The questionnaire results show a complex picture of movements in perception, seeming to indicate prejudice reduction in three of the four centre groups for which data are available. Many of the youth leaders found the whole exercise very educative, both in understanding the issues of racial prejudice and in implementing and evaluating the intervention.

The work describes a number of difficulties encountered, which had to be resolved both between youth leaders and between them and the youths attending the centres. In drawing on the results and experiences gained in carrying out this investigation, the authors offer valuable suggestions as to the pitfalls to be avoided in this kind of inquiry.

Coming from quite diverse academic backgrounds in history and science, Pat Whaley and Viv Shelley explore in Chapter 7 the issue of women's access to education and training in science and technology. Their common interest in opening up educational opportunities to all adults, both men and women, has underpinned their work in teaching, counselling and research over a number of years in higher education. In this study the authors examine the status of women in science, the factors influencing this state of affairs, the difficulties women experience in getting on science courses and the opportunities that could be created to attract more women into science and technology.

According to the authors, several social barriers prevent women taking up science and technology. Among these is the stereotype that science is a man's subject. Social stereotyping has, according to the authors, resulted in fewer women choosing or even having a choice to pursue studies in science and technology. Thus, the entrance of women into science and technology requires a great deal of courage and understanding on the part of the student and a great deal of understanding, encouragement and guidance on the part of the tutor. The authors offer some advice as to how this can be achieved.

To attract mature women into science, a pre-access course was designed exclusively for women at the University of Durham. The course was built around the themes of environment and health. Its aim was to attract mature women who had little or no previous experience into science by devising a suitably attractive course for them. Methods were devised – using informal and formal techniques – for assessing the progress of students. The course was designed to run over two terms of 10 weeks on one day a week, 10.00–12.00 a.m. and 1.00–3.00 p.m. Most of the tutors on the course were women. The course was delivered in an informal and interactive way, and drew on the experience and expertise of the students where appropriate. It was widely publicized in local newspapers, course leaflets, libraries and job centres, and a University of Durham Certificate was awarded on successful completion of the course. Assessment of the study was by pre- and post-course questionnaires. A follow-up questionnaire was also sent to all students six to nine months after the course ended, in an attempt to monitor their progression in higher education or the workplace.

The study indicates that it is possible not only to offer women a second chance to study science, but actually to recruit and retain them if the curriculum has been carefully thought through in order to meet their specific needs.

CONCLUSION

With the exception of Chapter 7, the contributions to this book have utilized mainly qualitative methods in order to investigate relatively common social and educational concerns.

It is hoped that the studies will provide the reader with some insights into what is involved in such inquiries and, more importantly, encourage them to undertake similar investigations into their own practice. The contributors were all concerned to improve their own practice, by their own endeavours and by means of research methods that helped them gather the evidence on which to base their judgement. It is to the investigations themselves that we now turn.

REFERENCES

Allen, V. L., and Wilder, D. A. (1975) Categorisation, beliefs, similarity and intergroup discrimination. *Journal of Personality and Social Psychology* **32**, 971-7.

Allport, G. W. (1954) *The Nature of Prejudice*. Cambridge, MA: Addison-Wesley.

Aronson, E. (1978) *The Jigsaw Classroom*. Beverly Hills, CA: Sage.

Blaney, N. T., Stephen, C., Rosenfield, D., Aronson, E., and Sikes, J. (1977) Interdependence in the classroom: a field study. *Journal of Educational Psychology* **69**(2), 121-8.

Boal, A. (1979) *Theatre of the Oppressed*. London: Pluto.

Brewer, J., and Hunter, A. (1989) *Multimethod Research: A Synthesis of Styles*. London: Sage.

Brigham, J. C., and Malpas, R. S. (1985) The role of experience and contact in the recognition of faces of own and other race persons. *Journal of Social Issues* **41**, 139-55.

Bryan, J. H., and Walbeck, N. (1970) Impact of words and deeds concerning altruism upon children. *Child Development* **41**, 747-57.

Burgess, R. G. (1984) *The Research Process in Educational Settings: Ten Case Studies*. Lewes: Falmer.

Burgess, R. G. (ed.) (1985) *Strategies of Educational Research: Qualitative Methods*. Lewes: Falmer.

Cohen, E. G. (1972) Inter-racial interaction disability. *Human Relations* **25**, 9-24.

Cohen, E. G. (1975) The effects of segregation on race relations. *Law and Contemporary Problems* **39**, 271-99.

Cohen, E. G. (1982) Expectation states and interracial interaction in school settings. *Annual Review of Sociology* **8**, 209-35.

Cohen, E. G., and Roper, S. (1972) Modification of interracial interaction disability: an application of status characteristic theory. *American Sociological Review* 37, 643–52.

Cohen, E. G., and Sharan, S. (1980) Modifying status relations in Israeli youth. *Journal of Cross-cultural Psychology* 11, 364–84.

Cohen, L., and Manion, L. (1989) *Research Methods in Education* (3rd edition). London: Routledge.

Cook, S. W. (1978) Interpersonal and attitudinal outcomes in cooperating interracial groups. *Journal of Research and Development in Education* 12, 97–113.

Davies, B., Corbishley, P., Evans, J., and Kenrick, C. (1985) Integrating methodologies: if the intellectual relations don't get you, then the social will. In R. G. Burgess (ed.), *Strategies of Educational Research Qualitative Methods*. Lewes: Falmer.

Deutsch, M. (1949) A theory of cooperation and competition. *Human Relations* 2, 129–52.

Elliott, J. (1980) Implications of classroom research for professional development. In E. W. Hoyle and J. Megarry (eds), *World Year Book of Education (1980) Professional Development for Teachers*. London: Routledge & Kegan Paul.

Elliott, J. (1983) Paradigms of educational research and theories of schooling. Paper presented at Westhill Sociology of Education Conference, January. Cited in A. Kelly (1985) Action research: what is it and what can it do? In R. G. Burgess (ed.), *Issues in Educational Research*. Lewes: Falmer.

Elliott, J. (1991) *Action Research for Educational Change*. Milton Keynes: Open University Press.

Epstein, J. L. (1985) After the bus arrives: resegregation in desegregated schools. *Journal of Social Issues* 41, 23–43.

Finemann, S. (1991) Getting involved. *The Occupational Psychologist*, August (14).

Fischer, W. F. (1963) Sharing in preschool children as a function of amount and type of reinforcement. *Genetic Psychology Monographs* 68, 215–45.

Fitz-Gibbon, C. T. (1983) Peer-tutoring: a possible method for multi-ethnic education. *New Community* 10, 160–6.

Freire, P. (1972) *Pedagogy of the Oppressed*. London: Sheed & Ward. Further Education Unit (FEU) (1988) *Staff Development for a Multicultural Society*. London: FEU.

Gredler, G. R. (1985) An assessment of cross-age tutoring. *Journal for Remedial Education and Counselling* 1, January, 226–32.

Hirst, P. (1990) A curriculum for social justice. *Australian Educational Researcher* 17(2), 43–50.

Johnson, D. W., and Johnson, R. (1981) Effects of cooperative and individualistic learning experiences on interethnic interaction. *Journal of Educational Psychology* 73, 454–9.

Johnson, D. W., and Johnson, R. T. (1982) Effects of cooperative, competitive and individual-istic learning experiences on cross-ethnic interaction and friendships. *Journal of Social Psychology* 118, 47–58.

Johnson, D. W., and Johnson, R. T. (1992) Social interdependence and cross ethnic relation-ships. In J. Lynch, C. Modgil and S. Modgil (eds), *Cultural Diversity and the Schools*. Vol. 2, *Prejudice, Polemic or Progress*. Lewes: Falmer.

Johnson, D. W., Johnson, R. T., and Maruyama, G. (1983) Interdependence and interpersonal attraction among heterogeneous and homogeneous individuals: a theoretical formulation and a meta-analysis of the research. *Review of Educational Research* 5(3), 5–54.

McCall, C. J., and Simmons, J. L. (1969) *Issues in Participant Observation: A Text and Reader*. Reading, MA: Addison-Wesley.

McFee, G. (1992) Triangulation in research: two confusions. *Educational Research* 34(3), 215–19.

Marks, G., Miller, N., and Maruyama, G. (1981) The effects of physical attractiveness on assumptions of similarity. *Journal of Personality and Social Psychology* 41, 198–212.

Nixon, J. (ed.) (1981) *A Teacher's Guide to Action Research*. London: Grant McIntyre.

Rudduck, J. (1985) The improvement in the art of teaching through research. *Cambridge Journal of Education* 15(3), 123–7.

Rudduck, J. (1989) Practitioner research and programmes of initial teacher education. *Westminster Studies in Education* 12, 61–72.

Sharan, S. (1980) Cooperative learning in small groups: recent methods and effects on achievement attitudes and ethnic relations. *Review of Educational Research* 50(2), 241–71.

Sharan, S., and Shachar, H. (eds) (1988) *Language and Learning in the Cooperative Classroom.* New York: Springer-Verlag.

Sharpley, A. M., and Sharpley, C. F. (1981) Peer-tutoring: a review of the literature. *Collected Original Resources in Education (CORE)* 5(3), 7–11.

Sherif, M. (ed.) (1966) *Group Conflict and Cooperation.* London: Routledge & Kegan Paul.

Sherif, M., and Sherif, C. W. (1953) *Groups in Harmony and Tension: An Investigation of Studies in Inter-Group Relations.* New York: Harper.

Sherif, M., Harvey, O. J., Hood, W., White, J., and Sherif, C. (1961) *Intergroup Conflict and Cooperation: The Robber's Cave Experiment.* Norman: University of Oklahoma/Institute of Intergroup Relations/University Books Exchange.

Slavin, R. E. (1980) Cooperative learning. *Review of Educational Research* 50, 315–40.

Slavin, R. E. (1983) *Cooperative Learning.* New York: Longman.

Slavin, R. E. (1985) Cooperative learning applying contact theory in desegregated schools. *Journal of Social Issues* 41(3), 45–62.

Stephan, W. G., and Stephan, C. W. (1985) Intergroup anxiety. *Journal of Social Issues* 41, 157–75.

Topping, K. (1987) Peer tutored paired reading: outcome data from ten projects. *Educational Psychology* 7(2), 133–47.

Warring, D., Johnson, D. W., Maruyama, G., and Johnson, R.T. (1985) Impact of different types of cooperative learning on cross-ethnic and cross-sex relationships. *Journal of Educational Psychology* 77, 53–9.

Weigel, R. H., and Howes, P. W. (1985) Conceptions of racial prejudice: symbolic racism reconsidered. *Journal of Social Issues* 41(3), 117–38.

Weiner, G. (1989) Professional self-knowledge versus social justice: a critical analysis of the teacher-researcher movement. *British Educational Research Journal* 15(1), 41–50.

Chapter 1

Can Monolingual Teachers Teach Language Awareness Successfully to the Benefit of All Children?

Wendy F. Reeds

The works of Edwards (1983), Merchant (1990) and Hawkins (1984) have suggested that the teaching of language awareness in schools has raised the self-esteem of bilingual children, increased knowledge and helped to reduce racial prejudice. Research by Houlton (1985) shows practical ways of carrying out the teaching of language awareness in primary schools.

This study is an attempt to investigate the teaching of language awareness to monolingual and bilingual pupils by monolingual teachers in an inner-city primary school. Although this study did not follow the methodology of the studies cited above, it does show how a team of English as a second language support teachers initiated a project in order to investigate language awareness by involving the teaching staff in planning, initiating, evaluating and appraising the investigation.

The study shows how monolingual teachers can teach language awareness successfully and also shows the difficulties and constraints involved in doing this kind of research. The study concludes by drawing the reader's attention to the improvements which can be made to this kind of research and so make the project beneficial to all children.

The benefit of this investigation is clear. It gives insight into the advantages both of undertaking the teaching of language awareness in schools and of using action research as a research model; it also shows how the investigation has been beneficial to the staff and school in which the study took place.

INTRODUCTION

My own previous research revealed that staff in this inner-city primary school had little knowledge of how the recognition of community languages aids the bilingual child's cognitive development, the learning of English and the raising of self-esteem; and of how the recognition of community languages can become an anti-racist strategy. (The phrase 'community languages', languages spoken within the community of the children, is explained more fully below.)

Staff felt that they had little knowledge of the languages spoken, written or read by the children in their class. This lack of knowledge meant a reluctance by class teachers to attempt any work involving the community languages. The school participating in this research had no staff who spoke the community languages of the school. Strategies developed by other schools using bilingual staff to prepare materials and to teach in the community languages were not appropriate. A programme of work which raised the awareness of many languages, including English, the community languages of the school, world languages and dialects of English, seemed appropriate.

I am a member of a team of teachers in the school who teach English as a second language. I approached my team colleagues to find out their views on language awareness and to see whether they were in favour of supporting staff and children in this type of programme. After a series of interviews and discussions with these colleagues we decided to approach the headteacher, deputy head and class teachers with a view to carrying out a language awareness project. We obtained permission and co-operation, and in January 1991 we began the Language Awareness Project. The project lasted for six weeks, and during that time class and support teachers worked together to teach an awareness of language to all pupils. Strategies used were surveys of the classroom languages, teaching of languages by children and staff, language activities relating to topic work, practice of various scripts, recognition of other languages using audio-cassette tapes, and investigations into the relationship between languages.

Data were collected by pupil questionnaires, field notes by the teachers and staff discussion. The data were then presented to the staff for their comments, which are recorded in the conclusion to this study. The data show that the levels of self-esteem and knowledge of community languages at the beginning of the project were high, that attitudes to languages other than European languages were changed by the project, and that the various languages were moving towards equality after the project. The staff believed that the project helped children to have greater pride in their community language and led to an increase in awareness by all children about languages. The problems encountered during the project included the difficulty of eliciting individual responses to the questionnaire rather than group collaboration, and difficulties experienced by the younger children in reading the questionnaire.

Some teachers were not able to find time during the lessons to complete the field notes, which led to a time lapse between the event and the recording of it. The difficulty experienced during the class discussions was due to limited time and to other demands on staff meetings time; more time would have given the opportunity for considering related issues, such as parental involvement and future policy documents.

This study shows the development of language awareness as a teaching strategy and discusses action research as a method of conducting research; it reviews the practical literature on language awareness and analyses the data collected so that a conclusion on the project's success can be made by the staff involved. The study is examined under five headings:

- Towards language awareness.
- Review of literature on language awareness.
- Action research.
- Initiating the project.
- The Language Awareness Project.

Definition of terms

In the literature relating to bilingualism and multicultural education, a number of terms are used to refer to the languages of a nation's minority groups. The linguistic background of pupils from ethnic minority groups may often be extremely complex.

Tansley *et al.* (1985, p. vii) define *community languages* as the languages spoken by or associated with a particular ethnic minority community. This term is seen as having advantages over others in common use. It avoids the ambiguity of terms such as 'home language' and 'mother tongue' in respect of the pupils of Islamic background, where the language of the home is Punjabi and is of less importance in terms of the community than is Urdu. The term 'community language' includes 'mother tongue', but in addition provides access to speech communities and cultures across the world. The 'mother tongue' may be a dialect but the preferred language of literacy will be the standard language: for example, the 'mother tongue' may be the dialect of 'Sylhet' but the standard language is Bengali. Alternatively, parents may prefer children to learn a language which has religious significance for them, rather than, or in addition to, the languages spoken at home: for example, Malay speakers learn Malay and also Arabic, the language of Islam.

In this study the term 'community languages' is used to refer to Arabic, Bengali, Malay, Punjabi, Pushtu and Urdu; the pupils are of Islamic background.

I am also indebted to Tansley for the definition of *bilingual*, which is 'used to describe all children whose first language is not English and who are at some stage along the English language learning continuum' (Tansley *et al.*, 1985, p. vii).

Fitzpatrick also discusses the term bilingual: 'It tends to take its definition from the particular context in which it is used and therein lies its usefulness and its complexity' (Fitzpatrick, 1987, p. 9). Fitzpatrick reinforces Tansley's definition by suggesting that the term is 'used to represent language use in a wide variety of social situations all over the world, as well as to represent a combination of abilities possessed by certain individuals' (p. 9).

Fitzpatrick further suggests that the ability to speak two languages or more seems to have peculiar status in our society, since 'while applauding the ability to communicate with foreigners provided other criteria for social esteem are met', it appears that schools do not value the many children who speak two or more languages fluently.

In this study *bilingual* will be used to refer to all children who speak a community language and who are learning English, at whatever level that English may be. The term *monolingual* will apply to staff and children who do not speak the community languages of the school (other than English).

TOWARDS LANGUAGE AWARENESS

The term 'language awareness' is used in a variety of teaching situations. Peter Garrett and Carl James in their paper 'Diversity and common ground in language awareness', based on the Bangor seminar on language awareness in April 1989, attempt to define the various meanings of the term:

- Some language awareness work is attempted by groups sharing a mother tongue; it aims to make the students more aware of the intuitions they have about 'their' language, drawing attention to specific language features, and 'raises the consciousness' of the learners with the focus on the first language.
- Some language awareness work is aimed at foreign-language learners. These programmes aim to make learners conscious of the specific relations between their mother tongue and the foreign language, and of how language in general works.
- Other language awareness work takes place with learners who do not share a mother tongue. The aim is to make pupils aware of their own knowledge of their first language, and also of *each other's* knowledge. Here, the emphasis is on language diversity and is perhaps a means of overcoming barriers between pupils in the same class. The teacher aims to increase the overall amount of knowledge in *each* individual.

This last aspect of language awareness is the one considered appropriate for work in this primary school. The children do not share a mother tongue. We aim not to raise awareness about the English language specifically, or its relationship with other languages, but to raise awareness of all languages.

Various projects, reports and initiatives have contributed to the growing awareness of the linguistic diversity of Britain. Until the Swann Report (1985), community language teaching received support from linguists, the Department of Education and Science, and educationalists. Swann, however, placed emphasis on using the community language to ease transition into school rather than as a skill in its own right, and suggested more work on language awareness. Since 1985 most primary school initiatives have been based on language awareness work for all children.

The Linguistic Diversity in the Primary School (LDIP) Project explored the implications of linguistic diversity for the training of primary school teachers. A network of tutors involved in pre-service and in-service training was established, and in-service courses on linguistic diversity were also organized in five participating LEAs.

The LDIP Project (1986–9) attempted to broaden professional understanding of linguistic diversity and the report *English for Ages 5 to 11* (DES, 1988) also drew attention to the significance of linguistic diversity in the development of individual, social and cultural identity. Bourne (1989), reviewing the present situation, suggests a wider receptivity to the benefits of linguistic diversity.

Using Garrett and James's (1989) definitions of language awareness, I have defined the term 'language awareness' for use in primary schools as work which takes place with learners who do not share a community language. The aim is to make pupils aware of their own knowledge of their first language and also of *each other's* knowledge.

There is much support for defining language awareness in this way, as a brief examination of the literature will show.

REVIEW OF LITERATURE ON LANGUAGE AWARENESS

There is literature available which is aimed at those teachers who are themselves bilingual; suggestions are made for teaching bilingual children the written form of their community language. There is also a wide range of literature available on the subject of language awareness, but much of it is written for secondary schools. A great deal of theoretical evidence exists concerning the 'why' of teaching about linguistic diversity. Houlton and Willey in *Supporting Children's Bilingualism* (1983) have included a table 'Why support bilingualism?' which clearly states the educational case for supporting home languages and dialects. Teachers need to seek help from the practical advice in the literature. I have used four criteria with which to assess this advice.

- Can the suggestions and ideas be used by *monolingual* teachers in primary schools?
- Can they be used *without* the aid of support from bilingual teachers, auxiliaries, nursery nurses, etc?
- Can they be used to reduce prejudice and for the educational achievement and advancement of *all* children?
- Is there a recognition of the part that dialect takes when discussing linguistic diversity?

Practical help for monolingual primary school teachers is provided by Houlton in *All Our Languages* (1985). It has many suggestions that give advice and guidance to the monolingual teacher in the primary multilingual classroom, trying to introduce language diversity into the curriculum or helping to extend work that is already under way.

Practical help can also be found in *Looking into Language: Diversity in the Classroom* by Gregory and Woollard (1984). This book shows the successful attempts made by some schools to question the use of English only in the curriculum. It shows how other languages can be an excellent resource to explore and tap into. The book gives case studies of work with children of all ages and has a good range of teaching ideas for all teachers no matter what sort of school they are teaching in.

The activities which the book outlines stem from the child-centred approach. Bilingual children's skills/abilities in their community languages have been recognized and allowed to develop. Underlying all the articles in the book is a concern with fundamental justice for all children and access to the curriculum for all.

The linguistic diversity of British schools is not often an educational problem. It is the attitude towards this diversity that is of great importance. Edwards in *Language in Multicultural Classrooms* (1983) attempts to show this and also stresses that the term 'multicultural' refers not only to bilingual children, but to speakers of non-standard dialects of English which have originated both in Britain and overseas. Unfortunately, some teachers in 'all white' schools will not appreciate this interpretation of 'multicultural' and they will not be aware that the book is relevant to their situation.

Dual-language books

Dual-language books as such have little use in primary schools where class teachers cannot speak the minority community language concerned. Many children are not literate in their community language and the books become merely reading books in English with the added interest of another language's script, instead of providing an opportunity for all children to gain knowledge of another language. Dual-language books with cassette tapes of the stories are ideal: they can be used by monolingual teachers, all children can listen to them, they give the opportunity for the bilingual children to make comparisons between languages, and they can be used as a 'way in' to the English language for elementary learners and as a means of supporting their self-esteem and pride in being bilingual.

Some of the best ones are those published by Harmony Publishing – *Topiwalo the Hat-maker*, *Sameep and the Parrots* and *Sonal Splash* – and by the Luzac Storytellers. The latter are stories which originate from countries where they have been handed down from generation to generation by word of mouth. Using these with all the children would fulfil the National Curriculum language guidelines, which support the idea that stories from other cultures and traditions should be used.

Material offered in the *Children's Languages Project* (University of London Institute of Education, 1984) provides starting points for children and monolingual teachers to explore their own linguistic diversity in school, at home and in the community. There are four activity cards focusing on language. Each card provides the children with activities, ideas and suggestions for extension. If teachers could be persuaded to use these materials, the children would learn from each other, and teachers would increase their own knowledge about the children's language and dialects. Looking at the diversity of the school will enhance its ethos and make the staff more aware of the cultural diversity and complexity of their children. This can only help them to be more effective in their class teaching and in developing the independence and self-awareness of the children.

The *National Writing Project* (National Curriculum Council, 1990) has involved hundreds of teachers and thousands of children. It gives teachers' accounts of practice in classrooms in which children have had very different language experiences. The project has been set up by the School Curriculum Development Committee and attempts to represent a broad view of language diversity for all teachers.

I refer back to the criteria by which the literature was to be evaluated at the beginning of this section. In reviewing the literature I have found that the third and fourth criteria have been fully explored and developed. I have found that teaching language awareness can reduce prejudice and help towards educational achievement and the advancement of all children, and that the literature explores the part that dialect plays when discussing linguistic diversity. However, it would seem from my review that the first two criteria have not been completely fulfilled. Only three books – the *National Writing Project* (National Curriculum Council, 1990), *All Our Languages* (Houlton, 1985) and the *Children's Languages Project* (University of London Institute of Education, 1984) provide any evidence that monolingual teachers, without the aid of bilingual support, can teach language awareness to *all* children.

Reviewing the literature which discusses language awareness has revealed that there is little of a practical nature to help monolingual teachers in the multilingual classroom, but the literature does suggest that celebrating linguistic diversity and increasing the language awareness of all children will result in greater knowledge which will advance educational achievement and lead to prejudice reduction. My own theorizing and reflection on this issue based on my experience within the school leads me to agree with the existing literature.

Guided by the existing literature on language awareness, I wanted to conduct an investigation into how teachers working without the benefit of bilingual support staff can teach an awareness of language successfully to the benefit of all children in a multilingual school. I decided after exploring various research strategies that 'action research' was appropriate for the purpose of this study.

ACTION RESEARCH

By 'action research' I mean a research approach that is in the control of the teachers conducting their own research. It is an on-the-spot procedure designed to deal with a concrete problem located in an immediate situation.

The basic premise of action research is that the teacher carries out the research. Stenhouse (1982) encouraged the 'teacher as researcher' movement, so that teachers undertaking a case study were themselves to become researchers, i.e. were developing a practical methodology. This alternative methodology had to be conceptually and linguistically accessible to the teacher. Not just any teacher will do, however. Stenhouse seems to have had the 'good teacher' in mind (see Stenhouse, 1982).

The school involved in this research has many good teachers, professionally aware and open to inquiry. Using a collaborative teaching method, support and mainstream teachers implemented various strategies in order to investigate linguistic diversity. These strategies were collected from the literature already reviewed by the research leader (myself). Teachers decided as a pair (support and mainstream) which strategies to implement. The data were collected by both support and classroom teachers acting as participant observers for each other.

The pairs of teachers were asked to make field notes during lessons. It was felt that this would avoid the time gap, suggested by Schwartz and Schwartz (1985), between the occurrence of an event and its recording. Discussions with teachers took place and questionnaires were given to the children before and after the research. These three different accounts of teaching acts in the classroom – field notes by participant observers, discussion with the teachers and questionnaires for the children – provided a multi-method approach called 'triangulation' developed by the *Ford Teaching Project* (Elliott and Partington, 1975). It was accepted that reliance on one method in action research may bias or distort the researcher's picture of the situation.

In my previous research I found that pupils and staff had a lack of knowledge about the linguistic diversity within our school community. This situation is not necessarily a problem, but it is an area which needs changing.

The primary school in which I work has set time aside on a regular basis in which problems are identified and discussed, ideas are tried and results are shared. They are already a research community and will, I feel, accept the value of further research.

The school: context of the inquiry

This school is situated in an inner-city area, and the population belongs to a low socioeconomic group. There is both council and low-cost private rented housing. One-third of the children are from ethnic minority groups, predominantly Asian;

the countries of origin are Pakistan and Bangladesh. Included in this third are the children of students from Malaysia and Indonesia studying at the university. The languages of the school are Punjabi/Urdu, Bengali, Pushtu and Malay. There are a small number of other children whose parents are also studying in England. Their languages are Spanish and Arabic. The school has a 'moving' population of white and black families.

The staff work hard to plan the curriculum to suit the needs of all children. Policies and strategies have been set up to deal with racial incidents under the guidelines of the LEA.

I am part of an ESL support team within this large primary school. There are two other teachers in this team. Previous research, when attempting to initiate an equal opportunity, anti-racist policy in the school, showed that they would be willing to help with this research project. All of us teach collaboratively with the mainstream teachers, and good professional relationships have developed between all teachers. On the basis of these good relationships, I decided to initiate a language awareness project.

INITIATING THE PROJECT

I decided not to approach the whole staff initially, but to try to set up a partnership with the two other members of the language support team. It was crucial to make sure first that they were in favour of trying to implement a language awareness policy.

There were other reasons for approaching the rest of the language support team. Research has shown (Tansley, 1986) that teachers of English as a second language have been innovative in other projects and in schools generally. We had all worked well previously. As all classes have one of us as a support teacher, we can cover the whole of the junior school with a language awareness policy provided that mainstream staff can be persuaded to support the project. So I planned three interviews with the language support team: the first to discuss issues and philosophy and to explore the idea of this policy with them; a second to discuss how to implement the policy; and a third to decide how to monitor its progress and evaluate it.

I decided to interview these two teachers separately to find out how they felt about the initiating of a language awareness policy; to find out their philosophy and ideas on the subject; and to ascertain whether they were in support of the rationale of supporting children's bilingualism.

During the first interview it became clear that the teachers were willing to work with class teachers and also to help initiate and implement the project. I found that their views were generally consistent with current theories about supporting bilingualism. I decided to supply relevant hand-outs from the current literature on language awareness to the team so that they would be prepared for the project and so that they could support the class teacher with information.

In the second interview the issues which arose during discussion were time for the support team to meet and talk with mainstream teachers, the need and desirability of a team effort, and ways of approaching the staff with a view to starting the project.

The final interview explored ways of monitoring and evaluating the project. This discussion forms the basis of the way the data were collected and evaluated.

THE LANGUAGE AWARENESS PROJECT

The sample

One hundred and sixty-one children took part in the project from Years 3 to 6. They were from seven different classes, three of which had mixed age groups. Ten teachers took part in the project, comprising seven class teachers and three language support teachers. This sample was chosen so that questionnaires could be used to determine attitudes at pre- and post-test. It was recognized that younger children would find it difficult to answer detailed questionnaires.

Aims

Houlton (1985) lists four aims on which we should base our teaching ideas for language awareness:

- They should be a natural and accepted feature of the classroom.
- They should permeate the curriculum as a whole, as well as being worthwhile areas of study in their own right.
- They should be something to which bilingual and monolingual children can contribute.
- They should help all children towards a greater awareness of their own and each other's language experience as well as the range of languages that go to make up our multicultural society.

Timetable

The project took place in the early part of the spring term 1991 over a six-week period. Classes had four morning sessions each where language awareness was the major focus. Each class teacher and their pupils conducted a survey of the languages spoken in their class. The data for this were recorded in pictorial histograms. This made a good beginning to the project. I shall now focus on the work of different year groups.

Year 6

The main focus of their work was in mathematics. It included work using number squares in community and other Asian number systems; making and using number lines in community and other Asian number systems; and mathematics games using these number squares and lines.

I compiled a languages tape which included community languages, Welsh, Doric dialect (north-east Scotland), London Afro-Caribbean, English and Geordie. The children listened to the tape and tried to guess the languages. Children who spoke a community language taught small groups in Urdu, Bengali and Malay. Chinese script was practised and easy sentences were compiled by the children using a set of interchangeable words. Year 6 had three class lessons in Hebrew, French and Italian taught by teachers in the school.

Years 4 and 5

These year groups incorporated work on language awareness into topic work on weather and the seasons. The children wrote work in Malay, Urdu and Arabic as well as English. A display was made where signs were also written in these languages. Lessons were given to small groups by the children who spoke the community languages. Collections of words were compiled, e.g. 'cat' in as many different languages as possible. The children investigated the derivation of English words such as 'bamboo', 'bungalow' and 'café'.

Year 3

These children collected ways of saying 'good morning' and illustrated this work by paintings of themselves. The work on language awareness was linked to a topic on journeys – they collected postcards and letters in other languages and discussed the need for knowing other languages when making journeys.

Problems which may be encountered

Houlton (1985, p. 40), reporting research findings, quoted a teacher involved in a language awareness project:

> We have had occasions when music from different cultural traditions has prompted embarrassment or ridicule, and given rise to stereotyped caricaturing. Reactions of children can be noted and, we feel, should be dealt with in smaller class groups. Classroom work can relate to the themes and images of the music to validate it, and by making cultural and language variety a constant, and so a natural part of the classroom, we are working to overcome negative reactions.

Children involved in our project may also become embarrassed or unwilling to speak either their own or another language. Although this project lasted for only six weeks, it was hoped that language diversity would become a natural part of the classroom in the future, and that negative reactions would be overcome by making language variety a constant rather than exotic. We anticipated criticism from parents, both monolingual and bilingual, who would object to the use of community languages in school.

The collection of the data

As previously stated, data were collected in three ways (see Figure 1.1).

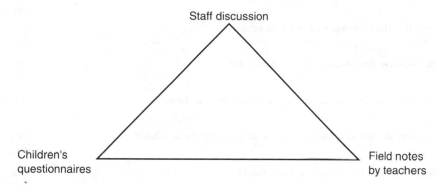

Figure 1.1 *The collection of data.*

Children's questionnaires

The aim was to be simple, unsophisticated and easily understood by primary school children. It was important that the questions should not be misunderstood owing to difficult or misleading phraseology. Each question had to be considered so that it did not give rise to unnecessary questions; but more than one question on a specific area had to be used in the attitude questions in order to try to determine a true picture of the attitudes of the children. It was thought that the respondents might give the answer they thought the teacher wished to hear. Questions were therefore used which, although about the same subject matter, were phrased differently or emphasized a different specific area. The questionnaire is shown in Figure 1.2.

The questionnaire was administered in the classrooms by class teachers working with support teachers. The older children were already familiar with using questionnaires before and after a topic in order for them to determine their progress within that area of work. One copy of the questionnaire was completed before the project began and another after the project finished. In this way it was hoped to determine changes during the project. There were 20 closed questions or statements and two open-ended 'offers of comment'. The questionnaires were not named and the children were asked to tick the appropriate answer or box in the closed questions and statements, and to write comments in the open comments section.

The questionnaire was divided into three areas – self-esteem, knowledge and attitude – and also had a section for comments. It had nine statements and questions which try to determine the attitude of the children towards community languages, the English language, European languages and learning languages in general. An example of the kind of questions asked in the questionnaire is: 'Item 1 Which language do you speak most at home?', which was included so that staff could determine whether the children knew the name of the home language. It was found at the pre-test that some children did write 'Pakistani', but very few at the post-test made this mistake.

What do YOU know about languages?

1. Which language do you speak most at home? ....

Please tick

2. Do you like the language you speak at home?

    Yes
    No

3. Is the language you speak at home important?

    Yes
    No

4. Should other children learn the language you speak at home?

    Yes
    No

5. Would you like the language you speak at home taught at school?

    Yes
    No

6. Is Bengali spoken by children in this school?

    Yes
    No

7. Is Malay spoken by children in this school?

    Yes
    No

8. Is Punjabi spoken by children in this school?

    Yes
    No

9. How many languages are spoken by children in Newcastle?

    1
    6
    29
    53

10. Which language is spoken by the most people in the world?

    Russian
    English
    Chinese
    Bengali
    Punjabi
    Malay

11. Which language has the same writing as English?

    Malay
    Urdu
    Bengali

12. Which language is the most important?

    Malay
    Urdu
    Bengali
    English

13. Which language would you like to learn?

    Bengali
    French
    Malay
    Punjabi

14. The best classroom is where everyone speaks only English

    True
    False

15. I believe that every language is a good language   ....

    I believe that only some languages are good languages   ....

    I believe that English is the best language   ....

16. Learning about another language is: *Please tick*
                       very important   ....
                       important   ....
                       not very important   ....

17. Learning about another language will:
                       help me a lot to make friends   ....
                       help me a little to make friends   ....

18. Learning about another language will:
                       help me to understand other countries   ....
                       not help me much to understand other countries   ....

19. Learning about another language will:
                       help me to understand other people   ....
                       not help me much to understand other people   ....

20. Everything in England should be written in English   ....
    Everything in England should not be written in English   ....

Write down anything special you would like to learn during your lessons on other languages

---

Write down anything you would like to tell your teacher about other languages

---

Figure 1.2 *The questions pupils were asked.*

Summary of the data collected

Analysis of the data in Table 1.1 shows quite clearly that levels of self-esteem at the beginning of the project were good, with small positive changes after the project. Knowledge of community languages was also good, but there were significant positive changes in knowledge of both community and world languages after the project. Attitudes to languages other than European languages have been changed by the project, although we must be aware that this change may be temporary. Children still thought that English was the superior language and French was their choice of another language to learn, but more children after the project believed that English was not the most important language and fewer children wished to learn French. Further items showed that the various languages were moving towards equality after the project.

Invitations for comment

The problem of coding responses to open-ended questions and comments is frequently discussed in the research literature (Cohen and Manion, 1980). Strategies for ensuring the reliability and validity of such data need to be developed.

In accordance with established practice, I have devised a coding frame by selecting categories that were typical of the response found in the sample. Quotations by the children are used to illustrate the categories.

The comments were invited to these statements:
Write down anything you would like to learn during your lessons on other languages.
and
Write down anything you would like to tell your teacher about languages.

At post-test the first statement was changed to:
Write down what you liked best in the language project and what else would you like to learn.

One hundred and twenty-three children were asked to offer a response to the open-ended requests; these were in Years 4, 5 and 6. The class and support teachers of Year 3 felt that this would be too onerous a task for their children and themselves to undertake.

The results of the open statements are listed in Table 1.2. The table shows the categories elicited from the open-ended comments section of the questionnaire and the number of responses by the children within these categories at pre- and post-test.

Analysis of the open statements

At pre-test, 72.3 per cent of the children stated that they would like to learn French, 13.8 per cent wanted to learn a community language and 24.3 per cent another language, either European or world (categories 1–4 in Table 1.2).

Statements such as 'I would like to learn French because everyone knows French in England, or German because that's a good language as well' corroborate item 13 in the structured/closed questionnaire statements, where 81.3 per cent of children

Table 1.1. *Questionnaire results: structured questions and statements.*

Question	Pre-test		Post-test	
	No.	%	No.	%
2 Y	154	95.6	155	96.2
N	7	4.3	6	3.7
3 Y	137	85.0	141	87.5
N	24	14.9	20	12.4
4 Y	121	75.1	133	82.6
N	40	24.8	28	17.3
5 Y	125	77.6	131	81.3
N	36	22.3	30	18.6
6 Y	145	90.0	156	96.8
N	16	9.9	5	3.1
7 Y	130	80.7	146	90.6
N	31	19.2	15	9.3
8 Y	135	83.8	150	93.1
N	26	16.1	11	6.8
9 1	12	7.4	7	4.3
6	45	27.9	18	11.1
29	36	22.3	30	18.6
53	65	40.3	104	64.5
10 R	9	5.5	4	2.4
E	137	85.0	111	68.9
Ch	3	1.8	39	24.2
B	4	2.4	3	1.8
P	0		2	1.2
M	8	4.9	1	0.62
11 M	91	56.5	124	77.0
U	36	22.3	14	8.6
B	30	18.6	22	13.6
12 none	0		10	6.2
M	13	8.0	14	8.6
U	13	8.0	17	10.5
B	12	7.4	14	8.6
E	122	75.7	102	63.3
13 B	6	3.7	13	8.0
F	131	81.3	111	68.9
M	13	8.0	21	13.0
P	11	6.8	16	9.9
14 T	49	30.4	24	14.9
F	112	69.5	137	85.0
15 a	91	56.5	130	80.7
b	28	17.3	17	10.5
c	39	24.2	14	8.6
16 a	121	75.1	129	80.1
b	36	22.3	24	14.9
c	4	2.4	8	4.9
17 a	142	88.1	151	93.7
b	19	11.8	9	5.5
18 a	148	91.9	156	96.8
b	13	8.0	5	3.1
19 a	150	93.1	156	96.8
b	11	6.8	5	3.1
20 a	92	57.1	68	42.2
b	69	42.8	93	57.7

Total number of respondents: 161

Table 1.2.   *Responses to requests for comments.*

Categories	Pre-test		Post-test	
	No.	%	No.	%
1 Desire to learn French	89	72.3	50	40.6
2 Desire to learn other European languages	20	16.2	17	13.8
3 Desire to learn non-European languages	10	8.1	8	6.5
4 Desire to learn a community language	17	13.8	31	25.2
5 Specific request for knowledge	11	8.9	18	14.6
6 Offers to share own knowledge	12	9.7	20	16.2
7 Positive attitude statement	12	9.7	19	15.4
8 Negative attitude statement	1	0.6	0	–
9 Desire to learn languages generally	6	4.8	11	8.9
10 Statements of own knowledge	5	4.0	17	13.8

Total number of respondents: 123

at pre-test chose French when asked which language they would like to learn and offered a choice of French or the community languages of the school.

At post-test, 40.6 per cent of children stated their continuing interest in learning French, a drop of 31.7 per cent; 25.2 per cent stated an interest in learning a community language at post-test, a rise of 11.4 per cent. This rise in interest in community languages corroborates item 13 at post-test, which also showed a decline in interest in learning French in favour of community languages.

The rise in interest in community languages after the language awareness project is corroborated by category 5 in Table 1.2, specific requests for knowledge. Specific requests were very small at pre-test: only 8.9 per cent wrote comments such as 'I would like to learn the alphabet in different languages' and 'I would like to learn to say "Hello" in other languages'.

At post-test, there was a rise to 14.6 per cent in requests for knowledge. Requests also stated the languages required e.g. 'I would like to write more in Chinese' and 'I would like to learn Malay, Punjabi, Bengali, Urdu and Fench'. Some children included what they had enjoyed specifically during the project: 'When Faizal learned us some Malay words', 'Learning the Bengali alphabet with Gulnahar' and 'The best part was learning to speak French, Hebrew, Malay and Urdu'.

At pre-test, 9.7 per cent of the children offered to tell or teach about their language (category 6). Comments ranged from 'I would like to tell my teacher about my language' (Pushtu) to specific offers to teach Scottish, sign language, Malay, Punjabi and Urdu.

At pre-test, 13 statements were made which reflected attitude (categories 7 and 8). The one negative response was 'I would like to know why do we have different languages, why can't we just learn one language?' by an English-only speaker. Statements reflecting a positive attitude included 'I would like to tell the teacher that it is important for children to learn different languages' (English speaker), 'I would like to learn how to help and make someone else understand me, so if someone is in trouble I could help' (Urdu speaker), 'I would like to learn Malay so I could speak to Zaid properly' and 'I think it would be fun to understand other people's language' (English speaker).

At post-test, 19 statements were made which reflected the children's attitudes. There were no negative statements. Statements reflecting a positive attitude were similar to the pre-test and included 'It's important to learn other languages' (English speaker) and 'more exciting than just speaking English all the time' (English speaker).

At pre-test only six statements of a general nature were made about language learning (category 9). They included 'I would like to learn other languages/write other languages'.

At post-test 11 statements were made, including 'I liked learning about other languages', 'I like language awareness' and 'I like learning how people talk to each other'.

The low percentage of comments in category 9 (4.8 per cent at pre-test and 8.9 per cent at post-test) reflects a low level of knowledge about languages generally in this inner-city school. Few children have had experiences involving the opportunity to learn a language; some have had holidays abroad and others have older siblings who are learning French at secondary school. I think this low response is due not to a disinterest in language learning, as Batters (1988) maintains, but to a lack of awareness generally about what opportunities are available for language learning.

At pre-test, 4 per cent of children showed their knowledge of language (category 10). Statements included 'We could not say some words in our language but in English you could', 'I know how to count in Malay' and 'Indonesian is written the same as English'.

At post-test, however, 13.8 per cent of the children showed their own knowledge. Their comments ranged from 'I can count in French' and 'I know how to write Arabic' to ' "Sun" in Malay is *matchari*' and 'In Indonesia we go to school at 6 o'clock'.

Summary of the invitations to comment

Analysis of the data concerning the children's comments in the open-ended section of the questionnaire shows a rise in interest in learning community languages and a decline in learning French at the post-test. There was also a rise at post-test in the number of children offering to share their knowledge with others. This would seem to validate the teaching of language awareness to raise the self-esteem and confidence of ethnic minority pupils. At post-test, there were also increases in positive attitude statements, no negative attitude statements and a significant increase in statements which reflected the children's own knowledge. This would lead me to conclude that the project helped children to have greater pride in their community language and led to an increase in knowledge about languages generally.

Difficulties experienced with the children's questionnaire

The major drawback we found with the questionnaire was the eliciting of responses individually. We asked the children to fill in the questionnaire by themselves without collaborating. Some of the children found this impossible to do. The school has a policy of encouraging children to work collaboratively and it is obviously very effective, since it was difficult for them to work alone. The lower-ability readers in Year 3 had to receive help in reading the questionnaire. Support teachers effected this help by working with the children in small groups; this method also led to collaborative work.

Occasionally, children missed out a question or spoilt their answer, so the total does not equal the sample of 161 children. This tended to happen when the answer was multi-choice and a child might have become confused. Simplicity was the aim in compiling the questionnaire but, even so, having a typed sheet before them was daunting to the younger children.

Some children did not write any comments at the end of the questionnaire. The majority of children made a limited response and wrote comments such as 'I would like to learn French'. Many children found it difficult to respond to these requests. This was the first time that such a project had been carried out, and they were not used to responding either specifically or generally when their opinions about language were asked for.

Field notes

These were used to record observations by class and support teachers during the language awareness lessons. A formula for these notes was provided; this enabled teachers to concentrate on salient points and also made data analysis more effective.

Teachers were asked to make notes recording instances of the following:

1a   Lack of awareness of other languages or speakers of other languages.
 b   Growing awareness of other languages or speakers of other languages.
2a   Negative remarks about other languages or speakers of other languages.
 b   Positive remarks about other languages or speakers of other languages.
3a   Instances noted of a lowering of self-esteem of speakers.
 b   Instances of a raising of self-esteem of speakers.
4a   Least successful aspects of the lesson.
 b   Most successful aspects of the lesson.

Here is a written appraisal given to me by one of the class teachers involved in the project:

> This has been a very useful exercise. I am sure it has raised awareness generally in the class. I know it has raised the self-esteem of some of the children and has created a great deal of interest. We have been able to incorporate this in our topic work on Weather and Seasons with children writing words in Malay, Urdu and Arabic as well as English.

She added that

> Various books have been brought in from home, one of them being a book with 'weather' pictures in Arabic. One boy went to great lengths to write a list of 'Winter' words in Urdu.

I asked him if all the spellings were correct and he said they were. We proceeded to display them, whereupon two Malaysian girls studied them carefully and told him he had got one of his spellings wrong. They can read and write Arabic! He went to look closely and decided they were right.

And finally,

All this has definitely improved communication between the children, and I have also learned a lot and thoroughly enjoyed it.

Teachers reported through their field notes a definite raising of children's awareness of their own, each other's and world languages. The children became more aware of the similarities and differences of languages and scripts. There was strong evidence of empathy as well as some evidence of ethnocentrism. Teachers noted many positive remarks about the language awareness lessons themselves. There was reported a gradual raising of self-esteem of some of the bilingual children and growing confidence in speaking their community language once they realized it would be valued. Teachers also noted many comments of admiration of children who were multilingual.

Difficulties experienced with using the field notes

Teachers and support teachers were able to keep these notes as the lesson was progressing because the team teaching situation allowed time for one teacher to take over the whole class for short periods. Teachers did not then have to write up the notes after the lesson. This worked well with the majority of staff, but two teachers found that they did not have the opportunity to write their notes in the lesson time. The problem of a time lapse occurring between the event and its recording may have arisen when their notes were completed after the lesson. 'The greater the time-lapse between the event and recording it, the more difficult it becomes to reconstruct problems and responses accurately and retain conscious awareness of one's original thinking' (Hopkins, 1985, p. 27).

For my part, as co-ordinator, it was very tempting to ask class teachers each week if the field notes were being completed, but I felt I could have been accused of 'hassling' them if I had done so. It was essential, however, that I checked with the other support teachers that the field notes were being filled in. It was easier to 'hassle' my own colleagues in the team than colleagues in the school.

Staff discussion

Purpose

The purpose of discussion by the whole staff after the project was completed was threefold:

- To make all staff in the school aware of the project.
- To share the strategies and teaching ideas used in the project.
- To give an opportunity for the staff involved to voice their reactions to the project generally.

The discussion took place during normal staff meeting time. I negotiated with the headteacher for this time. I asked a member of the management team not involved in the project to make notes. She agreed and I suggested that the notes could be made under two headings: positive and negative comments by the staff involved in the project. She was able to do this very effectively.

I compiled an agenda to lead the discussion so that everyone involved was given a chance to contribute as much or as little as they wished, and I suggested to the staff that we confine our discussion to strategies and feedbacks to the project rather than the ways of collecting data, as time was limited.

In conclusion, I drew the staff's attention to the resources now available and suggested that statements concerning the languages of the children might be included in any future equal opportunities policies drawn up by the school staff. The results are shown in Figure 1.3 below.

Difficulties experienced during discussion

The major difficulty was the limited amount of time owing to other pressing demands on staff meeting time. I felt the discussion could have gone on for longer and explored related issues, such as parental involvement in projects like this and policy statements which might be included in future policy documents.

Positive statements from staff during discussion
- 'Number line showed children working from right to left'
- 'Children enjoyed, and became engrossed in the activity'
- 'The children were interested and impressed that their peers can speak other languages'
- 'Self-esteem of bilingual children was raised'
- 'Since the project the bilingual children are more willing to talk'
- 'The children now know what their mother tongue is'
- 'They now know which language they speak in various locations'
- 'The project fostered co-operative learning'
- 'Children's writing [in any language] improved'
- 'Parents noticed labels in different scripts. This led to discussion'
- 'Staff awareness raised'
- 'Staff have learned from project'
- 'Staff and children enjoyed taking part'
- 'No one had an advantage [all beginners] when looking at Hebrew'
- 'Staff discussion of project raised other issues'

Negative statements from staff during discussion
- 'Monolingual children felt inferior'
- 'Children found copying the script difficult'
- 'Children were embarrassed at first, to talk about their mother tongue'

Figure 1.3 *Results from staff discussion.*

Summary of the analysis of staff discussion

The discussion revealed that there were overwhelmingly positive results from the language awareness project (Figure 1.3), the most satisfying being that staff awareness had been raised and that the teachers felt *they*, as well as the children, had learnt from this project.

There were three negative comments during the staff discussion. During the survey of languages in the classrooms, the monolingual children felt inferior until teachers included the use of dialect and 'holiday' languages in the survey. 'Holiday' languages were languages of which perhaps only a few words were known, but which were included in the surveys because of the need to make *all* children feel their languages were valued.

The second negative comment was due to teachers' lack of knowledge of the level of literacy in community languages for each child. Perhaps our survey into languages should have included the ability to read and write as well as to speak community languages. Teachers would then have been aware of the difficulties some children experienced in writing the scripts.

The third negative comment revealed embarrassment by some children to talk about, and in, their community language. Field notes also revealed this. Teachers reported growing confidence and raising of self-esteem, which points to a lack of confidence and lower self-esteem initially. As teachers become more aware of their children's abilities, and as community languages become valued in the classroom, so children will lose their embarrassment. It is to be hoped that languages will become part of the classroom curriculum and not something exotic or different.

Views of staff involved in the project

In accordance with the principles of action research, adopted for the purpose of this study, staff and management were asked to read the summary of the data collected and were invited to draw their own conclusions. These are some of their comments:

> *Headteacher:* I have enjoyed reading this. I think it has given the school a good yardstick to work by and has acted as a bench-mark on aspects related to attitudes among the mixture of children.

> *Deputy headteacher:* Integrated cross-curricular work on language awareness should be built into topic/curriculum each year and should be a natural part of the school year and school environment. Signs could be in different languages, those of the school and others. Staff respect the children more and vice versa if they know they speak more languages.

The deputy headteacher was very concerned about the self-image of monolingual children and would welcome more suggestions to enhance the self-esteem of monolinguists.

> *ESL support teacher A:* Should be ongoing throughout the school, beginning with the younger children. It should also be taught in a structured way, as are other areas of the curriculum, and not just left to chance.

> *ESL support teacher B:* Encouraging results at pre-test show that the children are receiving positive messages. Much groundwork has already been done in an area where prejudice

has been a problem in the past and still is in a number of cases. Are the children beginning to think for themselves?

Can we be sure however that some children answered the questionnaires honestly or were they writing answers that they thought were expected of them?

It would be interesting to note any changes if the questionnaire was administered in an environment other than school.

One *class teacher* was quite sure that 'Data back up the staff comments and feelings. The data have helped to reduce racism and have been of value.' She went on to add:

I feel that this was a very valuable exercise that raised the children's awareness of the other languages spoken in their class. My class found the written work difficult but this more reflected the ability of my particular class than the level of the prepared work. I did notice that some of the white children felt slightly inferior when they realized that some of the other children could speak two or three languages [when filling in a graph]. It also raised the children's awareness of which languages they spoke – some of my ethnic children did not know which language they spoke. I think that it would be a valuable exercise to be repeated regularly, e.g. once a year. It certainly raised the ethnic children's self-esteem.

Another teacher stated:

It is quite obvious that the work undertaken in school for this project heightened the children's awareness of other languages and cultures. However, maybe it was only a short-term result. Might it not perhaps be worth thinking about having a regular time (maybe a week/2 weeks) each year, given over, at least in part of the school, to work which will heighten the children's and staff's awareness? In this way maybe any new members of staff can be introduced to our values regarding a very important part of the school's life.

Summary of staff conclusions

On the whole, members of staff thought that work on language awareness should be built into the curriculum, either as a short-term project or as part of the everyday life of the school. They generally felt that the project had raised the children's awareness both of other languages and of their own.

Concern was felt at the lowering of the self-esteem of the monolingual children; staff wanted more strategies to be worked out to counter this. One teacher wondered whether the questionnaires had been answered honestly, but other data, analysed from field notes and staff comments, showed that awareness of languages had been raised, that the self-esteem of the bilingual children was greater and that staff thought the project had been successful.

I would refer the reader back to the title of this study: 'Can monolingual teachers teach language awareness successfully to the benefit of all children?' I suggest that this investigation has shown that monolingual teachers *can* teach language awareness successfully. It appears, however, that this has not been to the benefit of all children, and further work must be undertaken to ensure that the self-esteem of monolingual children is not lowered during projects of this kind.

However, if better race relations can be fostered by knowledge of each other's languages then there *are* benefits for *all* children, and if projects like this are 'a means of bridging barriers between pupils in the same class' (Garrett and James, 1989) then all children will have benefited. Carrington and Troyna (1989) suggest that collaborative action research projects, as opposed to traditional research, may provide the basis for research on 'race'. Changes can be fostered during the course of the research process. They also maintain that 'in planning, evaluating and appraising an initiative *with* teachers, researchers would find themselves in a position where they could intervene directly to influence attitudes and behaviour' (p. 22).

I submit in conclusion an additional comment by the head teacher: 'I feel carefully monitored projects like this improve a school's opportunity to achieve equality in a relatively non-threatening way.'

REFERENCES

Batters, J. D. (1988) Pupil and teacher perceptions of foreign language teaching. Ph.D. thesis, University of Bath.

Bourne, J. (1989) *Moving into the Mainstream: LEA Provision for Bilingual Pupils*. Windsor: NFER/Nelson.

Carrington, B. and Troyna, B. (1989) 'Whose side are we on?' Ethical dilemmas in research on race and education. In R. Burgess (ed.), *Ethical Dilemmas in Educational Research*. Lewes: Falmer.

Cohen, L., and Manion, L. (1980) *Research Methods in Education*, London: Croom Helm.

DES (1988) *English for Ages 5 to 11* (Cox Report). London: HMSO.

Edwards, V. (1983) *Language in Multicultural Classrooms*. London: Batsford Academic.

Elliott, J., and Partington, D. (1975) *Three Points of View in the Classroom* (*Ford Teaching Project*), Cambridge Institute of Education.

Fitzpatrick, F. (1987) *The Open Door*. Clevedon, Avon: Multilingual Matters.

Garrett, P., and James, C. (1989) Diversity and common ground in language awareness. *Baal Seminar on Language Awareness*, University College of North Wales, Bangor.

Gregory, A., and Woollard, N. (1984) *Looking into Language: Diversity in the Classroom*. Stoke-on-Trent: Trentham Books.

Hawkins, E. (1984) *Awareness of Language: An Introduction*. Cambridge: Cambridge University Press.

Honeyford, R. (1988) *Disintegration towards a Non-racist Society*. London: Claridge Press.

Hopkins, D. (1985) *A Teacher's Guide to Classroom Research*. Buckingham: Open University Press.

Houlton, D. (1985) *All Our Languages: A Handbook for the Multilingual Classroom*. London: Edward Arnold.

Houlton, D., and Willey, R. (1983) *Supporting Children's Bilingualism*. Harlow: Longman, for Schools Council.

Luzac Storytellers (various) Young Storytellers series. London: Middlesex Polytechnic.

Merchant, G. (1990) *Report for the Linguistic Diversity in the Primary School Project (LDIP) 1986–1989*. Nottingham University.

National Curriculum Council (1990) *A Rich Resource: Writing and Language Diversity* (*National Writing Project*). Walton-on-Thames: Nelson.

Rudduck, J. (1982) *Teachers in Partnership: Four Studies in In-service Collaboration*. Harlow: Longman, for Schools Council.

Schwartz, S. M., and Schwartz, G. G. (1985) Problems in participant observation. *American Journal of Sociology* 60, 343–54.

Stenhouse, L. (1982) The conduct, analysis and reporting of case study in educational research and evaluation. In R. McCormick (ed.), *Calling Education to Account*. London: Heinemann.

Swann, M. (1985) *Education for All*. London: HMSO.

Tansley, P. (1986) *Community Language in Primary School* (Report of SCDC Mother Tongue Project). Windsor: NFER/Nelson.

Tansley, P., et al.(1985) *Working with Many Languages*. London: SCDC [School Curriculum Development Committee] Publications.

University of London Institute of Education (1984) *Children's Languages Project*. London: Philograth Publications/Schools Council.

Chapter 2

Personal and Social Education: A Vehicle for Prejudice Reduction?

Lynn Powell

Research by Cook (1971), Leslie *et al.* (1972), Katz and Zalk (1978), De Vries and Slavin (1978), Aronson and Osherow (1980) and Sharan (1985) seems to indicate that interventions involving behavioural modification may reduce racial prejudice. Carrington and Short (1991) suggest that teaching the principles of stereotyping, rather than teaching directly against racism, may be successful in reducing prejudice in children. Balch and Paulsen (1979) suggest that the optimum gains in prejudice reduction are likely to occur when the child is most malleable: that is, during the early years. However, Aboud (1988) contends that this may not necessarily be so, provided that the strategies employed are pitched at the appropriate level of cognitive development.

This study takes account of previous research and attempts to investigate the effectiveness of a module in personal and social education (PSE) in reducing racial prejudice in a group of 14-year-old pupils in an almost all-white urban comprehensive school. The module comprises active learning techniques and acknowledges the self-concept of the pupil as a starting point for any learning situation focusing on personal development. Both cognitive and affective strategies were involved, and much of the intervention was focused on the pupils' acquisition of principles and the ability to transfer the learning to other contexts.

The results of the investigation seem to indicate that this type of intervention, employing the chosen methodology and relating it to PSE, may be successful in reducing racial prejudice in some pupils of this age.

INTRODUCTION

The research project was carried out in 1991 in Larkhill School – a 10-form entry 11–16 urban comprehensive in a largely white catchment area in the north-east of England, drawing from both private and council housing developments and a run-down mining community.

The school equal opportunities working party has produced a policy for dealing with racist incidents and has also worked with staff on raising awareness of race and gender stereotyping, and examining course materials for race and gender bias. The school's aims reflect this concern, and, to quote the school brochure, are based on 'the principles that all pupils are valued equally and are entitled to a maximum sense of success; that they are afforded equality of opportunity regardless of class, race, colour, gender, religion or disability . . .'.

The pastoral system in the school is a 'year' system, with a head and two assistant heads of year attached to each academic year.

Most of what is generally described as personal and social education (hereafter referred to as PSE) is delivered in the tutorial period between 9.00 and 9.30 a.m. on four days each week. This accounts for 10 per cent of the timetable, and includes registration and administration time plus a weekly assembly for each individual year group.

There is little in the school's five-year PSE programme relating directly to equal opportunities or issues of stereotyping or bias; nor is there anything directly aimed at increasing tolerance or reducing prejudice. Previous research by the school's equal opportunities working party indicates that, although there is some factual multicultural content in certain curriculum areas, little is done to tackle issues of prejudice and racism.

The log-book for recording incidents of a racist nature (kept by each head of year) testifies to the incidence of racial prejudice within the school. Although there has been a decline in the number of such incidents since the development of the policy, there are still sufficient entries to suggest that not enough is being done to educate against such behaviour.

Because I regard PSE as the responsibility of all staff, and believe that issues such as tolerance, respect for others, justice and equality – although hopefully implicit in any 'good' education, and in the kind of caring community that we would like Larkhill to be – are too important to be transmitted via the 'hidden' curriculum alone, I decided to investigate the use of PSE as a vehicle for exploring the issue of stereotyping with my own tutor group. I hoped that it might effect a reduction in prejudice and an overall increase in tolerance levels in some pupils.

PERSONAL AND SOCIAL EDUCATION

The inquiry was set against the background of the Education Reform Act and the directive that PSE should pervade every area of the National Curriculum. However, there are many differing views of what actually constitutes PSE and it is only possible to discuss here a selection of the materials investigated. While writers such as Button (1982), Baldwin and Wells (1980) and Hopson and Scally (1986) stress actual skills, others, such as McPhail (1982) and Wakeman (1984), feel the need of a moral framework in PSE. Certainly there is a strong argument that, where attitudes and values are involved, then so, of necessity, is morality.

The DES publication *Personal and Social Education from 5–16: Curriculum Matters 14* (DES, 1989), while clearly defining the place of PSE in the curriculum and the responsibility of every teacher in its delivery, does *not* prescribe content. Instead it describes some of the teaching and learning styles to be experienced in the delivery of PSE and outlines a set of objectives. It lists the personal qualities and attitudes that schools should be seeking to foster in all pupils, and a set of cognitive, affective and conative aims related to personal, social *and* moral development.

Leicester has argued the case for an anti-racist perspective to the teaching of PSE. She describes the congruity of aims of PSE and multicultural education, and the need for a 'person-centred approach to education', since 'it is not minds but persons that we are educating' (Leicester, 1989). Perhaps more than any other writer in the field of multicultural education, she has seen the potential for working to change attitudes within the context of PSE.

In a later paper (Leicester, 1990) she suggests the need for synthesis – for integrating the core of PSE and multicultural education to produce a new perspective, which would teach pupils to understand how institutional racism and structural discrimination is (often unwittingly) perpetuated.

There are many similarities in the methodology recommended by anti-racist theorists and that in general usage in the teaching of PSE.

Mindful of the criteria identified in the literature surveyed and of the absence of any one published resource which would meet my needs, I devised a module for use with my own Year 10 tutor group, borrowing some materials from *Picturing People: Challenging Stereotypes* (Manchester Development Education Project, 1988), from *Teaching Against Prejudice and Stereotyping* (Evans and Thomas, 1986) and from *Family Lifestyles* (Braun and Eisenstadt, 1985).

RESEARCH DESIGN

Action research is a style of research which investigates problems/situations identified by practitioners with the aim of changing and improving practice. It is dynamic – the changing and researching are simultaneous processes. One of its chief characteristics is that it seeks to define a problem within a specific context and then attempts to solve it in that same context (see Cohen and Manion, 1980). It is concerned not with obtaining generalizable knowledge, but rather with the acquisition of precise knowledge for a specific purpose.

Action research utilizes both quantitative and qualitative data collection methods, which makes it an accessible research style for teachers like myself with no background in either statistics or experimental procedures. It does not have the limitations implicit in the grounded theory of ethnographic research, which relies on hypotheses being derived from the data. It allows for hypotheses to be formulated at the outset, as well as the possibility of their subsequent modification during the research project (see Altrichter and Posch, 1989).

To me as teacher-researcher in my own school, therefore, an action research model was the most obvious style of research, since it would allow for ongoing review and modification during the teaching–learning process. Larkhill School already has an established teacher-researcher tradition and action research models have been used previously in curriculum development and review, so my decision was not likely to be running counter to the school's culture. The collaborative nature of this style of research and the scope it offers for self-evaluation made it all the more attractive.

The aim of the study was to provide both a knowledge input and an experiential input via PSE on the subject of stereotyping. The method used, presupposes that pupils will learn to transfer the knowledge acquired in one specific context to other contexts and arrive at an understanding of the underlying principles of stereotyping.

The research was more exploratory than hypothesis testing in nature, but nevertheless I had certain expectations with regard to its outcome:

- That the factual knowledge input would have an effect on reducing prejudice.
- That there would be an overall increase in tolerance levels.
- That principles learned from a specific context would then be applied to other contexts.
- That there would be an increased understanding of the role of the media in the process of stereotyping.

A mixture of qualitative and quantitative data collection methods was chosen, to try to ensure reliability and rigour and to give a degree of triangulation. The research design comprised the following components:

- Questionnaire on PSE to staff.
- Group interviews on PSE with tutor group.
- Attitude measure pre-test.
- Intervention – PSE module.
- Attitude measure post-test.
- Evaluation of module by tutor group.
- Discussion by pupils of video recording of a lesson.
- Interview with colleague who taught module.
- Field notes, both subjective and descriptive.
- Documentation.

RESEARCH METHOD

Questionnaires

Questionnaires seemed to offer the quickest method of obtaining information about staff perceptions of PSE within the school. Previous experience had shown that my colleagues were very willing to provide information by this means (provided that they are sure of the purpose behind the exercise) and that they would be interested in the findings. I had also found that they respond most positively to open-ended questions. The only real difficulty experienced previously was ensuring that they all met deadlines, but since only nine were involved, this was not to be a problem.

The questionnaire was administered first in a pilot form to two male and two female staff in the Year 10 pastoral team. I received returns from three of them and, on the basis of some very detailed and constructive answers to one item, I rephrased the question to give additional guidance. The questionnaire in its final format was given to the remaining staff in the year group – two male and three female – all of whom returned completed questionnaires.

Since the content of the questionnaire was not changed radically from the pilot to the final format, the information given by all eight respondents was used in the analysis.

Pupil evaluation

I decided to use a variation of the questionnaire format with my tutor group to evaluate the module *after* teaching. Similar evaluations had previously been used with the group after tutorial work on drugs and AIDS.

Interviews with pupils

In order to balance the staff views obtained in the questionnaire on PSE, and to add a qualitative dimension to the data, I interviewed members of my tutor group. I selected a group interview format as this might encourage pupils to be more responsive than on their own (see Woods, 1979).

I recorded two interviews, the first of which had been intended to be a pilot. However, because the second interview was identical in format to the first, and because the first had yielded the more interesting results, I utilized the information from both.

Sample

The first group was selected as follows: first and last boys, first and last girls on the register. The second group was selected as follows: class list in alphabetical order (*not* boys then girls), every fifth pupil selected (two boys and two girls).

Discussion of video recording of a lesson

Two boys and two girls were selected and asked to record a discussion while watching the video recording of a lesson filmed by my colleague a couple of weeks previously. Briefly, the lesson involved brainstorming the class's own images of Holland and the Dutch; brainstorming what images they thought the Dutch might have of Britain and the British; checking out the latter by reference to duplicated sheets of images of Britain produced by Dutch teenagers; and then comparing and discussing the different images and where they had come from. The pupils controlled both the cassette recorder and the video recorder themselves, and were thus able to pause/rewind the video and edit the cassette recording as they wished.

Field notes

Since I was working in a subjective capacity as teacher-researcher, I decided to record my observations on the module. I made jottings directly after each session, comprising comments made by individuals and a note of how successful or otherwise a particular session had been, and typed these up every evening. I also kept a log of the progress of the research, recording dates, methodology, communication with colleagues and constraints.

Replication

Full-scale replication of the process with another tutorial group was not viable, but I accepted a colleague's offer to use my PSE module with her own group.

Attitude measure

Despite the well-documented difficulties associated with measuring attitude accurately (see Oppenheim, 1966; Henerson *et al.*, 1978), I nevertheless felt it necessary to use a fairly objective method of assessing levels of prejudice.

I eventually decided to use a five-point Likert scale with statements relating to prejudicial views and stereotypes as both pre- and post-test. Not finding one suitable to my purpose in time, I was compelled to construct my own (see Powell, 1991).

Having decided that the main focus of my teaching should be to work on stereotypes, it seemed logical that my construct should relate to the readiness with which my pupils adhered to/accepted stereotypical views. A person displaying strong racial prejudice would, in the terms of my attitude measure, display ethnocentricity, a tendency to agree with generalizations and stereotyped views, and a disinclination to view people as individuals.

Attitude measure pilot

To define the area of my construct I isolated 10 areas which feature in ethnocentric comments and stereotypes indicative of racial prejudice. These were as follows:

* Religion.
* Family life.
* Culture/life-style.
* Clothes.
* Education.
* Employment.
* Housing.
* Crime rate.
* Numbers of ethnic minorities in this country.
* Exploitation of the welfare states.

I devised 60 statements – 30 with a positive and 30 with a negative bias (i.e. 30 where 'strongly agree' would be indicative of a high level of prejudice and 30 where 'strongly disagree' would indicate a high level of prejudice).

The pilot was administered by the assistant head of Year 10 with the tutor group of a friend (in an attempt to reduce the 'experimenter effect') who had shown an interest in my research and agreed to co-operate. This group is the same age and of a similar social mix to my own.

Twenty items were identified for the pre-test. Interestingly, after all the time spent producing a balanced pilot with an equal number of positively and negatively weighted statements covering the 10 areas I had identified in proportion to their (assumed)

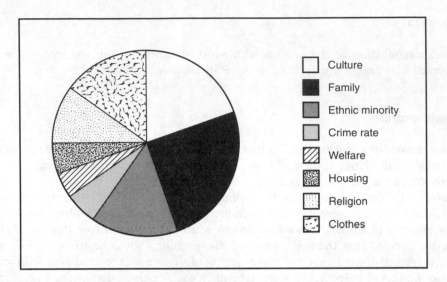

Figure 2.1 *The eight areas of content to be covered in the attitude measure pre- and post-test, indicating the proportion of the questionnaire devoted to each.*

significance, the resulting set of statements now contained *14* where 'strongly agree' indicated a high degree of prejudice and only *6* where 'strongly disagree' was indicative of a highly prejudiced attitude.

Attitude measure pre-test

The 20 statements used in the pre-test were those which had discriminated best in the pilot. The pre-test was administered under similar conditions to the pilot, but this time with my own tutor group. (Figure 2.1 shows areas of content of attitude measure pre- and post-test.)

Attitude measure post-test

The post-test, used to assess whether there had been any reduction in prejudice after the teaching of the PSE module, was identical in content and format to the pre-test, and was administered under similar conditions.

Intervention

The intervention, whose effects on the attitudes of my tutor group I sought to measure, consisted of a PSE module of some 21 sessions (only 20 of which were actually used, since I decided, after I had started teaching, that session 6 was not likely to be successful with my tutor group at this stage).

The whole inquiry took from November 1990 to October 1991.

Table 2.1. *Itemized breakdown of scores in attitude measure pre-test.*

Item	SD	D	U	A	SA
1	6	8	2	4	3
2	0	2	2	10	9
3	2	2	3	9	7
4	2	5	5	9	2
5	2	4	12	4	1
6	4	2	12	5	0
7	1	4	10	6	2
8	2	4	5	7	5
9	0	3	12	4	4
10	2	4	10	5	2
11	0	9	7	6	1
12	11	8	1	3	0
13	10	4	2	5	2
14	1	4	2	9	7
15	9	8	4	1	1
16	4	10	7	2	0
17	4	3	12	2	2
18	1	8	5	6	3
19	1	1	15	5	1
20	0	4	6	8	5

SD = 'strongly disagree'; D = 'disagree'; U = 'uncertain'; A = 'agree'; SA = 'strongly agree'.

RESEARCH RESULTS

Results of questionnaires given to Year 10 tutorial staff

The analysis of the questionnaires revealed that Year 10 staff felt a dissatisfaction with the resourcing of PSE and a general lack of confidence in their ability to deliver a subject for which most had received little or no training.

Results of racial attitude pre-test

There were 20 questions on a five-point Likert scale, which had the following categories: strongly disagree, disagree, uncertain, agree, strongly agree. The scores were calculated for each member of the group, according to the wording of the question. (Some questions required a 'strongly disagree' answer to indicate a high level of racial prejudice, while others required a 'strongly agree' answer.)

Each individual question was marked on the basis of 1 to 5 points from the least to the most prejudiced (see Appendix for a list of questions). On questions 1, 4, 5, 6, 8, 9, 10, 12, 13, 15, 16, 17, 18 and 19 'strongly disagree' represents a low level of prejudice, and on questions 2, 3, 7, 11, 14 and 20 'strongly agree' equates with a low level of prejudice. (Table 2.1 gives a breakdown of pre-test scores.)

The following questions proved to be the best discriminators, yielding results which covered the full range on the 1 to 5 point scale: 1, 3, 4, 5, 7, 8, 10, 13, 14, 17, 18, 19.

Since there were 20 questions, the lowest possible score was $20 \times 1 = 20$ and the highest possible score was $20 \times 5 = 100$. The lowest score achieved was 36 and the

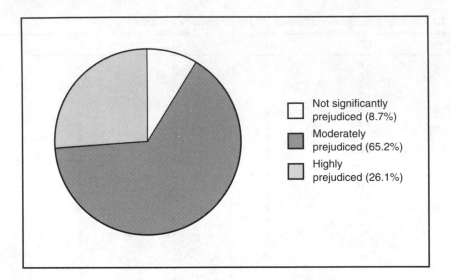

Figure 2.2   *Results of the attitude measure pre-test expressed in percentages.*

highest 77. Seventeen pupils achieved a score of less than 60. The mean score for the group was 53.4 $\left(\bar{x} = \dfrac{\Sigma x}{n} \right)$.

The categories used to differentiate pupils were as follows:

20–40 indicates not significantly prejudiced.
41–60 indicates moderately prejudiced.
61–80 indicates highly prejudiced.
81–100 indicates very highly prejudiced.

The results were as follows:

20–40	41–60	61–80	81–100
2	15	6	0

Calculated on a percentage basis, therefore:

 8.7% came out as being not significantly prejudiced.
65.2% came out as being moderately prejudiced.
26.1% came out as being highly prejudiced.
 0.0% came out as being very highly prejudiced.

Nearly two-thirds of the class (i.e. 15 pupils) were identified as being in the 'moderately prejudiced' category, none came into the 'very highly prejudiced' category and there were three times as many (6) in the 'highly prejudiced' category as in the 'not significantly prejudiced' category (2). (See Figure 2.2.)

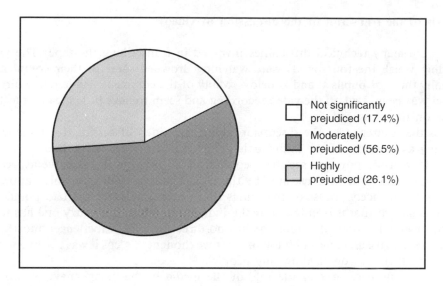

Not significantly prejudiced (17.4%)

Moderately prejudiced (56.5%)

Highly prejudiced (26.1%)

Figure 2.3 *Results of the attitude measure post-test expressed in percentages.*

Results of racial attitude post-test

The lowest score achieved was 30 and the highest was 75. Seventeen pupils scored below 60. The mean score for the group was 51.9 $\left(\bar{x} = \dfrac{\Sigma x}{n} \right)$.

The same categories were used to differentiate as in the pre-test and the results were as follows:

20–40	41–60	61–80	81–100
4	13	6	0

This shows that there were now 4 pupils out of 23 in the 'not significantly prejudiced' category (compared with 2 in the pre-test), 13 in the 'moderately prejudiced' category (compared with 15 in the pre-test), 6 in the 'highly prejudiced' category (the same as in the pre-test) and 0 pupils in the 'very highly prejudiced' category (the same as in the pre-test).

Calculated on a percentage basis, therefore:

17.4% came out as being not significantly prejudiced.
56.5% came out as being moderately prejudiced.
26.1% came out as being highly prejudiced.
 0.0% came out as being very highly prejudiced.

Slightly over half the class (i.e. 13 pupils) were identified as being in the 'moderately prejudiced' category, none as being in the 'very highly prejudiced' category, and there were two-thirds as many in the 'not significantly prejudiced' category (4) as there were in the 'highly prejudiced' category (6). (See Figure 2.3.)

The difference in the mean scores shows a reduction of 1.5.

Analysis of the transcript of the discussion of video

There were many technical difficulties involved in transcribing the tape. The video recording which the four pupils were watching drowned some of their comments – especially those of pupils **C** and **D** below. Many of the comments made relate directly to what was being said on the video recording and seem to have little meaning as they appear on the transcript.

From the transcript of the discussion about the video of session 16, I made the following assessments of the individuals involved and of their attitudes.

A, a 15-year-old boy, can see that people tend to focus on the negative aspects of a different culture, as demonstrated by the Dutch images of Britain which appeared on the printed sheets. 'Most of the things that's been said's like the bad points.'

He is adamant that it is unfair to make judgements about a country one has never visited, or about people of whom one has no direct personal experience: 'most of us couldn't really give an honest opinion of what we thought . . . 'cos it was . . . like – we'd never been there . . . don't know any people'.

He shows an awareness of the role of the media in the 'image-making' process, and lays much of the blame for the negative images held by the Dutch teenagers on the unfavourable coverage given to Britain and the British in the press. He is able to relate this particular lesson to other work done on stereotypes: 'like when they were on about the drugs and that. It'd only be a few people, but they base that on all teenagers, don't they?'

He realizes that stereotyping in this way is unjust, and apparently he feels strongly about it because during the group role-playing activity of session 9 he pointed out that he did not agree with people who claimed that black people were taking over the country. He said there were very few of them over here, and that it was rubbish to suggest that they should be 'sent back to where they had come from' because most of them were born here anyway. (Further information may be found in field notes to session 9 in Powell, 1991, Appendix 18.)

B is a girl aged 14 years. She realizes that people's images of another culture or country are based on what is well known or well publicized and not necessarily on the truth: 'They all seem to pick on one point and that seems to be things that are in London . . . things that are well known.'

She has grasped that people find 'strange' and view negatively that which differs from their own culture or experience, and she explains to **C** that this is why the Dutch have singled out school uniform as one of their 'images' of Britain: 'They don't wear uniform, though. That's why they think that we're strange.'

She points out that the images put forward by the class as shown on the video are stereotyped, traditional features of Holland, and that there is more to the Dutch than this: 'The things that we've picked on have been traditional, if you like, for years – like clogs . . . and that's not the half of it.'

C is a boy aged 15 years. He makes the point that the images of Britain put forward by the Dutch will necessarily be inaccurate, as they are not based on personal experience. Equally, he accepts the fact that the views of his own classmates are limited by the same absence of direct personal experience. This relates back to the work done in sessions 6 and 7 on the uniqueness of every individual and the necessity of basing one's judgements on one's own experience of an individual. The point had been made in the discussion at the end of session 7 that the fact of actually *knowing* someone was what made the difference between having a negative and a positive view, and that the positive view was generally reserved for individuals while the negative view was applied to groups. **C**, more than the others in the group, found the comments by some of the Dutch teenagers about the way British teenagers dress unacceptable: 'I didn't like the images the Dutch had of you. Actually, I find that *very, very* offensive . . . but they were *wrong*.'

This seems to have made quite an impression on him, since he also refers to it on the evaluation sheet. He makes the connection between the various forms of stereo-typing in the different sections of the module and relates this to the issue of racism: 'I think that all people, if there's something bad about a black person in the news, they brand everybody that's black with the same mark.'

D is a 15-year-old girl. Like the other three, she has no illusions about the role of the media in perpetuating national stereotypes: 'If there was something in the news about somebody and it was bad, then everybody else thinks that the rest of the people are like that – the lot of them are bad.'

She has been able to transfer the learning about bias in the press from the specific context of young people as examined in sessions 13 and 14 to a different context, and has therefore learned to generalize – to take the knowledge acquired in one specific context and reapply it to a different context (see Bruner, 1960).

Analysis of pupil evaluation of the PSE module

What have you enjoyed in this module and why?

There were 6 negative responses. The other responses were all fairly positive and some were quite specific. Several seemed to have enjoyed most of the module. One person particularly enjoyed the 'games' – presumably the labelling and the role-playing of sessions 7, 8 and 18.

How much have you learned from this module?

Ten pupils felt that they had learned very little; 11 pupils felt that they had learned a fair amount; 2 pupils felt that they had learned a lot. Just over half the group seemed to think that they had gained in knowledge during the course of the module.

Is there anything that you have learned in this module that you found surprising or interesting?

One pupil had been struck by what she had learned from the evidence work of the final session: 'I found it quite surprising that if a black child has the same amount of qualifications as a white child, the white child gets the job and the black child is discriminated against.'

Table 2.2.   *Mean scores by category in pre-test and post-test.*

Category	Pre-test	Post-test
Not significantly prejudiced	38.0	34.5
Moderately prejudiced	50.3	49.7
Highly prejudiced	66.2	68.2

Has anything in this module made you change the way you think/behave?

Eleven pupils responded negatively to this question. The boy who wrote in his answer to question 4 that he had been surprised by what he had learned about nicknames and name-calling, has been made either to rethink or to modify his behaviour in this respect, as he refers to it again in his reply to this question.

The evidence work featured in the final session was apparently effective in the case of two people, who have absorbed the facts presented in the reports: 'I thought there was more blacks in this country than there is.' 'I think it is unfair on black people that they get turned down for so many interviews.' One of the girls was obviously moved to consider her own behaviour as a result of the 'Outsider' simulation exercise in session 18: 'when we did the work on putting people in different groups'.

Another of the girls, who during the course of the module had made some quite revealingly racist remarks, wrote: 'I don't think I'm quite as racist as I used to be.' This is particularly interesting, since at no time during the teaching of the module was the word 'racist' used by me; and, as far as I am aware, no one ever suggested that anyone in the group was guilty of racist attitudes or behaviour. It would appear that this pupil has come to an appreciation of her own attitude and has been aware of some modification taking place, during the course of the module. Another pupil wrote: 'The way I think about ethnic minorities has changed slightly.'

Discussion of results of the post-test

The mean scores for each of the categories in which pupils were included in both the pre-test and the post-test are shown in Table 2.2. It can be seen from the table that, while there is a *significant drop* in the mean score of the pupils in the 'not significantly prejudiced' category and a *slight drop* in the mean score of the pupils in the 'moderately prejudiced' category, there is a *gain* in the mean score of the pupils in the 'highly prejudiced' category. It would be interesting to speculate on reasons for this, but presumably the intervention is responsible for these changes. It is not unreasonable to assume that the type of intervention used raises the level of consciousness of the 'highly prejudiced' individuals, and causes them to reflect on their attitudes in a way which they may not have done previously. They may feel that their position is being questioned or even threatened, and this may cause them to 'dig their heels in'.

The significant drop in the mean score in the 'not significantly prejudiced' category (from 38.0 in the pre-test down to 34.5 in the post-test) may also be due to individuals reflecting on their attitudes, particularly if they have (a) deduced what my attitude is

Table 2.3. *Itemized breakdown of scores in attitude measure post-test.*

Item	SD	D	U	A	SA
1	4	7	2	7	3
2	2	1	3	4	13
3	1	4	4	9	5
4	2	7	9	4	1
5	2	2	14	4	1
6	5	3	6	5	4
7	0	2	4	12	5
8	3	11	2	2	5
9	2	3	12	3	3
10	1	5	8	2	7
11	1	6	6	8	2
12	6	11	4	0	2
13	10	8	1	1	3
14	1	2	3	7	10
15	10	8	4	0	1
16	7	8	8	0	0
17	5	7	8	2	1
18	1	6	4	5	7
19	2	3	12	5	1
20	3	2	7	7	4

Note: The above table, when compared with Table 2.1, shows quite clearly the gains and reductions on individual items.

vis-à-vis stereotyping and rasicm, and (b) if they perceive me as being 'a trustworthy source with high credibility' (see Thomas *et al.*, 1980).

It is evident that, while an intervention of the kind used may produce *some* change, it may be only temporary. It is possible that both the 'not significantly prejudiced' and the 'highly prejudiced' groups may return to their former scores after a longer period of time (see Katz and Zalk, 1978).

It is also evident that something other than a short-term intervention is necessary to effect a reduction in prejudice in those in the 'highly prejudiced' category – possibly an intervention involving some form of interdependent inter-ethnic contact and working towards common goals (see De Vries and Slavin, 1978; Sherif, 1956; Cook, 1971).

Comparison of pre- and post-test scores for individual items, and discussion of findings

As can be seen from Tables 2.1 and 2.3, some items demonstrate an overall reduction in prejudice, some an overall gain, and some a change at either extreme of the continuum.

I have assumed for the purpose of this analysis that, where scores differ between pre- and post-test, there is a minimum of movement of any one individual. I have assumed that any change in scores is likely to be as a result of a minimal attitude shift, rather than a radical change. It seems unlikely that an individual scoring 5 points in the pre-test will score only 1 in the post-test, whereas it seems quite feasible for an individual to have moved from an 'uncertain' to either an 'agree' or 'disagree' position.

While this would seem to be a fairly logical assumption, it does not take account of the fact that research into Festinger's theory of cognitive dissonance suggests that there may be a greater change in attitude by those whose initial position is at the greatest distance from the (perceived) position of the communicator (see Thomas *et al.*, 1980). Furthermore, as individual scores and levels of prejudice were not the focus of this study, there is no factual evidence on which to base this assumption.

Although it is difficult to draw any hard and fast conclusions on the basis of the above results, there appears to be some evidence that issues that were dealt with directly in the module and which offered definite factual evidence have had an effect on the attitudes of some pupils. There also seems to have been a slight increase in tolerance generally, with regard to issues such as life-style and religion, which may be as a result of an increased understanding of the process of stereotyping and its dangers. However, there is also a possibility that, despite the increase in the overall level of awareness of the role of the media in stereotyping, the press reporting on the Gulf War may still have had some influence on pupils' attitudes.

In sum, the major findings of the quantitative aspect of this study are therefore as follows:

- Factual evidence seems to have some effect on reducing prejudice in certain pupils in this age group.
- There has been some increase in overall tolerance in some pupils.
- Some pupils appear to have absorbed and understood the principles of stereotyping, and their ability to apply this learning to other issues has resulted in a reduction in prejudice.
- Despite a good grasp of the role of the media in perpetuating stereotypes, there is no guarantee that pupils will not fall prey to media influence.
- With regard to certain issues, pupils already demonstrating a high level of prejudice may suffer a hardening of attitudes after this type of intervention, particularly where a strong emphasis is placed on knowledge acquisition.

Evaluation of the findings from the analysis of the video discussion

It seems from an analysis of the transcript that some learning did take place during the teaching of the module. As evidence of this, I would draw attention to the following points which emerge from the analysis:

- The understanding of the role of the media in creating and furthering stereotypes.
- The understanding of the images put forward by both their own classmates and the Dutch, and where these images have come from.
- The recognition that the stereotyped views are inaccurate and based on deficient and second-hand information.
- The recognition that direct personal experience is the fairest way of assessing people.
- The ability to make the connection between the various forms of stereotyping and groups studied ('non-specific transfer': Bruner, 1960).

It may be that their own emotional response to the Dutch teenagers' opinions helped them to grasp the injustice of making judgements without direct personal experience, and the danger of basing one's opinions on the views and images portrayed in the media. I feel that this experience – Lynch's 'affective' learning (Lynch, 1987) – brought home the inaccuracies and generalizations inherent in stereotyping far better than any purely cognitive method would have done.

What has become apparent to me is the value of using video in this way, for a group to review its own behaviour and reflect on its own learning. Not only does it re-air the issues of the lesson in question, but it also heightens pupils' awareness of what has been learned and makes them more self-critical. I think that the four pupils involved in this session had their learning from the module itself reinforced in a way that the rest of the group did not.

THE REDUCTION OF PREJUDICE THROUGH PSE – THE MAIN FINDINGS OF THE INQUIRY

The findings of the research seem to suggest that the type of PSE module described, avoiding *direct* teaching against racism or reference to oppressed groups, but teaching the *principles* of stereotyping in other contexts, and employing both *cognitive* and *affective* learning strategies, may be successful to some degree in reducing prejudice in some pupils of this age (13–15). This also appears to be corroborated by recent research by Carrington and Short (1991) with children in primary schools.

While the intervention described did achieve a small measure of success, it may be more fruitful, with regard to the most highly prejudiced pupils, to use the module in conjunction with behavioural measures: for example, those described by Cook (1971), where prejudiced white individuals were required to work alongside and co-operate with black individuals. The research of Aronson and Osherow (1980), De Vries and Slavin (1978), Sharan (1985) and Johnson and Johnson (1975) variously seems to indicate that co-operative learning strategies in multi-ethnic classrooms bring about both improved academic development and an improvement in intergroup relations.

In a review of strategies for the modification and prevention of racial prejudice in children, Balch and Paulsen (1979) suggest that the earlier in a child's life prejudice reduction strategies are introduced, the more successful they are likely to be.

There is, nevertheless, a case to be made for using strategies with children of secondary age, provided that they are pitched at the appropriate level of cognitive development. In a recent study, Aboud (1988) argues that children up to the age of 7 are inevitably prejudiced because of their cognitive limitations, and that active educational intervention should begin as children reach that age, rather than before.

As a teacher of PSE to my own tutor group, my position is not dissimilar to that of the class teacher in the primary school, in that I see my tutor group every day and provide a focus for their learning. Work done by Carrington and Short (1991) with primary school pupils on promoting social justice was sufficiently encouraging to suggest replication on a larger scale, and perhaps curriculum interventions such as my own, following similar principles and over a sustained period, would also be worth replicating on a larger scale. My own experience leads me to conclude that PSE may well be a suitable vehicle for reducing prejudice.

The findings of the inquiry were encouraging, but one of the most exciting parts of it was collaborating with colleagues and pupils. The support, interest and help given throughout made the whole project a rewarding experience in terms of my own personal and professional development – worth undertaking for this reason alone.

APPENDIX

The 20 items used in the racial attitude measure pre- and post-test

1   Black people wear weird clothes in loud colours.
2   I wouldn't avoid making friends with someone who was a non-white.
3   Non-Christians should not be forced to attend Christian worship in schools.
4   Blacks, Asians and Chinese are swamping the country.
5   They cost us a fortune in social benefit.
6   Jews are greedy and mainly interested in making money.
7   If a black family moves into the street, it doesn't have any effect on house prices.
8   Anyone who lives in Britain should be made to conform to our way of life.
9   Afro-Caribbeans have great big families.
10 Asian food is disgusting.
11 The average non-white family is about the same size as the average white family.
12 Asians, Chinese and black people should be refused entry into Britain.
13 If they want to live in our country, they should wear the same kind of clothes as we do.
14 Everyone should be allowed to follow their own culture and way of life.
15 I don't think people should inter-marry; they should stick to their own kind.
16 They should be made to adopt the Christian faith, if they intend to stay in this country.
17 I would only marry a white person.
18 Asian girls should be made to wear the same clothes as English girls in school.
19 Jews are renowned for being dishonest.
20 We have no right to stop any ethnic group from coming to this country.

REFERENCES

Aboud, F. (1988) *Children and Prejudice*. London: Blackwell.
Altrichter, H., and Posch, P. (1989) Does the 'grounded theory' approach offer a guiding paradigm for teacher research? *Cambridge Journal of Education* 19(1), 21–31.
Aronson, E., and Osherow, N. (1980) Co-operation, prosocial behaviour, and academic performance in the desegregated classroom. *Applied Social Psychology Annual*, Vol. 1. London: Sage.
Balch, P., and Paulsen, K. (1979) Strategies for the modification and prevention of racial prejudice in children: a review. Paper presented at 59th Western Psychological Association Meeting, San Diego, California.
Baldwin, J., and Wells, H. (1980) *Active Tutorial Work*. Oxford: Blackwell/Lancashire County Council.
Braun, D., and Eisenstadt, N. (1985) *Family Lifestyles*. Milton Keynes: Open University Centre for Continuing Education/Health Education Council.

Bruner, J. (1960) *The Process of Education*. New York: Vintage Books.
Button, L. (1982) *Group Tutoring for the Form Tutor: A Developmental Model*. London: Hodder & Stoughton.
Carrington, B., and Short, G. (1991) Unfair discrimination: teaching the principles to children of primary school age. *Journal of Moral Education* 30(2), 157–76.
Cohen, L., and Manion, L. (1980) Research methods in education. In J. Bell *et al.* (eds), *Conducting Small-Scale Investigations in Educational Management*. London: Croom Helm.
Cook, S. W. (1971) *The Effect of Unintended Interracial Contact upon Racial Interaction and Attitude Change*. Boulder, CO: Colorado University Press.
De Vries, D. L., and Slavin, R. E. (1978) Team-Games-Tournament (TGT): review of 10 classroom experiments. *Journal of Research and Development in Education* 12(1), 28–38.
DES (1989) *Personal and Social Education from 5–16: Curriculum Matters 14*. London: HMSO.
Evans, R., and Thomas, O. (1986) *Teaching against Prejudice and Stereotyping: A Practical Handbook for Use with the 15–19 Age-Range*. Oxford: Oxford Development Education Unit.
Henerson, M. E., Lyons Morris, L., and Taylor-Fitzgibbon, C. (1978) *How to Measure Attitudes*. New York: Sage.
Hopson, B., and Scally, M. (1986) *Lifeskills Teaching Programmes*. London: Lifeskills Associates.
Johnson, D. W., and Johnson, R. (1975) *Learning Together and Alone: Co-operation, Competition and Individualization*. Englewood Cliffs, NJ: Prentice-Hall.
Katz, P., and Zalk, S. R. (1978) Modification of children's racial attitudes. *Developmental Psychology* 14(5), 447–61.
Leicester, M. (1989) *Multicultural Education: From Theory to Practice*. London: NFER/Nelson.
Leicester, M. (1990) Pastoral care and anti-racist education: interface and synthesis – preliminary remarks. *Pastoral Care*, March.
Leslie, L. L., Leslie, J. W., and Penfield, D. A. (1972) The effects of a student-centred special curriculum upon the racial attitudes of sixth graders. *Journal of Experimental Education* 41, 63–7.
Lynch, J. (1987) *Prejudice Reduction and the Schools*. London: Cassell.
McPhail, P. (1982) *Social and Moral Education*. London: Blackwell.
Manchester Development Education Project (1988) *Picturing People: Challenging Stereotypes*. Manchester: Manchester Development Education Project.
Oppenheim, A. N. (1966) *Questionnaire Design and Attitude Measurement*. London: Heinemann Educational.
Powell, L. (1991) A study of the development and implementation of a PSE module aimed at reducing racial prejudice in 13–15 year olds in a comprehensive school with a low ethnic minority intake, and an investigation into its effectiveness. Unpublished M. Ed. dissertation, Sunderland Polytechnic.
Sharan, S. (1985) Co-operative learning effects on ethnic relations and achievement in Israeli junior high school classrooms. In R. E. Slavin *et al.* (eds), *Learning to Co-operate: Co-operating to Learn*. New York: Plenum Press.
Sherif, M. (1956) Experiments in group conflict. *Scientific American* 195, 54–8.
Thomas, S., *et al.* (1980) *Techniques of Behaviour Change: Review of Theories and Research*. Florida State University, Tallahassee, School of Home Economics.
Wakeman, B. (1984) *Personal, Social and Moral Education: A Source Book*. London: Lion Publishing.
Woods, P. (1979) *The Divided School*. London: Routledge & Kegan Paul.

Chapter 3

Experiencing Temporary Disadvantage through Drama as a Means of Prejudice Reduction

Carol Bianchi-Cooke

In this chapter the target group and college are described, the relevant literature on multicultural education is reviewed, and some claims made for drama in education are outlined. The method of Forum Theatre is then described and interviews are documented and discussed. The results appear to suggest that the interviewees found the Forum Theatre of value in experiencing temporary disadvantage.

Recommendations are made as to the suitability and value of using drama in this context, although doubts are expressed as to the efficacy of prescriptive methods of evaluation and alternative methods are suggested.

INTRODUCTION

The social context of the college

Redstone College of Further Education, in the north of England, employs 379 full-time and approximately 120 part-time staff, enrolling a total of 18,224 full- and part-time students in 1989–90. During this year the college was reorganized to include the education of former sixth-form students in the borough. The college moved from being a marine and technical college to a tertiary college. This process involved both an increase in staff and students, and also a considerable rejigging of existing staff and systems.

It was during this academic year that the institution began a programme of multicultural education for college staff. At its inaugural stage, the model for this programme was diffused and although the will to succeed was evident, and the steering committee was personally committed, the direction of the programme was non-specific. The programme started life in this non-prescriptive way in order both to meet the needs of the community which the college serves and to discover the needs of the staff working within the college. An internal college report of 1991 outlined the profile of the ethnic community in the area served by the college, as follows:

- Bangladeshi.
- Iranian.
- Indian subcontinent other than Bangladeshi.
- Arab.
- Others – people who do not form part of the other groups.

This categorization serves to illustrate the point that there are many different groups which make up the ethnic community in the area; each group requires different responses and provision from the college.

The multicultural weekend

The year's work in multicultural education culminated in a residential weekend with the stated aim of creating an equal opportunities policy, and developing awareness of prejudice and stereotyping present in staff thinking and institutional practice. It was agreed that the most useful way forward for the college as a whole lay in addressing these two issues. The conference would examine both institutional and personal racism and attempt to identify a way forward on both fronts. I was invited by the committee to conduct a practical workshop using experiential learning methods, with the specific aim of giving participants the experience of temporary disadvantage, and working towards prejudice reduction.

This request arose out of another piece of work which I had undertaken for the local probation service and to which I refer in the results section. The work involved practical approaches to assist people to examine the attitudes and beliefs which they carried around, often without thought or reference to new experiences. A member of the steering committee had taken part in this workshop and found it effective in addressing prejudice reduction.

I agreed to conduct a workshop which would enable the participants to experience temporary disadvantage, ideally leading to an examination of thought. Dorothy Heathcote, lecturer and drama practitioner, has this to say on the subject:

> A leader who can help groups, made up of individuals, consider their personal life-view, is in my opinion one of the most important things a teacher (and drama experience) can offer to society, and in the end should sow seeds of small 'p' politics which may turn individuals into aware members of social communities.
>
> (1989, p. 39)

The workshop had a twofold purpose in that it was organized to offer the participants an experience, but it was also organized to enable the method to be used by tutors in the pastoral system.

Details of the participants

The group of lecturers from Redstone College were representatives from Humanities, Business Studies, Marine and Mechanical, Electrical Engineering, and Support Staff, who had been targeted by the committee and invited to the conference. There had been an attempt to invite staff from all departments of the college. However, attendance at the conference was not mandatory, so some staff had simply refused the invitation to attend. The workshop session was therefore composed of staff who had accepted the invitation to attend the conference and who were prepared to try out the practical session.

The workshop was viewed with trepidation by some staff, who warned me that they had never done drama before, and tried to ascertain that I was not going to make a fool of them. Neither item – doing drama or looking a fool – was on my personal agenda for the afternoon. The session was also seen as a break in the conference programme of lectures and seminars. It was important to me, however, that the session was not taken any less seriously than the lectures and seminars, and for this reason I was pleased that the session was planned for the afternoon rather than during the evening after dinner, as had been first suggested, when there was a danger of its being seen as a diversion from the serious stuff, rather than as a learning experience. The combination of anxiety and interest can be a volatile one, but it can also be a combination which assists learning.

Purpose of the study

At the initial stage, I viewed the workshop as an experimental process which I felt fairly sure would yield some interesting insights for the participants. Later, as a result of discussion and interviews, I became convinced that the drama workshop was worth documenting as the method would be useful to other tutors.

The workshop was based on the practice of Augusto Boal's Forum Theatre, details of which I will outline later in the chapter. The practical session was planned for an afternoon slot lasting two hours, followed by a break and a debriefing session.

REVIEW OF IDEAS AND LITERATURE WHICH INFORM MY PRACTICE

My workshop session in the multicultural programme was based on two premises: that racism is concerned with power and control; and that drama can assist people to experience temporary disadvantage. I will examine the literature, and describe the practice which results from these beliefs.

Racism as power and control

The idea of racism as a manifestation of power is not a new one: examples abound in literature, from Harper Lee's *To Kill a Mockingbird* to more recent books by black women writers such as Maya Angelou and Toni Morrison. Chris Brazier states that racism is more than individual prejudice: 'The racism . . . that hems black people in on all sides, is woven into the fabric of our societies' (1985, p. 8).

The Racial Harassment Project conducted in Sheffield in 1988, entitled *Because the Skin Is Black*, drew the same conclusion. In their report the writers said:

What is described here is, of course, not a problem of the individuals concerned, either victim, perpetrator or those in authority. It reflects totally the low status given to black people living in this predominantly white culture. Responses and remedies therefore need to be wide ranging and to focus on economic and social change.

(Sheffield City Council, 1989, p. 54)

Jon Nixon supports this view and argues that:

Racism perceived solely in terms of personal prejudice over-simplifies an extremely complex reality . . . it lays the blame for inequality at the feet of white, often working class, racists and thereby fails to perceive the importance of the relation between race, class and gender divisions in the construction of that inequality.

(1985a, p. 6)

Racism, according to these writers, is more than an individual knee-jerk response to a situation. It is systemic, feeding on the individual response, but also responsible for the individual response.

Racist behaviour

Racism, according to Nixon (1985b), whether individual or systemic, is more than a set of beliefs. Racism is displayed in behaviour:

Any adequate definition of racism would have to recognise the ways in which racism sets out to justify the unequal treatment of certain groups conceived of as distinct racial categories. What we are beginning to feel our way towards then, is an approach to racism which cannot be seen simply in terms of personal feelings detached from social structure. A redefinition of the personal element within the equation is required which embodies a condition whereby those defining themselves as superior also believe that they should put this belief into practice and so create and sustain a set of relationships based on domination and subordination.

(p. 35)

Nixon is suggesting that racism does not stop at thought, but that racist thinking offers the rationale and authority for racist behaviour.

Education to combat racism

If we accept that racism is individual prejudice reinforced by social structure and made manifest in a relationship based on domination and subordination, then as educators we may wish to address the problem both through the curriculum and via delivery of the curriculum. Bruner *et al.* (1980), quoted in Coffield (1983, p. 205), state that the 'best learning takes place when the learner takes charge', and Peter Brook says, 'For the first time this century . . . men are beginning to realise that if you want to say something, and if you say it in the form of a didactic proclamation, you arouse antagonisms rather than acquiescence' (1973, p. 15).

Bruner from the world of education, and Brook from the world of drama and theatre, make the point that the best learning takes place through a combination of thought and personal experience. Coffield (1983, p. 205) advocates a learning theory based on 'hot-blooded cognition', which he defines as a fusion of personality and intellect. He, like Bruner and Brook, calls for the use of 'participatory learning methods and democratic procedures' to be at the heart of the educational system, which will produce 'thinking, adaptable and socially committed people' (p. 205).

It would appear pointless, then, simply to tell our students about the problems of racism and go on to describe the iniquities inherent in racist ideology. We need a learning process which will combine information with thought, emotion and experience, and involve a degree of participation in the whole process.

Drama as a learning experience

Micheline Wandor (1981) advocates drama as a means of changing ideas; she states, 'polemic is about changing things in a direct political way. Drama is subversive' (p. 5). Wandor was talking about performance in the theatre, but if we turn to Dorothy Heathcote, we find a drama lecturer and practitioner who makes no divisions between theatre and drama as a learning medium.

Heathcote uses drama because she says that via drama she can 'expand awareness' (Wagner, 1979, p. 15). She says that learning, specifically through drama, involves the 'left hand of knowing' (Heathcote, 1984), which she defines as placing emphasis on applying experience, using emotion to aid understanding, challenging the teaching and taking decisions to modify its pattern. If drama does involve all of these activities, then it may be used to experience temporary disadvantage and to come closer to understanding another point of view.

Heathcote's drama sessions offer the participant the time to reflect: 'Play makes constructs of reality which are then available for examination by the spectator which exists in each participant'; and she also says that it is 'the digestion process of the arts, which creates the opportunity for reflection which is what education is all about' (1984, p. 35). This is the type of education proposed by Coffield, based on a critical understanding of our environment coupled with an emotional response to it, and I regard it as a way forward for multicultural work, combining information with an experiential, thoughtful response.

Different approaches to the use of drama

Nixon (1985a) advocates the use of drama in multicultural training, and states: 'Drama has an important contribution to make as a means of raising teachers' awareness of their own unintentional racism and of the institutional racism in which they are implicated' (p. 10). In the same article, he goes on to attack Gavin Bolton and Dorothy Heathcote, two respected practitioners of drama in education, for what he sees as their stubborn refusal to engage directly in the emotional issues at the heart of anti-racist teaching. Nixon feels that drama should be used to face a challenging issue directly, and disagrees with what he says are the indirect methods used by Bolton and Heathcote.

Bolton and Heathcote, until recently, held lecturing posts in drama in education. Their influence was and continues to be far-reaching and challenging. Both Heathcote and Bolton write and lecture across the world. More to the point, however, is the fact that both theoreticians continue to be practitioners, and use their methods to inform their theories, thereby creating a true praxis. Heathcote and Bolton are both concerned to encourage the students to face an issue squarely. This involves strategies which enable the student to deal with the issue in an honest and unembarrassed way. If an issue is dealt with directly, then the students are sometimes tutors forced to take refuge in laughter, or may trivialize the subject as a way of escape. Heathcote and Bolton sometimes approach a subject from a position which looks unconventional, but which will, paradoxically, bring the truth of the issue into strong focus.

An example of this technique can be found in an unpublished transcript of an interview conducted by John Hudson with Dorothy Heathcote in November 1985, on the subject of a drama about a missing child. She begins the drama, not with a mangled body or a court of justice, but with a piece of derelict ground in Africa which is overlooked by a factory full of pattern-cutters making children's clothing.

Similarly, Bolton (1984b, pp. 130–8) advocates strategies to edge closer to delicate issues. He suggests that analogy may be used. For example, racism can be dealt with by reference to Greeks and Romans, or drug abuse with reference to Odysseus and the Sirens. Bolton adds the proviso that the teacher has a responsibility to ensure that the students make the correct connections. My own drama sessions on racism rely heavily on analogy, in that I do not ask anyone to pretend that they are a black person in Soweto; rather I require people to work from their own experience of power-lessness and oppression. It is then my job to ensure that the right connections are made.

Gavin Bolton (1985) was offered the right of reply to Nixon's article, and said that, rather than 'protection from a delicate issue', he advocates 'protection into squarely facing it'. Bolton closes his article by raising the question of how far drama should be used 'as a springboard to help pupils to understand social and political issues' and how far the tutor is required to view drama 'as social and political'. My own view is that education is indirectly political and that drama can clothe issues and in doing so make them more explicit. This process does not necessarily make the issues easier to resolve, but it may enable the protagonists to view a problem more concretely. Bolton (1984b) claims that 'The dramatic event is a lens through which to search beyond the event to its social, anthropological, historical or aesthetic implications' (p. 167). He does not define a drama session simply in terms of what happens in that hour, but uses the session to draw out layers of meaning.

A description of the ideas which underpin Forum Theatre

The work of the theatrical practitioner Augusto Boal in creating and developing Forum Theatre, and the work of the educator and writer Paulo Freire, are of particular value when providing relevant experiences of disadvantage for tutors who are involved in a multicultural programme. Forum Theatre is described in detail in Boal's *Theatre of the Oppressed* (1979) and briefly consists of small groups enacting a scene of oppression. The audience is then given the chance to change the scene in such a way as to lessen the oppression. The change is then discussed and analysed as to its feasibility.

Paulo Freire, a friend of Boal, outlines his theories on the oppressed in his book *Pedagogy of the Oppressed* (1972). He offers a pedagogy for people in the Third World who are oppressed by both their society and their education system. Freire places learning in a direct relationship to the cultural situation in which people live, maintains a critical relationship with this environment, and uses language as a tool for liberation. According to Freire, 'The pedagogy of the oppressed is an instrument for their critical discovery that both they and their oppressors are manifestations of dehumanization' (p. 30). His pedagogy tries to make explicit the link between oppression and power. It is the same link made by Jon Nixon and quoted earlier in this chapter.

Freire deplores the 'banking' concept of education; the harder students work at depositing information, 'the less they develop the critical consciousness which would result from their intervention in the world as transformers of that world' (p. 52). This form of education never proposes that students 'critically consider reality' (p. 25). It is this critical analysis of society which Gavin Bolton upheld when he called for the kind of drama 'which enables the individual to feel free to know his political self and to know how to look at society' (1982, p. 17).

Augusto Boal developed Freire's pedagogy of the oppressed and translated it into dramatic practice. It is this model which I have used in my work, linking drama with the participants' lives, while maintaining a critical relationship with society. Freire sees education as being concerned with the struggle against 'oppressive and dehumanizing structures' (1972, p. 70). Boal uses theatre in the struggle to educate: 'theatre can be placed at the service of the oppressed, so that they can express themselves and so that by using this new language, they can also discover new concepts' (1979, p. 121). The work of Boal, both in theory, in *Theatre of the Oppressed*, and in the practice of Forum Theatre, offers a way forward in terms of analysing reality and assessing the feasibility of change.

I will move now to a description of the work undertaken during the multicultural weekend.

METHOD

Before beginning the work on Forum Theatre I handed each participant a list of my objectives for the session. These were as follows:

- To base the work on personal experiences of power and oppression.
- To learn in an experiential mode.
- To use Augusto Boal's Forum Theatre to analyse the feasibility of change.
- To move from the particular towards the general, and to make the connection between particular incidents of oppression and systemic oppression.
- To create a piece of drama which unites reflection and action.
- To consider critically and deconstruct a piece of Forum Theatre on oppression.

Boal's practice of Forum Theatre starts from the experience of the participants, who are asked to tell a personal story about a political or social problem which left them feeling powerless. I divided the large group into three smaller groups in a random fashion. I did, however, ensure that each group contained both men and women. Then I asked every member of the groups to tell their story of personal oppression. The group members then decided which story they would use for the next part of the Forum.

The stories were not tales of grand derring-do or protracted heroism; small incidents often make the best theatre. One group worked on a story from Central America concerning the oppression of a woman by her husband. Another group concentrated on a story of oppression at work. The third group used a story about Greenham Common. It is perhaps worth mentioning here that, for some members of the group, the experience of retelling the tale of oppression was a particularly powerful and cathartic one.

As none of the participants had a great deal of experience of drama, I tried to structure each stage precisely, so that people were sure of what they had to achieve. It was interesting to observe that the group depicting the Greenham story worked in a polarized fashion. The group consisted of equal numbers of men and women. The women played the roles of Greenham women and the men played the roles of the oppressors. It became apparent, to me as an observer, that planning for the play was developing in two distinct strands. The women were planning their bit of the play and the men were planning their roles. It was becoming less and less a play and more and more a war-game.

Once each group had decided on the story, they were told to make a still picture which showed the moment of severest oppression. Each picture was shown to the other groups in the workshop, who were invited to place a hand on the person who appeared to them to be the main protagonist. If the picture was not clear, the group worked on it until the main focus of the story emerged. The group made two more pictures, one depicting the moment just prior to the first picture, and one depicting the moment after the point of oppression. Each group then showed the three pictures to the other members of the workshop, adding words where appropriate if they wished. The next stage brought together the pictures into one continuous piece of theatre, telling the story of the oppression.

The piece of theatre, developed from one person's story of oppression, was performed for the spectators. Then the piece was performed again, and this time the spectators were invited, by myself as the person in charge (called by Boal 'the Joker'), to interrupt the play at the moment when they felt that the action could be changed to give a more positive response to the oppression. The play was repeated, and the spectator who offered the alternative entered the play and took the place of the main protagonist who had suffered the oppression: 'the poetics of the oppressed focuses on the action itself. The spectator ... assumes the protagonic role, changes the dramatic action, tries out solutions, discusses plans for change – in short, trains himself for real action' (Boal, 1979, p. 122).

The original picture was presented again and the other groups were asked to give the picture a name. The three groups operated independently until the time came to perform the pieces of theatre and consider the possibility of change.

The Joker encouraged the spectators to discuss the feasibility of the change, since as Boal says, 'It is not the place of the theatre to show the correct path, but only to offer the means by which all possible paths may be examined' (1979, p. 141). The protagonist in each play was required to act out the scene without accepting the repression, rather fighting to impose his or her will. It is a rehearsed resistance to oppression.

During the performance and discussion the whole group was encouraged to 'ascend from the phenomenon towards the law' (1979, p. 150), i.e. from the phenomenon present in the plot of the story towards the social laws which govern the phenomenon. The protagonist was encouraged to look at the possibility of change, but also to look outside of the personal situation to the external situation which caused the oppression. The personal experience was 'made the basis of the collective experience of Forum Theatre' and raised to the point of 'social and collective consciousness' (Boal, 1984, p. 41). It is important, from the point of view of the mental health of each group, that the protagonist and the oppression are not seen in isolation from the social laws which govern or condone the oppression, as this leads to a reinforcement of powerlessness rather than an affirmation of strength.

RESULTS

Prior to the multicultural weekend three tutors were interviewed on the subject of using the pastoral system, already operational in the college, as a vehicle for work on prejudice reduction and multicultural education. The tutors, who were already involved in the pastoral system, were asked for their views, but there was no attempt to make them stick to the point or only answer in a way which was germane to the questions. The questions, and part of the answers are as follows:

Pre-weekend responses

Is it possible to change or modify attitudes as a result of a pastoral care programme on anti-racism?

> *Lecturer C:* The process of socialization and growing up will create a set of prejudices and opinions which will be with them [the student tutor group] for the rest of their lives. You might modify them slightly. People aren't open books. . . . I willingly admit to a certain amount of prejudice, some might even call it racism. . . . I don't feel I've gone down that road. . . . Let me give you an example. Last night there was a programme on television about three and a half million people that some say we should give jobs to in Britain. For practical purposes I would keep them away . . . or for reasons of conscience should we let them in? The practical purposes could be put down to racism.

> *Lecturer D:* If you bring an issue out into the open and discuss it, then the student's opinion is valued.

> *Lecturer E:* If the tutor regards the tasks as worthwhile then the students will regard them as worthwhile.

C was justifying the right to 'let them in' or 'keep them away'. The logic implicit in this language was that he had the right to decide. His language suggests that he defined himself as able to decide owing to birth and race, and may have been prepared, should the opportunity have presented itself, to put these theories of domination and submission into practice. Tutors **D** and **E** appear to feel that there is value in raising issues in an attempt to modify attitude.

In what way do you think tolerance and empathy could be encouraged?

> *Lecturer C:* If they move into our society and move into our culture they should drop a great part of their culture and assimilate into ours. Not in private, but they should adopt our culture. The subculture is alien to the main culture, deviant to the main culture. They don't weaken [their] culture, they go the other way for defensive reasons, they strengthen the culture and that makes them alien.

> *Lecturer D:* A lot of people attach a blame to them [ethnic minorities], a fault to them which they don't really deserve . . . fault and blame are two words that you don't need to use.

> *Lecturer E:* Challenging social myths is wonderful, it makes people think . . . they move away from fact-based learning to learning which is thoughtful and analytical.

Tutor **C** does not appear to think that there is much point in encouraging tolerance and empathy as this tutor has adopted the view that 'they' should fit into 'our' culture. Tutors **D** and **E** again broadly concur that discussing issues with students may be productive.

Do you think there is value in activities designed to enable students to experience temporary disadvantage?

> *Lecturer C:* Those people who don't experience disadvantage will not know how ethnic minorities feel. I don't believe in artificial games, I don't think they work. But experiencing a disadvantage may be profitable. The pure disadvantage of being black or coloured or whatever is the disadvantage of stereotypes. If you're 55, female and black you've got no chance. Do away with yourself.

Lecturer **D** made the point that discussion and debriefing were all-important after the work:

> It [temporary disadvantaging] does work to a certain extent . . . you need a lot of discussion afterwards. You can't feel the long-term day in, day out wearing down when people are disadvantaged. They see their family and people they love being disadvantaged. Imagine if that were to go on forever in everything you did . . . the whole concept of being disadvantaged is difficult to imagine on a long-term basis.

Lecturer **E** said 'I don't think that the leap done in class and life outside is very easily made. It's a hard leap to make', but also added, 'Learning can take place when people are put off stroke.'

Despite the gloomy prognosis for any black, middle-aged woman, tutor **C** highlighted a problem: that of games and simulations dealing largely in stereotypes. I suggest that drama can avoid this pitfall by dealing with real people's stories and real responses (see method). Tutor **D** made the point that work on disadvantage could only go so far. This point was reiterated by tutor **E**.

Given the very real problems associated with experiencing temporary disadvantage, it is clear that all tutors quoted felt that some positive learning could take place.

Do you think students can understand the concept of stereotyping and labelling?

> *Lecturer C:* We can hope to achieve a modification of attitudes.
>
> *Lecturer D:* The only experience I can discuss with them is being female ... They [the students] aren't encouraged to be interested in the people next door. We are so frightened of asking a question, we're so frightened of showing ignorance.
>
> *Lecturer E:* If you refuse to stereotype you get a much more genuine response. You are helping people to think. You have to face the fact that they might not turn out like you want them to. You have to defend people's rights to draw their own conclusions.

The last lecturer quoted was expressing the view that a genuine experience of disadvantage may encourage an honest response that eschews the stereotypic reaction.

Post-weekend responses

I questioned three lecturers on their experience of Forum Theatre. The questions were as follows:

* Was the experience vivid or otherwise?
* Did you learn anything from the experience and make any connections between the experience and the multicultural programme?
* Was there an opportunity for one's views to be challenged?

I have reported extracts from the interviews as a continuous piece of narrative and not as discrete answers to discrete questions; the responses have more impact when read in this way.

Lecturer **C** chose not to attend the multicultural weekend. His views cannot then be canvassed on the value of the workshop, although this does not make his thoughts and views any less important or relevant for the programme as a whole.

Lecturer **D** attended the workshop and said that she found the Forum Theatre of value. She said:

> It's good to realize that you were in the position where you couldn't do anything. Talking about it that weekend was the best therapy ...
>
> It was very vivid, I remember having to recall it, I could still feel the way I felt that day, it wasn't just telling about something that had happened in my past. I could really feel how angry and hurt and upset I was. I could still feel the colour in my cheeks and we were talking twenty years later.

She went on to add:

> I think what it did was it put it [my experience] into context, because at first when it happened I thought it was a personal thing, you know, they don't like you. And then I realized very quickly that it wasn't my problem, although I suffered because it was those people who forced that on me. I realized that weekend, having discussed lots of issues and been put in positions of disadvantage just what it feels like to be like that.

And that:

> It was good to go through it again and realize that it wasn't me but someone else's prejudice that's forcing the situation. It's good to realize that you were in the position

where you couldn't do anything. Talking about it [the experience of disadvantage] that weekend was the best therapy. I can tell people and laugh about it now. I think the weekend did help me to realize that it does happen and not just to me.

Lecturer **E** said, 'It was very vivid, in fact it was so vivid that it upset me so much that it made me cry later on' and continued:

I made connections because the experience that I had which was enacted that particular time, while it was only a temporary feeling of powerlessness for me, I hadn't had the experience of years and years of discrimination. I did have a tiny insight into what it must have been like for someone who, since they have been born, because of the colour of their skin, have been treated in a way which denies them their humanity . . .
It came as quite a shock to me. I should have been debriefed. It should be borne in mind that it can be quite a disturbing thing for people to go over things in their past, and I don't know how you get round that. Maybe warn someone that it might be upsetting.

Lecturer **F**, not previously quoted but included here because the response was apposite, said:

Those of us who went on the Alnwick course, being reasonably aware and sympathetic, still found that there were things we had missed . . .
Having a policy doesn't change a thing. Drama can give you a fuller experience than a simulated experience. You can debrief afterwards. The tensions you experience are for real at the time.

All of the last three lecturers stated that they had gained from the drama, but they did not suggest that the drama itself was totally responsible; rather that the workshop consolidated previous thoughts and experiences.

EVALUATION AND DISCUSSION

Problems

Evaluating something like experiencing temporary disadvantage in Forum Theatre is not easy, for the basic reason that it is difficult to pinpoint what is worth evaluating. One model of evaluation, established in 1949 by Ralph Tyler (see Jackson, 1980), sets out objectives and then devises a programme to fulfil these objectives. It is then possible to evaluate to what extent the objectives have been covered. However, the effects of an educational programme may be unexpected; and the aims and objectives may not remain constant, but may be modified in response to audience participation, ability and interest. Using the objectives method to quantify and qualify drama encourages a static approach to both long- and short-term learning. Learning in the field of experiences and responses can be the culmination of thoughts, ideas and discussions held over days, weeks or even months.

The prescriptive model, then, is inadequate in evaluating the effects of experiencing temporary disadvantage, largely because it is impossible to predict what sort of learning or reinforcement will take place, in part because of the varying degrees of thought and experience brought to the workshop by each individual. Elliott Eisner (1969, quoted in Jackson, 1980, p. 91) distinguished two types of learning objectives: the first is instructional, and specifies skills and objectives to be learned; the second

Eisner calls 'expressive objectives' which identify the learning situation but not what learning should take place. This second learning objective allows the learning area to be explored in a way that is meaningful to the participants. A drama session which I conducted with young offenders may illustrate this point.

The group were brought to the college by their probation officers, who were keen for them to work on their self-confessed and demonstrably racist attitudes. I worked with the whole group, offenders and officers, using an analogous situation which was supposed eventually to demonstrate to the group the error of their attitudes. The sessions were amiable and violence-free, and the officers felt that lessons had been learned – so much so that they were eager to repeat the exercise with another group of young offenders. I felt that little had been learned on the anti-racist front, but that the group had demonstrated an ability to work together and value the contributions of others. The learning area had been prescribed and, although the actual learning was meaningful, it was difficult to quantify and qualify. The evaluation in this case was, of necessity, less prescriptive, more descriptive and dependent on the group members. Eisner's second model, then, is closer to the type of evaluation which would have relevance to the Forum Theatre workshop.

The process of evaluation presupposes that there is something in the workshop which is worth evaluating. Again the problem arises of defining what is worth evaluating; this may vary from person to person. The evaluation process must take into account the responses and values of all those involved. For example, if lecturer **C** had attended the multicultural weekend then his learning curve would have begun at a different point from that of lecturer **D**, presuming that the initial interviews had accurately demonstrated the state of mind of each lecturer.

Michael Scrivens (1967) describes two sorts of evaluation: 'formative', which shapes the development of a programme; and 'summative' which reflects its overall effect. Tony Jackson (1980, p. 93) quotes Scriven's evaluation models then adds another model of his own, which he calls 'reflexive evaluation', described as a two-way process. He is talking specifically of evaluating Theatre in Education, but I feel that this is an appropriate model to use when attempting to evaluate the Forum Theatre workshop. He suggests that the work is performed, then the information gained from the audience, and the Theatre in Education team's evaluation, are fed back into the work to inform the next programme. This type of evaluation combines personal perception, prior experience and analysis of both the process and the product. It links theory and practice, action and reflection in a spiral, creating praxis.

One answer – reflexive evaluation

In view of comments made by the participants after the Forum Theatre, and bearing in mind my own experience of taking part as well as running a Forum Theatre, I feel that the workshop offered the opportunity to achieve the following:

- Discover what we think.
- Try out emotions.
- Investigate society.

Discover what we think

This discovery is a useful starting point for growth (see earlier references to the work of Freire). Boal's Forum Theatre can raise issues which are usually dismissed or abandoned as being too painful to discuss. There is value in making explicit the implicit personal values by which we live. The 'Joker' in Forum Theatre should assist the participants in finding out what they really think, with the aim of reviewing that opinion in the light of new data and experiences.

Finding out what we think can, in itself, be challenging and not always welcome. For example, I was invited to prepare a session of Forum Theatre for another college in the locality, as its multicultural officer had attended a previous session and enjoyed the experience. The lecturers at this second college were wary of experiential methods, but could possibly be won over, she thought, if I was extremely cautious in my approach. I promised to try, and proceeded to plan as cautiously as possible. However, she contacted me soon after, and informed me that the lecturers had voted with their feet and decided not to attend that session.

New methods of working, and ways of finding out, are threatening for people with a relatively insouciant view of the world; how much more frightening must this type of learning be for people like our students, many of whom are unsure of themselves and of their place in the world.

Try out emotions

Forum Theatre gives the participants the opportunity to try out a range of emotions in the make-believe world of the drama. Gavin Bolton says that the experiences 'exist in actuality if not in reality and our reflection upon those experiences is the basis of learning through drama' (1986, p. 166). In Forum Theatre, experiences and emotions can be repeated to assess the feasibility of the proposed change. Although art mirrors life in that the drama is dependent on real-life stories, the learning takes place at the point of departure from real life, where participants can discuss, act, become involved, then step back for a reassessment. Boal's theatre offers the participants the opportunity to experience disadvantage, and its attendant emotions.

Investigate society

Personal experiences of disadvantage tend to be minimized, although they are rarely forgotten. Forum Theatre offers participants the space to retell their stories. A fairly high level of personal confidence in each participant is assumed, and it may be significant that the only time I have met with absolute failure in Forum Theatre was during work with some young men on probation (not the group previously referred to). Their level of confidence was low. This meant that they could not admit to themselves, let alone the group, that they had ever experienced even temporary disadvantage. Forum Theatre acts as a laboratory where we can look at society from a personal standpoint, but also from the position of being a member of society. However, in this case it failed because the group members were unable to step back from their own permanent state of disadvantage, and look analytically at their position.

CONCLUSIONS

It would be pointless to attend a multicultural weekend, spend time participating in Forum Theatre and then forget the whole experience. The value of drama in such a programme, as far as I can see, is that it combines the skills of critical analysis and understanding with the vividness of a real, emotional experience. The work which I have documented shows that feeling, alone, is not enough; it is the link between thought and feeling which can energize and motivate, so that the learning achieved in the programme can be utilized in our colleges.

There is, demonstrably, a place for drama in a programme of prejudice reduction. The method which I have used, that of Forum Theatre, is just one way in which drama can be put to the service of multicultural education. Other types of drama, including drama in education, theatre in education, and plays which address racial issues, are also used. Forum Theatre is effective because it enables people who have little or no experience of drama to become engaged in a meaningful experience which may lead to a change in perception. For some participants, this is only the start; but in my opinion, and judging by experience, it is a good start.

REFERENCES

Boal, A. (1979) *Theatre of the Oppressed*. London: Pluto.
Boal, A. (1984) *Documents on the Theatre of the Oppressed*, ed. by Anthony Hozier. London: Red Letters.
Bolton, G. (1982) TIE for political growth. Unpublished paper at Newcastle University quoted by E. van Ryswyk in *2D* 2(2) (Spring 1983), 15–21.
Bolton, G. (1984a) Teacher-in-role and the learning process. *SCYPT Journal* 12, 21–6.
Bolton, G. (1984b) *Drama as Education*. Harlow: Longman.
Bolton, G. (1985) A reply to Jon Nixon. *Curriculum* 6(39), 13–14.
Bolton, G. (1986) *Selected Writings*, edited by D. Davis and C. Lawrence. Harlow: Longman.
Brazier, C. (1985) The white problem. *New Internationalist* 145, 8.
Brook, P. (1973) Politics of sclerosis: Stalin and Lear. Interview with A. J. Liehm in *Theatre Quarterly* 3(10), 13–17.
Bruner, J. S., Donaldson, M., and Papert, S. (1980) *Mindstorms*. Hemel Hempstead: Harvester.
Coffield, F. (1983) Learning to live with unemployment: what future for education in a world without jobs? In F. Coffield and R. Goodings (eds), *Sacred Cows in Education: Essays in Reassessment*. Edinburgh: Edinburgh University Press for University of Durham.
Coffield, F., Borrill, C., and Marshall, S. (1986) *Growing Up at the Margins*. Milton Keynes: Open University Press.
Eisner, E. (1969) *Instructional and Expressive Educational Objectives: Their Formulation and Use in the Curriculum*. Chicago: Rand McNally. Cited in Jackson (1980).
Freire, P. (1986) *Pedagogy of the Oppressed*. London: Sheed & Ward.
Heathcote, D. (1984) *Collected Writings on Education and Drama*, ed. by L. Johnson and C. O'Neill. London: Hutchinson.
Heathcote, D. (1989) Commentary on Geoff Gillham's article. *2D* 8(2), 39.
Hudson, J. (1985) A child goes missing. Unpublished interview with D. Heathcote.

Jackson, T. (1980) *Learning through the Theatre: Essays and Casebooks on Theatre in Education*. Manchester: Manchester University Press.

Nixon, J. (1985a) Drama and anti-racist teaching: guidelines for action. *Curriculum* **6**(3), 5–12.

Nixon, J. (1985b) Education for a multi-cultural society: reviews and reconstructions. *Curriculum* **6**(2), 29–36.

Scrivens, M. (1967) *The Methodology of Evaluation in Perspectives of Curriculum Evaluation*. Chicago: Rand McNally. Cited in Jackson (1980).

Sheffield City Council for Racial Equality and the Police and Community Safety Unit (1989) *Because the Skin Is Black*. Sheffield: Sheffield City Council.

Wagner, B. J. (1979) *Dorothy Heathcote: Drama as a Learning Medium*. London: Hutchinson.

Wandor, M. (1981) *Understudies: Theatre and Sexual Politics*. London: Eyre Methuen.

Chapter 4

Using Curriculum Material and Teaching Methods to Reduce Prejudice and Maintain Academic Standards in an A Level Human Geography Course

Anna Schlesinger

Contemporary research in the teaching of 'Geography for Prejudice Reduction' favours using curriculum material in a direct 'cause and effect' approach (Gill, 1983; Marshall, 1985), with methods that involve co-operative tasks and discussion in groups (Hicks, 1981; Richardson, 1982). This investigation seeks to discover whether there is a particular combination of curriculum material and teaching approach that would be more effective than others in reducing prejudice in A level students in a 'mainly white' tertiary college.

Curriculum material was chosen with the following objectives in mind:

- To promote equality to counter injustice and bias.
- To encourage a global perspective in solving specific problems.
- To meet the need for 'change' in attitude.

The same material and 'value-inquiry' approach (Banks, 1984) was used with three parallel groups of second-year A level students of human geography, the only variable being the teaching method. Methods chosen were *collaborative group work*, *didactic teaching* and *paired peer-tutoring*. A racial attitude test was given before and after the project to establish any change in attitude, and a questionnaire mid-term and at the end of the project for responses to curriculum material and methods.

The main findings suggest, first, that it is misleading to assume all students are prejudiced and, second, that to increase favourable attitudes the curriculum material should emphasize a *positive* image of developing countries and a *solution* to inequalities. Conclusions drawn from the project favour a mixture of methods with an emphasis on group work and student-led discussion. Future work in this area should include a further review of materials, including games and simulations, and collaborative work with colleagues.

INTRODUCTION

Teacher, examine thyself.
(Katz, J., 1978)

This research project was carried out in a tertiary college during January–March 1991, and is concerned with improving both curriculum material and learning styles for the teaching of human geography to second-year A level students. Its overall aim is to reduce prejudice and to maintain academic standards; and it does this by giving three groups of students the same selected subject material and approach, while combining them with a different teaching–learning method in each group.

Preparation and planning for the project was during the period of the implementation of the National Curriculum (1990–1), when the educational climate was concerned with reviewing practice in order to improve standards. A government White Paper (20 May 1991) gave support to an approach for geography teaching similar to that adopted by the project: to interrelate the core themes of human, physical and environmental geography, and to use a case study approach to represent each topic at a local, national and global scale. At the time of writing (1992), teaching methods for students of all ages are under scrutiny in a drive to cut the cost of provision (Ward, 1992), which makes relevant an investigation of methods.

The college in which this research took place is situated in the north-east of England and will be called MC College. In 1989 it was reorganized to become a tertiary college, which involved an increase in staff, in 16–19-year-old students and in economic resources. It concerned me that, for much of the time, I along with colleagues still 'stood in front of students in a classroom *telling* them' (Waterhouse, 1990). This relates to Norman Graves's observations made 10 years earlier when he said, 'many teachers assume that their jobs are essentially to get the students to learn the content of the syllabus' (1979, p. 21).

Now, in the early 1990s, the content of the geography syllabus has changed and does somewhat reflect the multi-ethnic nature of societies, although it is not necessary to stress the need for equality of opportunity, nor to view information from a global perspective. But teaching methods for 16–19-year-olds have changed little, and humanities subjects are generally taught using a didactic approach, despite the continuing popularity of student-centred methods in primary education. These situations and a personal need to investigate and improve my own practice are the reasons for this investigation.

RELEVANT LITERATURE AND RESOURCES

The fight to end racism in education must be concerned with changing the content of education, changing the pedagogy and the curriculum.
(Brandt, 1985, p. 71)

A prejudice reduction approach was adopted in the choice of curriculum material and teaching methods, accepting the premise expressed by the social geographers John Cater and Trevor Jones that 'the existence and extent of racial discrimination [is apparent] from the overwhelming body of evidence confirming both its presence and its intractability' (1989, p. 164).

Before attempting to change prejudiced attitudes it was necessary to clarify what these attitudes are. The Swann Report defines prejudice as a 'preconceived opinion or *bias* for or against someone or something where the opinion has been formed without *adequate information* on which to base a rational judgement' (DES, 1985, p. 18, emphasis added). Mal Leicester adds two other factors, 'irrational beliefs' and 'harmful discriminatory behaviour' (1989, p. 18), and argues that the education process is a vehicle for disseminating as well as reducing prejudice. To counter prejudice she quotes C. Glock (1986) in suggesting that students need 'to think, reason and question clearly about prejudice', which concerns both the teaching approach and method.

The geography syllabuses provide a good opportunity to do this, as illustrated by a recommendation in the Swann Report: 'A good education must reflect *the diversity of British society* and indeed *the contemporary world*' (DES, 1985, p. 318). But it is widely understood that correct knowledge is only one step to reducing prejudice (Singh, 1989; S. Catling, quoted in Hackett, 1990); it is also necessary to examine values and attitudes (Allport, 1958; Lynch, 1987). Therefore the first objective when selecting curriculum material is to make sure it *pursues equality and justice to counter the existing inequalities expressed by omission, bias and stereotyping*.

Guidelines for making changes are found in Boardman's *Handbook for Geography Teaching* (1986), which includes recommendations from the Geography Inspectorate, and an anti-racist policy statement from the Geographical Association. Researchers in multicultural education stress the need for a *global* context (Lynch, 1989; see also Brandt, 1985; Shallice, 1984), and the second objective in choosing curriculum material for topic areas is to promote *global perspectives as opposed to ethnocentric ones*.

The curriculum material is communicated through the teaching approach and method, which are both controversial areas. The neutral-chairman approach of the Schools Council Humanities Curriculum Project (Beddis, 1970) is no longer supported, since it is impossible to counter inequality in the form of bias and stereotyping by remaining neutral (Singh, 1989; Klein, 1986; Hicks, 1984; Gill, 1983). Today educational institutions have equal opportunities policies, and researchers support a holistic approach, referring directly to inequality by combining selective content with student-centred methods in an endeavour that 'action in the classroom will reflect the policy of the institution' (Lynch, 1987). Research by CARE (Stenhouse *et al.*, 1982) and Allen (1987) provides evidence that a 'direct' approach can reduce prejudice. Multiculturalists agree on the need to change *self* (Lynch, 1987; Banks and Banks McGee, 1989) and the third objective pursues this by questioning existing values and attitudes. Its strategy is to emphasize the need for *change in the relationships within and between countries to counter existing power structures* through a careful choice of curriculum material.

The overall approach is structured to incorporate all three objectives and to encourage the students to make connections between the values discussed and their own personal attitudes and behaviour.

OTHER RESOURCES RELEVANT TO THE INQUIRY

Especially relevant to geographical education are techniques and materials which may encourage involvement in matters of local, national and global concern.

(*Contemporary Issues* 1(1), p. 7)

The six-week MC College Project took place during normal timetable time with three parallel groups of second-year A level students who were taught a module from the University of London 210 syllabus. As explained, the *same* curriculum material (topics and case studies) and direct teaching approach were used with all three groups. Preparation focused on seeking resources appropriate to the aims and objectives of the project to add to my existing materials. It is possible here to discuss only a selection of the geographical books, journals and films that were investigated when planning the module.

Approaches to teaching geography

The implementation of the National Curriculum revived the controversy of whether it is better to teach geography using a thematic or a regional approach. The lobby wanting a return to an ethnocentric 'regional' approach is supported by Dr S. Lawlor, Deputy Director of the Centre for Policy Studies (Hackett, 1990), while a process-based (thematic) and developmental geography is promoted by the team of Norman Graves, Michael Naish, Francis Slater, Ashley Kent and Keith Hilton, who work at the Institute of Education, University of London. They expressed their views in an article in *Teaching Geography* (Graves *et al.*, 1990), and this approach is followed by most A level textbooks. It is supported by researchers whose work is in seeking equality and correcting bias and stereotyping (Hicks, 1980, 1981; Klein, 1986) and for all these reasons it is used in the MC Project.

Resources for teaching geography

Of the textbooks available, the two which best meet the criteria for prejudice reduction, and which combine human and physical geography and use a thematic approach illustrated by case studies, are Brian Knapp's *Systematic Geography* (1986) and David Waugh's *Geography: An Integrated Approach* (1990). Waugh's warns of the limitations of textbooks which 'are out of date even before their publication', and most of the material used in the project was therefore gathered from journals, newspapers and video film. For instance, land use and economic development in countries receive only limited explanation in textbooks, so articles were sought in *Contemporary Issues in Geography and Education*. Here researchers such as Dawn Gill and Ian Cook discuss causes of the unequal division of the world's wealth, and stress the importance of viewing people in developing countries positively (Gill, 1983).

Two models of economic development looking at the legacy of colonialism and the economic power of transnational companies, rarely found in textbooks but necessary in meeting the project's criteria, were contained in the *Geography Review* 1(1), a relatively new publication specifically for A level students. Indeed most of the material for the theme on trade, aid and transnationals in the project was found in journals and newspapers, such as the (Education) *Guardian*, the Development Education Project (Manchester Polytechnic) *Panoscope* (Panos) and the *New Internationalist*.

Video film is particularly useful. Its information is often more topical and the student retention rate is considered to be 20 per cent greater than that from reading

(National Training Laboratory, Massachusetts). Graham Butt (1991) considers film a builder of positive or negative images, as 'pupils tend to assume the images presented before them represent the objective truth'. It was the most effective resource for portraying case studies: for example, in J. N. Sayo's life, which was interspersed throughout the series *Reclaiming the Earth* (Channel 4, 1984) – films made from an Afrocentric perspective. These films had other advantages, such as an equal gender mix of 'authority' figures, and people from all income groups being interviewed.

The 20-minute BBC 2 educational films are limited in their range of topics, but have excellent case studies to illustrate their themes (e.g. *Skyscrapers and Slums*, 1987). Another advantage of films over textbooks and other publications is that they can more easily be edited if some of the material is incorrect or prejudiced. If not edited out, such misinformation or indoctrination can be used as a learning device in discussion (e.g. *Vanishing Earth*, BBC/TVE, 1987). For direct teaching on race, documentary television programmes, such as 'The Black Belt of Alabama' (*First Tuesday*, Channel 4, 1986), have made a great impact.These are simply examples of the wealth of material available for a direct and thematic approach to geography teaching.

Teaching methods for prejudice reduction

The three methods chosen for this research – didactic, small collaborative groups and peer-tutoring – represent a range (one teacher-centred and two student-centred) that could be accommodated within the existing structure of timetable, group size and impending A level examinations. It must be noted that 'didactic' here does not mean a totally teacher-centred approach; rather, it means 'whole-class teaching' with questions and discussion, which resembles my own current practice. The importance of co-operative and collaborative approaches for cognitive and affective learning is reflected in a wide range of literature (Brandes and Ginnis, 1986; Gibbs, 1981; Hammersley, 1986; Topping, 1988; Goodlad and Hirst, 1989), which identifies the interactive pair method of tutoring. This method was used in the project, as contributing to attitude change, self-esteem and a positive attitude to learning.

METHOD OF INQUIRY

The method used in this research inquiry closely resembles the Simple Action Research Model used in the Further Education Unit's RP390 Project, with two stages of 'plan, act, observe, reflect' (FEU, 1988), allowing for revision after reflection. This was because it shares the same aim and is concerned with testing and changing methods in the classroom. As much of the data would be of a qualitative nature, it was thought necessary to quantify in some way to assess for prejudice reduction (after Stenhouse and team at UEA), in addition to using reflection as part of evaluation (Elliott and Adelman, 1976; Kemmis and McTaggart, 1982).

An inductive approach was chosen for the MC Project because, by checking the findings at each stage, the teacher-researcher can change her practice so that the research becomes part of the process of her teaching (Glaser and Strauss, 1967; McCall and Simmons, 1969; Elliott, 1976; Kemmis and McTaggart, 1982). The subjective

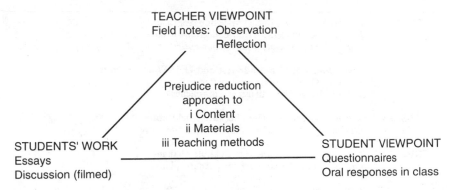

Figure 4.1 *Triad method of data collection: MC College. Adapted from Hopkins (1985, p. 80); used by kind permission of the Open University Press.*

nature of an inductive approach was checked by setting up a framework of 'triangulation' (Walker, 1985), which compares the reseacher's findings with those of at least two other people (e.g. observer, student). Hence the 'Triad' method was adopted. This is a multi-*method* means of corroborating evidence, as illustrated in Figure 4.1.

Participant observation (McCall and Simmons, 1969; FEU, 1988), which follows 'an agreed checklist with a coding schema and descriptive notes' (M. Schwartz and C. Schwartz, quoted in McCall and Simmons, 1969) was the principal teacher-researcher means of data collection. A checklist used in the FEU Project, which had been adapted from a model in Walker and Adelman's *Guide to Classroom Observation* (1975), was further adapted for the current project. It had columns for positive and negative instances in relation to the three objectives. Descriptive notes which include observations from the checklist were written as part of the field notes each day. The recorded notes and observations were then used to validate findings raised in the classroom situation, which is called 'saturation'. The saturation process revealed 'categories' emerging from the observations, which were checked for frequency with the other data. In summary, the Triad method involves validating the findings from one method or viewpoint with the findings from other methods for the same situation (Reid *et al.*, 1988).

Selected sessions in each group were filmed (Walker, 1985; FEU, 1988), and were useful for validation as they had the advantage of allowing 'the researcher to re-visit at later points in time' (Erickson and Wilson, 1982). This technique provides evidence for use in student discussion, and allows the researcher to make a 'pattern analysis of key moments in the transcripts' (Walker, 1985; in FEU, 1988), which compares with the coding paradigm of grounded theory (Strauss, 1987) using transcripts of interviews.

The 'passive interview' or questionnaire technique was chosen, as the total of 32 students (three groups) was not large enough for a sample study, yet not small enough for individual interviews. This technique also bridges the gap between qualitative and quantitative forms of data (Walker, 1985; Hopkins, 1985). Questionnaires on curriculum material and methods were given to the students mid- and post-project as in the *Ford Teaching Project* (Elliott and Adelman, 1976). The mid-project questionnaire was similar to one of Roger Bols quoted by Hopkins (1985), with the addition of 'further comments on methods, resources and organisation'. Student opinion on curriculum material and teaching methods was used to compare with teacher-researcher observations in the analysis of findings.

STAGE 1	PLAN	*Research method*: Inductive-action approach
		Research techniques: Triad collection of data
		Curriculum material: Plan resources/lessons
	ACT	*Distribute*: Racial attitude test and Gulf War questions
		Provide: Global curriculum material
		Teach: Using three different approaches
	OBSERVE	*Teacher-researcher*: Use checklists, field notes
		Students: Initial inquiry–discover questionnaire
	REFLECT	*On student questionnaires*: Possible changes
		On field notes/coding scheme: Adapt plans
STAGE 2	REVISED PLAN	*Prepare changes/additions to*
		(a) Teaching methods (b) Curriculum material
	ACT	*Implement changes*: Carry out new lesson plans; prepare whole-class discussion for filming
	OBSERVE	*Teacher-researcher*: Monitor changes and lessons
		Student: Final inquiry–discover questionnaire; post-racial attitude test
	REFLECT	*Analysis/interpretation*: Of Triad data findings; of TARAT responses
		Make changes to existing practice
		Communicate findings: To colleagues; make thesis available

Figure 4.2   *Implementation stages in research design: MC College.*

The *racial attitude test* given anonymously before and after the intervention was the Thomas Allen Racial Attitude Test (TARAT) (Allen, 1987), designed for 12–18-year-old white students in London. It was used because his research was similar to the MC Project, in that it investigated whether the teaching of Third World geography affected attitudes towards black people. The first TARAT test was given nearly three months before the intervention, in the hope that it would be given an honest response if construed independently of the project. The scoring for the test and how prejudice is reflected in the results is explained in the section on the results of the experiment.

The research design for the MC Project, based on the Simple Action Research Model of the FEU (1988), is shown diagrammatically in Figure 4.2.

How the content meets the objectives

The six-week module of selected areas from the University of London 210 syllabus was suitable for meeting the project's objectives of equality and justice, a global attitude and the need for change with the overall aim of reducing prejudice. The intervention was planned for six weeks starting in January 1991.

THE RESULTS OF THE EXPERIMENT

The aim of the experiment was to discover whether a combination of selected curriculum material and teaching methods could reduce prejudice as well as maintaining

Table 4.1. *Results of TARAT racial attitude tests.*

	Pre-test	Post-test	% change
Group C (didactic)	654	679	+3.8
Group B (peer-tutoring)	970	985	+1.5
Group D (collaborative)	749	731	−2.4

standards; and if one combination was more effective than the others. A total of 33 students from the three groups took the pre- and post-racial attitude (TARAT) tests. In the test scores, 4 points were given for strongly disagreeing with a statement demonstrating a favourable attitude, 3 for disagree, 2 for agree and 1 for strongly agree. Half the items represented an unfavourable attitude while the other half were favourable. Scoring needed to take into account that 'agree' could be favourable or unfavourable depending on the item, and a low total score indicated little prejudice. The scores were then statistically analysed to discover attitude change, either within or between the groups.

The group scores

Ten students in Group C (didactic) and Group D (collaborative), and 12 students in Group B (peer-tutoring) completed both tests. The maximum score for Groups C and D would be 1600 if each of the 10 students chose the column 'strongly disagree' (with a favourable attitude), for the 40 questions, as each in this column was given 4 points (see above). The minimum score for these two groups would be 400 if all 10 students chose the 'strongly agree' column for each of the 40 questions, as 1 point was given for questions in this column (see above). By calculating in the same way, the maximum score in Group B with 12 students would be 1920, and the minimum score 480. The results are shown in Table 4.1.

These totals indicate a slight increase in prejudice in Group C (didactic) and a slightly smaller increase in Group B (peer-tutoring). It is of note that Group C originally had the lowest score of the three groups (654 out of a max./min. 1600/400) whereas Group B originally had the highest prejudice score (970 out of a max./min. 1920/480). In order to test the significance of these results the Will Coxon Matched Pairs Ranks test and the Student test were applied to the results. An analysis of variance, which considers the amount of change between groups, was not possible owing to unequal numbers of people in each group.

The Will Coxon Matched Pairs Ranks Test

This test seeks to discover if there is any significant change in the scores *within* the groups. It takes each individual pre- and post-TARAT score, and applies the Will Coxon test to the data, which is fully explained in my own research report (Schlesinger, 1991, App. 18). The result for Group C (didactic) shows no increase in the mean score and therefore no change in attitude for this group.

The Will Coxon test was similarly applied to the scores of the 12 students in Group

Table 4.2.   *Results of the T test applied to pre-test scores between groups.*

	No. of subjects	Results
Groups C and B	10 and 12	T calc = 1.86
Groups B and D	12 and 10	T calc = 0.8214
Groups C and D	10 and 10	T calc = 1.078

Table 4.3.   *Results of the T test applied to post-test scores between groups.*

	Subjects	Results
Groups C and B	10 and 12	T calc = 1.778
Groups B and D	12 and 10	T calc = 1.167
Groups C and D	10 and 10	T calc = 1.586

B (peer-tutoring) (Schlesinger, 1991, App. 18), and the result shows no change or statistical difference in attitude. The same process was applied to the scores of the 10 students in Group D (collaborative) (Schlesinger, 1991, App. 18), which shows no increase in the mean scores. Although this test shows no *statistically significant* increase or decrease in prejudice within any of the groups, the *shifts* in individual student scores and in the total group scores are of interest and will be discussed later in the chapter.

The Student 'T' test

This test was used to discover whether there were differences *between* groups. The results of applying the Student *T* test to the pre-test scores are shown in Table 4.2.

The *T* test was similarly applied to the post-test scores between the same groups, and the results are shown in Table 4.3. The values in Table 4.3 all fall below the respective critical values obtained from statistical tables.

These two tests indicate that there has been no significant change which can be statistically measured either *within* the groups or *between* the groups. These results were disappointing, bearing in mind that the aim of the project was to reduce prejudice.

Trends in the shifts in individual and group scores

It is inappropriate to compare these scores with those of other research involved in changing attitudes because the variables are different. However, it is noteworthy that Carnie's research (1972) into prejudice reduction recorded no change in attitude; while Miller's 1969 research (reported in Allen, 1987), using a direct approach recorded an increase in prejudice. Allen's research (1987) into the teaching of geography in London schools was more similar to the MC College Project and important in that it recorded a *reduction* in prejudice.

Despite there being no statistical change in attitude, the individual scores and group scores reveal *trends* worth investigating. There was a marginal increase in prejudice of 3.8 per cent and 1.5 per cent in two groups, and a marginal decrease in prejudice of 2.4 per cent in the third group (Table 4.1).

Relative differences in scores for males and females

In the individual scores showing units of change (+ and −) for the 17 female and 15 male students, there was a higher overall increase in prejudice for *females* than for males, with the highest negative increase concentrated in Group C (didactic). Also of interest were the roughly equal shifts in attitude by student gender for the groups using student-centred methods, B (peer-tutoring) and D (collaborative). Bearing in mind the small sample of the study, it is interesting that the trend shown here is opposite to that of Verma and Bagley (1982) and Allen (1987), who both recorded a greater reduction in prejudice for females. It is perhaps noteworthy in this case that the teacher-researcher is female.

The fact that the statistical tests showed no significant change in attitude either within or between groups (despite the marginal increase in prejudice in two groups and decrease in one) indicates that there is no single accountable factor. Simply because the teaching methods were the only differentiating variable between the groups does not make them the dominant factor for attitude change. To get a clearer picture of the results it is necessary to investigate the combinations of the project's three component parts: the nature of its approach, the curriculum material and teaching methods.

DISCUSSION OF FINDINGS FROM CURRICULUM MATERIAL

> It can be argued that the main influence on attitude change arose from the kind of topics chosen for the programme and the kind of information used on each topic.
>
> (Allen, 1987, p. 191)

The project was extended by one week to complete the work, with each group taking part in a filmed discussion. As Figure 4.1 illustrates, a Triad method of data collection was used to ensure a balance of viewpoints. Each area was investigated to see if it achieved the three objectives, and the findings were interpreted in the context of each particular teaching method. Researcher opinion was gathered in field notes written after each lesson from observation based on a coding scheme (Schlesinger, 1991, App. 20). Students' opinion was gathered from questionnaires, essays, notes and filmed discussion. Only a judicious selection of work can be referred to here, with tables of findings wherever appropriate.

Findings from the use of films

The figures in Table 4.4 (overleaf) are the totals for each group, those in parentheses indicating mid-module totals. Some students ticked more than one resource. It is interesting to note that the two groups with student-centred methods (B and D) found films more effective than Group C with a teacher-centred method.

Despite the enthusiasm for this resource, the students' notes recorded little comment on the instances of prejudice and inequality. At best they made only short factual comments such as the following in reference to the film *The South: USA* (BBC2, 1990) which was chosen to further the students' understanding of equality (objective 1): 'Industry tends to avoid Black areas' (Sarah, Group B peer-tutoring).

Table 4.4.   *Groups' responses to choice of curriculum material.*

Which of the following resources do you find most educationally helpful?

	Video	Textbooks	Articles/handouts
Group C (didactic)	3 (2)	1 (1)	9 (7)
Group B (peer-tutoring	6 (5)	5 (3)	7 (3)
Group D (collaborative)	9 (8)	4 (5)	9 (3)

In all three groups only one student attempted to *reflect* on a situation, and he had low (unprejudiced) scores in the TARAT tests (47 and 57 out of a min./max. of 40/160). He observed: 'it may be argued that inequality is no longer an issue of race. Blacks are able to be affluent, Whites may well suffer poverty' (Lee, Group C).

Films using a thematic approach recommended for reducing ethnocentricity (Klein, 1986; Boardman, 1989) evoked a more opinionated response, although students tended to be confused by the moving back and forth between locations (*Vanishing Earth*, BBC/TVE, 1984). Two out of three sub-groups in Group D (collaborative) attempted to distinguish between Arizona and California by reporting back using a regional approach, which contradicted the object of the exercise and illustrates a difficulty with this approach on film.

Film was more successful than other curriculum material in meeting the second and third objectives (which seek a global perspective and an understanding of the need for change). Students in all three groups were enthusiastic about a series of films on Kenya, *Reclaiming the Earth* (IBT, 1987). Its narrator and interviewees were Kenyan, and it had an equal number of men and women from professions, politics, local farms and different tribes. Some of the phrases used in the films were quoted by the students in their essays and in discussion, such as 'wheat élite' (Clare, Group D discussion, 21.2.91; Paul, Group D essay) in reference to a monopoly of cash croppers in Kenya. A 'blueprint of colonialism' (Mark, Group B, 19.2.91) was used to explain the inappropriate multistorey buildings in Nairobi, and gathered licence for use in other examples of post-colonialism. The success of these films with regard to the objectives can best be judged by the number of students supporting Kenyan opinion in their essays: for instance, that a preference for cash crops over staple crops was the chief problem of the country, *not* population growth as expressed in many traditional A level textbooks.

Findings from the use of publications

Articles from geographical journals and newspapers were not my preferred materials for achieving the objectives, but they were popular with the students and widely used in the second half of the module for topics on trade, aid and multinationals, where there are few good films or textbooks.

The field notes indicate a livelier and less inhibited discussion if the issue/topic for discussion was at a geographical distance from the college. For example, the students felt more comfortable discussing inequalities in developing countries than prejudice in the locality. In Group B (peer-tutoring) with the highest pre-TARAT test score (Table 4.1), three students undermined a discussion on a newspaper article when it became critical of the maltreatment of Black Americans; there were audible asides such as '*They* [Black Americans] can be prejudiced as well you know' (Paul) and 'I never think about racism or prejudice – I'm just worried about myself' (Derek in a stage whisper to Anthony, 13.2.91). Discussion of the same article in the other two groups took the form of intellectualizing. The women in Group C (didactic) were quick to point out that 'Black Americans would be the inevitable targets for misuse today' (13.2.91) as a result of former slavery. But they were surprisingly unresponsive when I queried whether this thinking could be applied to Commonwealth citizens in the UK today as a result of colonialism. The only contribution on this point came from Group D (collaborative), who expected 'Arabs' to become a target of criticism through the heightened ill-feeling towards Iraq prior to the Gulf War (January 1991).

A mid-module and post-module questionnaire, adapted from one of Roger Bols quoted by Hopkins, highlighted the value of articles (see Table 4.4). One student's request at the end of the questionnaire was for 'a better use of articles [e.g. Education *Guardian*] with discussion and group work' (Graham, Group D).

The most popular articles were 'Our daily bread' (11.12.90) and 'When a charity nose best' (12.3.91) from the Education *Guardian*, chosen for their global perspective and suggestion of 'change'. Materials which I thought important to illustrate the developing countries' request (and need) for a 'new world order' came from 'The global economy: trade, aid and multinationals', *Contemporary Issues in Geography and Education* 1(3), the Development Education Unit at Manchester Polytechnic (Food: Section 3, Aid and Development, Section 7, 1986), and from various issues of the *New Internationalist* ('Planting poverty', June 1987; 'Land rights and wrongs', November 1987).

Issues arising from curriculum material

Although all the above resources met with the objectives, I became conscious of a viewpoint which was consistently *critical* of the practices of northern countries towards those of the South (particularly the practices of advanced market economies (AMEs), which include the UK). It concerned me that this would create not only a negative picture of the developing countries (with 'problems'), but a feeling of guilt for belonging to a country which is being criticized. This situation is thought to be counterproductive to changing attitudes.

Issues emerged from the findings that were common to all the groups. The students' disinclination to discuss prejudice in the UK (and particularly in north-eastern England) could be interpreted as 'denial' of their real feelings (Allport, 1954). To test whether the low-prejudice pre-TARAT test scores were accurate, teacher-pleasing or an example of denial, the findings of a questionnaire on the Gulf War were investigated. This questionnaire had been given by my colleagues to disassociate it from myself. Despite the fact that 3.6 per cent of MC College students come from countries of the Middle East and that there is an established Yemeni population in the local town, little hostility towards 'Arab' peoples was recorded. And this was so despite the negative media coverage at the time, which Carnie (1972) believed influenced attitudes. It could be said that the findings from the Triad method of data collection on the curriculum material (Figure 4.1 and Schlesinger, 1991) supplied no conclusive evidence to suggest that the students were in a state of denial and that their responses in the TARAT test were not accurate.

Table 4.5.   *Comparison of pre- and post-TARAT scores with their rank in their group, of students who quote negative images.*

	Pre-test	Post-test	Rank
Group B	95	90	3
Group C	86	86	3
Group D	98	95	1

FINDINGS FROM STUDENTS' WORK: ESSAYS, NOTES, DISCUSSION

To test the students' understanding of the objectives, an essay was set which involved studying the factors contributing to the disparity of food supply in different countries, and the range of opinion to account for this.

Despite students being provided with selected resource material emphasizing the amount of land in developing countries under cash crop production, and the increased power of the transnationals (Carr, 1987; Knapp *et al.*, 1989), one student in each group suggested population growth as the main cause of food shortage in developing countries. This could be construed as a conditioned response to the 'negative image' of these countries in textbooks and the media. It was interesting to note that each of these students had a high ranking in the group's scores for prejudice, as shown in Table 4.5.

I was interested to see how many students, and from which groups, made the connection between ex-colonial countries and those using land for commercial plantations, in place of traditional staple crops. The greatest number came from Group B (peer-tutoring), although the significance of this was lessened because they were the *only* group *not* to make the same connection in the filmed discussion. In the essays, only two students in each of Groups C and D spotted a cause and effect link, and surprisingly it was one of the less academic students who produced this impressive evidence: 'In 1990 there were 36 less developed countries in the world – almost all were ex-colonial countries' (D., Group D, naming his source as *The Least Developed Countries* (Geofile, 1986)).

Although Group C's essays contained little analysis, as a group their contribution in the filmed discussion (on the same topic) at the end of the project showed the greatest understanding of 'inequality'. One student was even able to quote from memory from the film *Reclaiming the Earth*:

> *Bob*: These countries [developing] should not have to follow a blueprint like ours starting with agriculture, then industrializing . . . who is to say our style is *right*?

This illustrates the thought-provoking nature of the film. To help the students understand a global perspective (second objective), I had pointed out local farmers and nomadic herdsmen being interviewed on film. And in evaluating how the students rated 'grass-roots opinion' I had counted the number of essays mentioning the concept. The numbers in each group were compared with that group's percentage of change in its racial attitude test. The comparisons for each group are set out in Table 4.6.

It is interesting to note that Group C, with the lowest percentage of students referring to the concept, had the largest increase in prejudice. This information was then compared to the transcripts of the filmed discussion on the same topic.

Table 4.6.   *Trends in progress in groups mid-term.*

% mentioning concept	Post-TARAT test swing
Group B (peer-tutoring) 64%	+1.5% increase in prejudice
Group C (didactic) 33%	+3.8% increase in prejudice
Group D (collaborative) 67%	−2.4% decrease in prejudice

Group D (collaborative), who had been strong in supporting grass-roots solutions in their essays (67 per cent) were equally strong in discussion. For example, Nicola supported a 'top down' approach to educating local farmers in this way: 'I think by education, teaching them how to use the land.' Graham opposed her indignantly: 'I think they do know how to look after the land as they have been doing it for hundreds of years . . .'

ISSUES RAISED BY STUDENTS' WORK

Is the nature of globalcentrism a political stance?

An analysis of the transcripts of the filmed discussion on 'Aid and Development' (Schlesinger, 1991, App. 22) indicates an understanding of a global perspective in Groups C and D. The information quoted in the essays was considered satisfactory in Groups B and C, which makes further investigation necessary to understand why the TARAT tests do not show a statistical reduction in prejudice.

It is possible to speculate that what could be perceived as a *political* stance (or one biased towards developing countries and critical of developed countries, including one's own) has had a counterproductive effect. In the inquiry–discover questionnaire given to students, two questions asked whether the 'perspective' of the resources helped them to understand issues. A majority of the replies were in the affirmative, although a few mentioned that the opinion expressed was not an 'establishment view'. Some educationalists suggest that a dilemma is created for students when 'a multiethnic perspective challenges the existing power structure' (Banks, 1982; Walford, 1981). It is also noteworthy that Banks stresses the importance of finding a teaching approach and method that build confidence, so that emotional difficulties that arise can be overcome.

Should the approach create a positive or a negative image?

If a direct approach is counterproductive, and a neutral approach ineffective, it poses the question of *what* approach should be used. Allen's (1987) research into the teaching of Third World geography in London schools confirmed the opinion of some geographers for using *positive images* (Hicks, 1984; Gill, 1983; Marshall, 1985), which achieved a reduction in prejudice.

The MC College Project focused on the *causes of the problems* of developing countries, as recommended by the Schools Council in its Assessment in a Multicultural Society Project (1982), but on reflection, it would appear that this emphasis could create a negative image of developing countries (and by implication of developed countries as well), if not carefully balanced by a study of positive sociocultural factors. I started to question my emphasis on negative images and recorded this in my field notes on Group C. It appears that I should have taken more notice of the research by Davy, Goodman and Milner recorded by Klein. It states that attitudes are formed by the age of 3 years, and to counter established negative images, stronger positive images are needed. Marshall's (1985) research suggests that one way to do this is to emphasize how 'well off in spiritual terms if not in material terms these countries are', but this seems too general and controversial in my opinion.

To summarize briefly: the data collected on the curriculum material show Groups B and C preferring the use of articles and handouts to films (with equal votes in Group D). Films were seen as a popular resource in the student-centred groups. Textbooks were seen as a less popular resource in all three groups.

DISCUSSION OF FINDINGS FROM THE TEACHING METHODS

> I know I cannot teach anyone anything. I can only provide an environment in which he can learn.
>
> (Rogers, 1969, p. 389)

Peer-tutoring (Group B)

In Group B, the most prejudiced of the three groups, the pre-TARAT test score for 12 students was 970 out of a possible 1920, and the post-test score of 985 indicated a 1.5 per cent *increase* in prejudice. This compares with a 3.8 per cent increase for Group C (didactic) and a 2.4 per cent decrease for Group D (collaborative).

Group B was dissatisfied with the teaching approach from the beginning and, despite changes in the method after three weeks, the group was unanimous in wanting a return to didactic teaching at the end of the project. Lessons had been planned for a balance of independent work, followed by peer-tutoring sessions with a regular partner of their choice. The first pair peer-tutoring session was planned for 10 days into the project, and it appeared to be successful with every student present and co-operating. On reflection it is interesting to note that I ignored an initial warning hand vote of 8–4 in favour of the didactic method taken at the end of the lesson, and concentrated on responses concerned with *improving* rather than *questioning* the method. The group complained about the amount of work the method created in note-taking, and I agreed that they could photocopy their partner's notes, not realizing that they would then think the 'tutoring' unnecessary.

Before I could introduce a third session, one girl's father at a parents' evening asked me if I would return to normal teaching, as his daughter was anxious about the examinations, and the new method was causing strain. I changed the method to 'co-operatively working in pairs', thinking that by doing so I would satisfy the students, and still retain a student-centred method appropriate to the project's design. According to the Further Education Unit (1988) and other literature cited above, a change of method should come about or be introduced only as a result of negotiation *with* the students. If changes are made after a negative response and without negotiation, 'adverse consequences' (FEU, 1988) could result. It was not surprising, therefore, that despite the change there was little evidence of co-operation.

The field notes bear witness to my concern and preoccupation with this group in comparison with the other groups, and the video transcripts provide further evidence of this. However, *my* perceptions may not be entirely accurate, for in the student questionnaires a question was asked on 'whether the teacher was too dominant': of the *three* out of 12 students who thought so in the mid-term replies, only *one* did at the end of the project. However, a majority wanted a return to didactic teaching in both the mid- and post-module questionnaires.

Didactic teaching (Group C)

As explained, this group continued with its normal teaching style for the project, which more aptly should be described as 'mixed' rather than didactic. Like the others it had the addition of a filmed discussion during the final week. Group C had the *least* prejudiced score in the pre-TARAT test as well as the highest average mock examination result (60.6 per cent). But at the end of seven weeks it had the *highest* prejudiced score and the average essay mark lay between those of the other two groups, indicating that the group had not maintained its previously higher academic standard. With regard to teaching method, the majority opinion was for a change to a mixture of methods, the following comment being typical: 'if it [didactic method] was combined with another method it would be helpful' (Alan, Group C).

The field notes indicate that I was not as dominant with Group C as with Group B. In fact I felt sufficiently confident to allow an argument between two boys about the film's content to resolve itself amicably (Schlesinger, 1991, App. 22). The following comment is one of several of a similar nature made after the filmed discussion, which was encouraging: 'When the discussion on aid was under way, I personally understood the concept of aid much clearer' (App. 22.) Such comments were validated by the inquiry–discover questionnaire, and requests for more frequent use of discussion doubled to four, from mid- to post-project returns for this group.

The fact of A level examinations being three months away affected all three groups' choice of method. The two groups experiencing different methods had a majority vote in favour of didactic teaching for passing A level examinations, although neither chose it as their preferred method of learning. The reasons for this are a matter of conjecture, not least because of the difficulty of making changes, considered by Donna Brandes and Paul Ginnis as 'a tough challenge for any of us' (1986, p. 167).

There is very little support for solely didactic approaches in recent research and literature, and none with regard to prejudice reduction. Lynch considers the didactic approach a contradiction to 'the development of a reflective commitment to the values of a democratic cultural diversity' (1987, p. 113). Taking this together with counter-productive factors such as using a direct approach (anti-racist perspective) and negative images (problems in developing countries), perhaps it is no surprise that Group C showed a marginal increase in prejudice.

Collaborative group work (Group D)

At the start of the project Group D had the *lowest* average percentage of marks in the January mock A level examinations (46.75 per cent), and their average essay mark during the project was the *lowest* for the three groups (17/25). Group D's pre-TARAT test score lay midway between those of Group B and Group C, but its post-TARAT test score was the only one to record a *decrease* in prejudice (2.4 per cent).

It is fair to assume that the teaching method contributed to the positive attitude change, as the curriculum material and direct approach were the same for the other groups which recorded a negative attitude change. Owing to this being a short project and because of the pressure of the syllabus, the collaborative group work method was not carried out to full advantage. A pattern evolved where I set the tasks and the self-chosen sub-groups decided on how to divide and carry out the work. An important outcome was my improved relationship with this group, which increased my confidence in using the method.

Both myself and the students identified similar difficulties with this method. The problem of *time*, for students to record all the information that was engendered by the sub-groups, had also been recorded by Group B (peer-tutoring). A particular difficulty lay in the negative effect any one student could have on a sub-group. For instance, Claire had erratic attendance and Nicola from her sub-group complained that 'current group teaching method is not very organised, some people end up doing all the work and others don't do very much' (Schlesinger, 1991, App. 21D).

Despite this complaint, the field notes also recorded positive incidents regarding individual students. Two students attended more regularly during the project, lapsing back to their old habits when it ended, and a student who had moved his seat to make a sub-group remained with them at the end of the project.

An analysis of Group D's assessment of the collaborative method recorded 3 out of 11 students feeling dissatisfied with it, and eight thinking they had gained knowledge from it. However, they were unanimous in thinking that the method had helped them understand issues, an opinion supported by the literature and research on teaching for prejudice reduction (Lynch, 1987; Brandt, 1985).

SUMMARY OF STUDENTS' RESPONSES TO THE METHODS

Teacher-led *whole-class* discussion was incorporated in all three groups and was a popular technique. However, the request for more discussion (in the questionnaires) could have been a request for more *student-led discussion*, which researchers in 'multicultural geography' stress should take place *between students* in small groups of up to six people (Hicks, 1981; Richardson, 1982; FEU, 1980). Although the MC College research had some student-led discussion in Group D (collaborative), and between pairs in Group B (peer-tutoring) it was more concerned with the *organization* of tasks than with 'co-operative tasks where sharing information is vital' (Richardson, 1982). The development of co-operative tasks within group work will be part of my agenda for the future.

By comparing the findings of the questionnaires in all three groups, a picture of the students' attitudes towards the teaching methods emerges. Seven out of 10 questions

Table 4.7. *Groups' responses to teaching methods.*

	Total no.	For didactic	For more group work	For mixture	For discussion
Group B	12	11	0	0	1
Group C	11	4	4	1	2
Group D	10	0	4	2	4

in the mid-module questionnaire and 11 out of 16 in the post-module one referred to teaching method, and the general trend was a shift away from didactic teaching, with an increase in support for group work (Schlesinger, 1991, App. 21). A table of the groups' responses to the question 'Do you want to return to didactic teaching or do you want changes?' is found in Table 4.7.

Of the six students wanting changes in Group C (didactic), four specified more group work, and two more discussion. Similarly, of the six opting for changes in Group D (collaborative), four wanted more group work, four more discussion, and two a mixture of methods. Evidence from the essays showed that the student-centred methods produced a greater global awareness, indicating that this method was helpful in achieving the second objective. To conclude, the students' response to teaching methods can be summarized as follows:

- A positive attitude to group work, with a request for better organization.
- A favourable attitude to discussion in all three groups.
- A negative attitude to peer-tutoring, even though the group concerned improved its academic performance during the project.

TEACHER-RESEARCHER'S RESPONSE TO THE METHODS

It would seem that the skills needed for action research are perception and 'reflection in action' (Kolb and Fry, 1975; FEU, 1988; Kemmis and McTaggart, 1982; Boud *et al.*, 1985). Walker (1985) thinks an ability which he calls an 'intraview', meaning 'being *objective* about what is essentially subjective' (p. 150), is also necessary to the process. And all these recommendations were kept in mind in the analysis of findings. The seven weeks' data recorded in the field notes and observations were analysed for patterns of recurring situations, behaviour, etc., as recommended by the grounded theorists (Strauss, 1987; Altrichter and Posch, 1989), and the following categories emerged:

1. Too teacher-led; little student initiation.
2. Little time for discussion.
3. Good atmosphere.

Categories 1 and 3 can be validated in the transcripts of the filmed discussions (Schlesinger, 1991, App. 22), but they are my perceptions and are not necessarily shared by the students. For instance, while I considered my role too dominant in all three methods (category 1), all but three of the students circled 'enough' to the question: 'Is the teacher involved in the sessions . . . too much/enough/too little.' However, throughout the module efforts were made to involve the students more, helped by the student-centred methods in two groups.

The filmed whole-class discussion or 'active-learning method' (FEU, 1988) was planned for all groups in response to data in the field notes, suggesting that informal discussion was getting marginalized to the end of lessons. The topic 'Aid and Development' was chosen to cover all three objectives with a particular emphasis on the third objective, the need for change. While chairing the discussions and helping students understand the concept of change, I was mindful of Lynch's advice when he quoted Kohlberg, an American, who suggested that students should be 'introduced to moral dilemmas which are solved by applying reasoning one stage *above* their existing reasoning' (Kohlberg, 1984, p. 91). The students, in being asked to comment on the strategies taken to solve a country's problems, were encouraged to examine their own attitudes and value system, which is a long-term aim of the project.

Through sifting the findings into categories, it was hoped to discover why the TARAT test scores revealed no statistical change (i.e. no reduction in prejudice). The evidence repeatedly returned (although often by a process of elimination) to the direct teaching approach. This is supported in the literature and research for use in prejudice reduction, although inadequately used to date in teaching political geography.

James Lynch describes the anti-racist phase of the mid-1980s as a 'rough shod approach of condemning white racism and building on the guilt of the majority community to train teachers and pupils out of their prejudice' (1989, p. 37). If by teaching political geography *directly*, there is a reflection of this 'rough shod approach', one could deduce that it could have a similar counterproductive effect. Could it be that it is not the direct approach that is culpable, but the *style* of that approach?

The main findings from the investigation of the curriculum material, teaching approach and three methods can be summarized as follows:

- It is misleading (and in this case unproven) to make assumptions about people's attitudes, including prejudice.
- A *positive* image of developing countries is a necessary precursor to a reduction in prejudice towards their peoples.
- The ethos of direct teaching is important in attitude change, and anti-racist teaching and political geography are counterproductive to prejudice reduction if focused on *blame and guilt*.
- Negotiated student-centred teaching methods are an essential part of a democratic classroom and could help towards attitude change.
- Teaching methods that build confidence (self-image, empowerment) are necessary in the process of change.

CONCLUSIONS AND LOOKING TO THE FUTURE

A teacher-researcher has an opportunity for autonomous, professional self-development through systematic self-study, through the study of the work of other teachers and through the testing of ideas of classroom research procedure.

(L. Stenhouse, article in *New Society*, 1975)

By combining the component parts of this small-scale project, a series of discoveries emerge which suggest the need for changes in my own current practice. The first objective, promoting equality and countering injustice and bias, had shortcomings as the curriculum material concentrated on the existing *inequalities* and suggested few solutions. The literature and research suggest that this approach would create a negative rather than positive image of developing countries, which is counterproductive to prejudice reduction.

It is less easy to assess how far the second objective, encouraging a global perspective of the world, had been achieved. The 'Observation Coding Charts' revealed more examples of ethnocentric thinking than global perspectives. Perhaps a contributory reason lay in there being a lack of suitable curriculum material. Material showing an Afrocentric viewpoint was used, but although informative in portraying another point of view, it did not represent a global perspective. Similar difficulties were recorded by Paul Grey when he quoted a State Education Commissioner's comments on a history curriculum in the USA: 'It is difficult to imagine what a global perspective might be, given the report's vague prose' (1991, p. 4). In future, I intend to increase the use of case studies relating to different societies, to emphasize particular cultural attributes and values. More research and information are needed on this area of the geography curriculum.

Conclusions have been drawn from qualitative results to assess whether the third objective, which stresses a need for change in the relationships between countries, was successful. The content of the essays and the trend of the discussion were convincing in that the majority of students supported a *need* for change in the balance of power within and between countries.

Taking a holistic view of the project, I regret sincerely the added stress that a sudden change of teaching method put on the students particularly in Group B (peer-tutoring), when they were all pressurized by impending public examinations. As mentioned earlier, all future investigations will be made with first-year A level students to avoid this problem. With an increase in adult education in tertiary colleges, the future points to further investigation of individual methods, such as supported self-study and the use of the Open College.

The findings from the field notes (Schlesinger, 1991, App. 20) indicate teacher dominance also occurring with student-centred methods. Although this was addressed in the project, it will continue to be part of my future agenda since it smacks of authoritarianism. As explained by Allport, 'if authoritarianism and hierarchy dominate the system the child cannot help but learn that power and status are the dominant factors in human relationships' (1954, p. 395).

What other researchers should bear in mind

Although one of the advantages of action research is that plans can be altered mid-project after reflection, the MC College Project suffered through insufficient planning at the outset, particularly in its limited choice of curriculum material (insufficient positive images and global material), and in the organization of small collaborative group work.

Accepting the evidence and the results of the research was difficult and I found myself wanting to distort them by rationalization, denial, etc. Other researchers should be aware of this pitfall in any research of a qualitative nature. In looking for positive aspects to these disappointing results, I am reminded of Rogers's words: 'they [results] do *not* demonstrate the existence of a teacher-expectancy effect' (1986), which is surely reassuring, considering my concern about teacher dominance.

The project has left me very conscious of stressing the positive aspects of developing countries, and of discussing solutions to problems, avoiding blame and not causing guilt. My teaching method at present is 'a composite strategy rather than a single approach' (Nixon, 1985), which allows me 'to use the insights gained from them all' (Waterhouse, 1990).

To improve the curriculum material for 'affective learning' (Lynch, 1987) new resources need researching, particularly for using in small groups – such as the board games and simulations which were lacking in the project. Packs of cards on appropriate topics are recommended to stimulate student-led discussion, a noteworthy example being Starkey's *The Rich and the Poor* (1979), with Kidron and Segal's *State of the World Atlas* (1981) for reference.

The MC College Project points to a future agenda involving small-scale changes on a daily basis, and the possibility of future experiments involving colleagues. At a meeting where the results of the project were explained to six members of the section staff (Geography, History, Government and Politics) I was hopeful. In the words of Philip Waterhouse, 'methods are an ongoing process' (1990) and I am seeking opportunities for co-operative work with colleagues in monitoring peer-group tutoring sessions between first-year A level and GCSE students, and in exploring flexible learning approaches that could include supported self-study and possibly 'supplemental instruction' (Kingston University). Indeed, it would be essential to work co-operatively if a change to another A level syllabus were thought necessary (the new JMB A level syllabus proposed for 1994 was discussed at a 16–19 conference in Newcastle upon Tyne in June 1991).

Above all, A level students need to feel secure that they are being provided with a quick access to knowledge, to enable them to achieve what R. F. MacKenzie calls 'the acceptable mark-earning answers that will gain them high grades in the certificates' (in Hammersley, 1990, p. 10). For high grades in human geography, it is also necessary to understand and explain situations in different countries, a task which requires a self-critical awareness and a personal value system.

Although I have been fairly disappointed with the curriculum material and teaching approaches adopted for this small-scale project, which did not result in a reduction in prejudice, there have been important personal benefits. These are well summarized by Jean Rudduck as follows: 'reflective classroom-focussed research is a way of building *personal excitement, confidence and insight* – and these are important foundations for career-long personal and professional development' (1989, p. 67, emphasis added).

REFERENCES

Allen, T. N. (1987) An investigation into the attitude of white secondary school pupils towards black people and an assessment whether geography teaching about the Third World modifies such attitudes. Ph.D. thesis, University of London.

Allport, G. W. (1954) *The Nature of Prejudice*. Cambridge, MA: Addison-Wesley.

Altrichter, H., and Posch, P. (1989) Does the 'grounded theory' approach offer a guiding paradigm for teacher research? *Cambridge Journal of Education* **19**(6), 21–31.

Banks, J. (1982) Reducing prejudice in students: theory and research practices. *Conference Papers* 65-9. Seattle.

Banks, J. (1984) Multicultural education and its critics: Britain and USA. *New Era* **65**(3), 58-65.

Banks, J., and Banks McGee, C. (eds) (1989) *Multicultural Education: Issues and Perspectives*. Boston, MA: Allyn & Bacon.

Beddis, R. (1970) Schools Council Geography for the Young School Leaver Project. *Teacher's Guide: Cities and People*. London: Nelson.

Boardman, B. (ed.) (1986) *Handbook for Geography Teaching*. Sheffield: Geographical Association.

Boud, D., Keogh, R., and Walker, D. (eds) (1985) *Reflection: Turning Experience into Learning*. London: Kogan Page.

Brandes, D., and Ginnis, P. (1986) *A Guide to Student-Centred Learning*. Oxford: Basil Blackwell.

Brandt, G. (1985) *The Realization of Anti-Racist Teaching*. Lewes: Falmer.

Butt, G. (1991) Have we got a video today? *Teaching Geography* **16**(2), 51-5.

Carnie, J. (1972) Children's attitudes to other nationalities. In N. Graves (ed.), *New Movements in the Study and Teaching of Geography*. London: Temple Smith.

Carr, M. (1987) *Patterns and Process and Change in Human Geography*. Basingstoke: Macmillan.

Cater, J., and Jones, T. (1989) *Social Geography: An Introduction to Contemporary Issues*. London: Edward Arnold.

DES (1985) *Education for All* (Swann Report). London: HMSO.

Elliott, J., and Adelman, C. (1976) Classroom Action Research. Unit 2. Research Methods. In *Ford Teaching Project*. Cambridge: Cambridge Institute of Education.

Erickson, F., and Wilson, J. (1982) *Sights and Sounds of Life in Schools: A Resource Guide to Film and Videotape*. Michigan State University.

Further Education Unit (1988) *Staff Development for a Multicultural Society*: 3 *Curriculum Change*. 5 *Teaching and Learning Strategies*. Video: *Looking At Learning*: 4 *Classrooms in Action* (RP 390). London: FEU.

Geofile (1986) *The Least Developed Countries*. London: Mary Glasgow.

Gibbs, G. (1981) *Teaching Students to Learn: A Student-Centred Approach*. Milton Keynes: Open University Press.

Gill, D. (1983) Education for a multicultural society. *Contemporary Issues in Geography and Education* **1**(1), 24.

Glaser, B., and Strauss, A. (1967) *The Discovery of Grounded Theory*. Chicago: Aldine.

Glock, C. (1986) *Adolescent Prejudice*. New York: Harper & Row.

Goodlad, S., and Hirst, B. (1989) *Peer Tutoring: A Guide to Learning by Teaching*. London: Kogan Page.

Graves, N. (1979) *Curriculum Planning in Geography*. London: Heinemann Educational.

Graves, N., Kent, A., Lambert, D., Naish, M., and Slater, F. (1990) First impressions: A discussion of the Interim Report of the Geography Working Group for the National Curriculum. *Teaching Geography* Jan., 2-5.

Grey, P. (1991) *Time*, 8 July.

Hackett, G. (1990) Teaching barricades go up over the matter of facts. *Guardian* (Education Guardian section), 17 April.

Hammersley, M. (ed.) (1986) *Case Studies in Classroom Research*. Milton Keynes: Open University Press.

Hammersley, M. (1990) *Classroom Ethnography*. Milton Keynes: Open University Press.

Hicks, D. (1980) *Images of the World: An Introduction to Bias in Teaching Materials*. Report for Centre for Multicultural Education, Institute of Education, London.

Hicks, D. (1981) Bias in geography text books: images of the Third World and multi-ethnic Britain. *Working Paper No. 1*. Institute of Education, London.

Hicks, D. (1984) Geography. In A. Craft and G. Bardell (eds), *Curriculum Opportunities in a Multicultural Society*. London: Harper & Row.

Hopkins, D. (1985) *A Teacher's Guide to Classroom Research*. Milton Keynes: Open University Press.

Katz, J. (1978), in J. Twitchen and C. Delmuth, *Multicultural Education*. London: Harper & Row.

Kemmis, S., and McTaggart, R. (1982) *The Action Research Reader*. Research 5:67 (RP 390). London: FEU.

Kidron, M., and Segal, R. (eds) *State of the World Atlas*. London: Heinemann.

Klein, G. (1986) *Reading into Racism: Bias in Children's Literature and Learning Materials*. London: Routledge & Kegan Paul.

Knapp, B. (1986) *Systematic Geography*. London: Unwin Hyman.

Knapp, B., Ross, S., and McCrae, D. (1989) *Challenge of the Economic Environment*. Harlow: Longman.

Kohlberg, L. (1984) Essays on moral development. In J. Lynch (ed.) (1989), *Multicultural Education in a Global Society*. Lewes: Falmer.

Kolb, D., and Fry, R. (1981) Experiential learning theory and learning experiences in liberal arts education. In *New Directions for Experiential Learning*. San Francisco: Jossey-Bass.

Leicester, M. (1989) *Multicultural Education: From Theory to Practice*. Windsor: NFER/Nelson.

Lynch, J. (1987) *Prejudice Reduction and the Schools*. London: Cassell.

Lynch, J. (ed.) (1989) *Multicultural Education in a Global Society*. Lewes: Falmer.

McCall, C. J., and Simmons, J. L. (eds) (1969) *Issues in Participant Observation*. Reading, MA: Addison-Wesley.

Marshall, L. D. (1985) An analysis of factors influencing the nature of Third World studies in the geography curriculum. M.Phil. thesis, University of London.

Nixon, J. (1985) *A Teacher's Guide to Multicultural Education*. Oxford: Blackwell.

Reid, K., Hopkins, D. and Holly, P. (1988) *Towards the Effective School*. Oxford: Blackwell.

Richardson, R. (1982) Geography. In A. Craft and G. Bardell (eds), *Curriculum Opportunities in a Multicultural Society*. London: Harper & Row, 1984.

Rogers, C. (1969) *Freedom to Learn*. Westerville, OH: Merrill.

Rogers, C. (1986) Research into teachers' expectations and their effects. In M. Hammersley (ed.), *Case Studies in Classroom Research*. Milton Keynes: Open University Press.

Rudduck, J. (1989) Practitioner research and programmes of initial teacher education. *Westminster Studies in Education* 12, 61–72.

Schlesinger, A. (1991) An investigation into the use of selected curriculum material and teaching methods for an A level human geography module with an aim to reducing prejudice and maintaining academic standards. M.Ed. dissertation, Sunderland Polytechnic.

Shallice, J. (1984) *Challenging Racism*. London: Altart.

Singh, B. (1989) Neutrality and commitment in teaching moral and social issues in a multicultural society. *Educational Review* 41(3), 227–42.

Starkey, A. (1979) *The Rich and the Poor*. Pack of 100 cards. Available from EARO. The Resource Centre, Cambridgeshire, CB7 4DA.

Stenhouse, L., Wild, R., Verma, G., and Nixon, J. (1982) *Teaching about Race Relations: Problems and Effects*. London: Routledge & Kegan Paul.

Strauss, A. L. (1987) *Qualitative Analysis for Social Scientists*. Cambridge: Cambridge University Press.

Topping, K. (1988) *The Peer Group Tutoring Handbook: Promoting Co-operative Learning*. Beckenham: Croom Helm.

Verma, G., and Bagley, C. (eds) (1982) *Self-Concept, Achievement and Multicultural Education*. Lewes: Falmer.

Walford, R. (1981) *Signposts for Geography Teaching*. Charney Manor Conference. Harlow: Longman.

Walford, R. (ed.) (1985) *Geographical Education for a Multi-cultural Society*. Report of the Working Party set up by the Geographical Association. Sheffield: Geographical Association.

Walker, R. (1985) *Doing Research: A Handbook for Teachers*. London: Methuen.

Walker, R., and Adelman, C. (1975) *A Guide to Classroom Observation*. London: Methuen.

Ward, D. (1992) When sir takes a back seat. *Guardian*, 28 July.

Waterhouse, P. (1990) *Classroom Management*. Teaching and Learning Series. Stafford: NEP.

Waugh, D. (1990) *Geography: An Integrated Approach*. London: Nelson.

Chapter 5

The Effects of Cross-ethnic Tutoring on Interracial Relationships and Academic Achievements

Cecilia J. Datta

This chapter focuses on a study of a system of cross-ethnic tutoring that was initiated as a means of promoting collaborative and co-operative learning between peers in an inner-city multicultural comprehensive school. The objectives of fostering interracial relationships and academic achievement were identified.

After the pre-study interview, 27 pupils were selected. From these, nine pupils of mainly Bangladeshi origin, who were still in the process of acquiring English as a second language, were paired to work with nine monolingual pupils in the experimental group. The control group consisted of nine bilingual pupils who were matched on similar variables with bilingual pupils in the experimental group. Conditions for interactive work were established in subject areas for English, drama, geography, modular technology or science. Pupils in both the experimental group and the control group had their attitudes and behaviour monitored by a mid-study interview and a post-study interview.

The major findings that emerged from this study demonstrated social gains and the development of a measured degree of interracial friendship for the bilingual and monolingual tutors and tutees. In contrast, the control group made slightly lower educational gains and their social progress was significantly less. Although the evidence from a series of interviews showed that cross-cultural relationships did not extend beyond the school boundaries, the development of some degrees of friendship between pupils in the experimental group was observed to occur across the curriculum.

INTRODUCTION

Children from the New Commonwealth and Pakistan receive support in mainstream classes to help them acquire English as a second language (ESL). I was in post under section 11 of the 1966 Local Education Act. The post was financed by government (75 per cent) and the local authority (25 per cent). Home visits were made regularly on language concerns, to ascertain parents' expectations and to keep them informed of the developments of the National Curriculum.

The local authority implemented national guidelines on race and language development, providing training to staff at all levels. Specifically, the Calderdale Report (1986) facilitated the dismantling of language units. As a consequence, ESL pupils gained access to the full curriculum; here they studied along with their indigenous peers. All pupils were working towards common goals, notably the gaining of qualifications. The parents of the ethnic minority, by sending their children to the school of their choice, were also eligible to become school governors.

The Swann Report (1985), *Education for All*, highlighted the necessity for schools to provide 'good education' and to take measures 'to challenge racism'. Institutional support came from the local authority but, as will be explained later in the chapter, this support was minimized to some extent because of the prevailing local climate.

At the 'chalk face', mainstream teachers and language support teachers worked collaboratively in team teaching situations in those classes where there were bilingual pupils. The term 'bilingual' refers to those pupils whose mother tongue is not English; they are in the process of learning English.

This study was designed to foster the bilingual pupils' acquisition of English, and to examine the effects on inter-ethnic relations and on the academic standards of the pupils involved. Peers were interacting in tasks which involved the skills of speaking, listening, reading and writing; additionally, cognitive demands included making inferences, explaining, instructing, analysing and evaluating. As they worked co-operatively, they shared ideas and resources. The presence of two teachers contributed to the standardization of the language. The local dialect was so strong that methods for second language acquisition were also appropriate for the ethnic majority.

Research undertaken here has its origin in contact theory (Cook, 1978, p. 97). In this theory, a favourable outcome is predicted, fostering equal status, maintaining contact so as to disconfirm the prevailing stereotypical beliefs of the disliked group, promoting co-operation in achieving a joint goal, revealing individual characteristics of the persons contacted, and governing the contact situation under conditions which promote equality and egalitarian association.

There is nothing new about children learning from their peers. Wagner (1990, pp. 21–37) outlined the historical context in which students have taught other students in settings directed and planned by the teacher. Aristotle is reported to have used peer-teaching (Wise, 1964), and Quintilian pointed out how younger children could learn from the older ones in schools of oratory (Kennedy, 1969). Wagner quoted Comenius' famous phrase: 'He who teaches others, teaches himself' (1990, p. 24).

'Teaching as reinforcing one's own learning' is a principle which has been acknowledged by many educators (Topping, 1988, pp. 1–26). That a co-operative structure encourages achievement has been verified by Sharan (1980) and Johnson *et al.* (1983). However, meaningful systematic studies of different forms of co-operative learning were influenced by Allport's premise (1954, p. 281) that prejudice is decreased by equal status, close contact and co-operative efforts towards a common goal (Ziegler, 1981, p. 264).

This study contained some of the elements of the classical form of co-operative learning strategies, but also differed in certain aspects as stated below. As such, the cross-ethnic tutoring which is described here can be termed a variant of co-operative learning.

Throughout the 1960s and 1970s, interest in co-operative learning accelerated in many situations. Lippitt and Lippitt (1968) had multiple goals of stimulating older tutors, providing academic and motivational help for younger children, and developing friendship and mutual regard among students of different ages. Cloward (1967) was responsible for a carefully designed programme for homework helpers, as a result of which the tutors' reading ages improved significantly. Mollod (1970) did a study to control the total amount of instructional time. Even when the experimental group was peer-tutored for only half of the allotted lesson time, gains were made for tutees and tutors. Further examples have been referenced by Gredler (1985), Devin-Sheehan *et al.* (1976) and Topping (1987).

It is a well-researched topic and numerous studies of co-operative learning have produced a wealth of data. Co-operative learning, particularly the peer-tutoring or cross-age version of it, in its simplest form refers to the tutoring or teaching of pupils by older pupils on a one-to-one basis after the older pupil is taught a subject (Fitz-Gibbon, 1983, p. 160). Various forms have been adapted to satisfy the needs of educationally, physically and socially disadvantaged pupils.

Positive outcomes of co-operative learning have been found to be related to academic gains, race relations, mutual concern, self-esteem, school liking, and the ability to take another person's perspective (Slavin, 1980, p. 323).

SOME RESEARCH ON PEER-TUTORING

The four principal models – teams games tournaments (TGT), student teams academic divisions (STAD), jigsaw, and small group teaching – are well-defined and well-researched techniques which have been influential in affecting academic progress and cross-racial interactions. The use of the small group teaching technique (Sharan and Sharan, 1976) was characterized by a high degree of student autonomy and task interdependence within the group, but it involved little group interdependence or sharing between the groups. By this method, learning occurs through co-operative group inquiry, data gathering and group discussions. These processes enable the development of linguistic skills among second language learners, and yet relatively little work has been done using this technique.

A study (Hertz-Lazarowitz *et al.*, 1978) indicated increased co-operation and altruism, and decreased competition and vengefulness, among the experimental group compared to the control group judged on a reward-allocation task. The personal qualities fostered in their study have social relevance in multi-ethnic situations.

Glynn (1985) has emphasized the importance of a wider social context for peer-tutoring. It has been argued that if peer-tutoring occurs within a responsive social context then this will permit individuals to acquire not only specific skills but also generic knowledge about how to learn.

A research review of 82 studies of peer-tutoring by Sharpley and Sharpley (1981) highlighted several important points:

- The range of students that can acquire benefit from tutoring.
- The importance of relative competence between the tutor and the tutee.
- The effectiveness of sex pairing.
- The question of optimum period of tutoring.

- The effectiveness of tutoring on racial and socioeconomic issues.
- The nature of interaction.
- The tasks and activities included in various programmes.

Sharpley and Sharpley came to the conclusion that social, academic and cognitive benefits can be imparted to students who are high achievers, low achievers or poorly motivated.

The majority of the research reviewed by Sharpley and Sharpley showed that cognitive gains achieved were invariant of the size of tutor–tutee age difference. The conclusion was that same-age tutors were as effective as the different-age tutors in inducing cognitive gains in the tutees; but for the gain of tutors, same-age tutoring was more effective.

In recent years the scope of application of peer-tutoring has been extended to include a wide age range, a variety of tutors and tutees – underachievers and those with behavioural and emotional problems – and new subject areas: modern language teaching (Fitz-Gibbon and Reay, 1982, pp. 39–44), chemistry (Bland and Harris, 1988) and spelling (Oxley and Topping, 1990).

CHARACTERISTICS OF THIS STUDY

The main characteristics of this study are as follows:

- A small group was used.
- A range of subject areas was selected.
- The students remained in the mainstream class with the exception of drama/English, which was a cross-aged group.
- No selection was made on the basis of ability.
- Class level was mixed-ability.
- Method of evaluation was by interview and 'tests'.
- Both academic and social effects were assessed.
- Assessment was made of the prevailing cross-racial relationships both in the school (outside the tutoring group) and in the community.

The study was designed to avoid a competitive structure. It began with an observation and planning period of half a term, and the study's duration was 10 weeks. Before and after this period the teacher-researcher was actively involved with colleagues in team teaching situations. The type of learning strategy employed included some of the elements of the classical forms of co-operative learning, e.g. small group, heterogeneous group and defined task. However, the method adopted here differed from the classical forms of co-operative learning in two respects: first, the use of normal examination tests, and secondly, the use of interviews for assessment of outcomes. The method provided information about academic achievement particularly on conceptual aspects, but most importantly they provided information about the development of cross-ethnic relationships outside the school environment.

What follows is a brief description of the subjects of the study, their background and the existing level of interracial relationships in the society in which they lived and in the school where they studied.

The 'subjects': composition and history

Most of the 60 bilingual pupils in this school had come from Bangladesh within the previous three years. Their fathers came in the 1960s to work in the steel industry or in weaving. Since the decline in manufacturing, a few have turned to the restaurant trade, but most have taken early retirement. Their eldest sons have entered the restaurant business, while their wives are not in employment. They have extended families to maintain, and the oldest members of the families are not articulate in English; many attend English classes held locally. The Muslim religion is very important, and their homes tend to be in the vicinity of the mosque. Most of the children attend classes on the Qur'an after school hours. Unfortunately, racism is very prevalent in the areas where they live. Various fascist organizations have been identified as promoting racial violence (Director of Recreation and Leisure, November 1989). Although anti-racist organizations, the police and the local authority actively try to prevent racial attacks, these still persist.

The school

The school maintained a record of racial incidents. All racial incidents, whether intentional or unintentional, verbal, written or physical, were investigated with great thoroughness by the school's managers. This school enjoys a particular reputation for teaching English as a second language. For many years it has been one of the schools which have attracted children of Asian origin from the neighbourhood.

METHOD OF THE STUDY

This section outlines the experimental technique, and describes how the experimental group was formed and matched with the control group.

The experimental technique

The experimental technique was chosen as a tool for monitoring, evaluating, tracing influence on outcomes, and verifying inferences (Gopal, 1964, pp. 218–25). It involved selecting pupils for the experimental group and for the control group. The former group worked in conditions which were recognized as fostering educational and social attainment. Simultaneously, the control group was taught by methods that class teachers preferred. To cover the 'whole school' in the study, pupils were selected from each year group. Collaboration between mainstream staff and language support teachers was an integral part of the study. An initial decision was the selection of bilingual pupils and their monolingual partners, then came the planning of lessons which would enable qualitative interactive strategies for language acquisition.

The pairing of a bilingual pupil with a peer whose mother tongue was English was a break from the philosophy prevailing in some areas of the school, which allowed children to sit with friends of their own choice. One significant reason for its introduction was based on the observation that a bilingual pupil often had no English-speaking friend with whom to sit, so that teacher intervention could pre-empt isolation.

The design of the study

The study involved an experimental group of 18 pupils, 9 of whom were bilingual and 9 monolingual, and a control group of 9 pupils, all of whom were bilingual. It should be noted that all bilingual pupils in the school were of Asian origin, and that the unpartnered pupils in the control group were free to form friends in class. Their teachers were not asked to teach these pupils with particular strategies devised by the author.

Both groups had to be observed so that a check could be made on pupils' behaviour in lessons: that is, the extent of interaction, degrees of effort exerted, methods of recording information, and types of written and oral work undertaken. Both groups were to be monitored by a series of interviews to ascertain the impact of the teaching methods:

- *Pre-study interview*: to gain factual personal information covering social, academic and behavioural data. This would include pupils evaluating areas of difficulty on the curriculum, and providing the names of friends with whom they travel home.
- *Mid-study interview*: to gain rapport with each pupil on issues pertaining to classwork, friendship and other matters they might raise after five or six weeks.
- *Post-study interview*: to assess pupils' educational achievement in the subjects, and to elicit examples of social development.

The evidence thus ascertained would enable a check to be made that all pupils were being treated fairly and gaining equal access to the curriculum.

The whole-school policy

The whole-school policy of mainstream support meant that all pupils had access to the full curriculum. There were specialist teachers for special needs, hearing-impaired, referral (behavioural problems) and English as a second language. Occasionally, there were three teachers team teaching in a class. Thus teachers were accustomed to 'actively involving children in an engaging process of using language. Thereby linguistic competence was being developed' (Bazen, 1986, p. 117).

Permeating the curriculum

The approach adopted for the experimental group was cross-curricular, across the age range and cross-cultural. First, the pre-study interview elicited facts about 78 pupils. In the next stage, bilingual pupils were selected who were in classes supported by myself as the teacher-researcher. Then they were paired with a monolingual pupil in the class and also matched on similar variables with a bilingual pupil in the control group.

Pre-study interview

The pre-study interview was conducted individually with 78 pupils in classes from Years 7 to 12 which I taught. Data were obtained on their length of residency in Britain and their time in this school; languages spoken at home; subjects studied and in which year group; names of people they spoke to at break, and names of those with whom they travelled home; from the monolingual pupils only, the names of friends who spoke two languages; and from the bilingual pupils only, the names of friends born in Britain.

From these questions it was possible to clarify the expected level of language acquisition of the bilingual pupils once length of residency was confirmed. Questions on naming people gave information on the degree of cross-ethnic friendship.

Selection of the experimental group

At the outset 15 bilingual pupils were chosen from classes supported by the teacher-researcher. The pairing in Year 12 could not be sustained as monolingual pupils were finding jobs, while the bilingual pupils continued receiving one-to-one support. The study was therefore confined to Years 7 to 11.

The pairing of pupils in the experimental group

As pairing aimed to promote a social relationship, the English monolingual speakers were chosen carefully, maintaining the factors of age, gender, subject area and compatibility in ability. Some of these data were ascertained at the pre-study interview; the attitudes, behaviour and calibre of the pupils were familiar to the teacher-researcher.

Both pupils were primed for the partnership: reasons for the procedures were explained, and they were told that expectations were high that they would work co-operatively on tasks in their subjects. They were both of 'equal status', yet it was pointed out to the native speaker that his or her partner had less English and would sometimes need further clarification.

The matching of the bilingual pupils in the experimental group and the control group

The experimental design involved matching pupils in the experimental group with those in the control group. The variables included age, gender, mother tongue, religion, country of origin, length of time learning English, ability, and subject on the curriculum.

The matching provided a common denominator which would allow a meaningful comparison between experimental and control groups with respect to the bilingual pupils. The main difference was that the control pupils did not have a peer as a partner. Gross differences were avoided by checking out the individual variables.

It is suggested that the limitations to the technique were slight because the matching was very close.

Staff collaboration

The pairing was agreed upon by class teachers, the co-ordinator of the Support Service and the head of the ESL team. A general observation at the outset was that paired pupils reacted positively to the interest that was being taken in them.

The control group

The bilingual pupils in this group were made aware at the outset that their progress and welfare were being monitored, and that they would be given two subsequent interviews regarding their educational and social attainments. It is fair to point out that the control group received adequate teacher support, which was additional to the mainstream teacher, from other ESL staff and also learning support staff. The main differences were that they were not paired with a native speaker of English and they were not necessarily being taught by co-operative methods.

Subjects and staff

The interactive work was done in the mainstream subjects: English, science, modular technology and geography. There was an element of cross-age tutoring in drama/English, which consisted of eight pupils who were withdrawn from mainstream English for intensive language work. The pupils were from Years 7, 8 and 9. There was a two-year gap between oldest and youngest. Three were monolingual and five were bilingual pupils who were still acquiring English.

Collaboration between colleagues

Prior to the study, preparation time was used to plan and organize the group work with the mainstream teachers. At least 12 teachers of the experimental group were involved in a consultative process on how pupils would work interactively on projects required by the national curriculum in the chosen subject areas.

Pattern of the study

Five to six weeks of classroom interaction by all pupils in their science, English, modular technology, geography and drama/English were skilfully induced. Maximum input was given to encourage paired work and collaborative group work between black and white pupils.

Mid-study interview

All 27 pupils were interviewed half-way through the study at off-peak times, usually at break or in the lunch hour. The children were asked about their progress in lessons, relationships with peers and homework, and about general socio-affective aspects of life at school.

Later in this chapter the results of these interviews will be analysed along with class tests set by specialist subject teachers. In these ways intellectual gains were also ascertained and presented.

Work progresses and third interview occurs

The classwork continued in the five subjects with marks being allocated by the mainstream teacher. The concluding interview was given at the end of the tenth week – though it took a few weeks to complete. Pupils were asked about their work so that any benefits, whether academic or social, from the dyadic grouping would be ascertained. Further questions on developments outside school were included.

These interviews were structured to clarify the attitudes and behaviour of all 27 pupils towards self and towards each other.

RESULTS OF THE STUDY

Co-operative learning and peer-tutoring

The results of this study concurred with some findings confirmed by previous researchers. It can be concluded that social, academic and cognitive benefit can be facilitated to a broad range of students: low achievers, poorly motivated students and high achievers (Sharpley and Sharpley, 1981).

The results (through mid-study and post-study interviews) indicate cross-ethnic friendships, a breakdown of some inter-ethnic barriers and, in general, a more positive attitude and less stereotyping among peer groups (Fitz-Gibbon, 1983, pp. 160–5).

Results of the pre-experiment interview

Each of the 27 pupils answered questions orally before the study began. This section summarizes those responses.

How long have you lived in this country?

For the experimental bilingual pupils, the median was 3.3 years; for the control bilingual pupils, it was 4.2 years. The average for bilingual pupils was 3.8 years. As a contrast, the monolingual pupils had lived in Britain for 15 years as the median. The 11-year gap indicates the amount of 'catching up' required by the bilingual pupils to acquire proficiency in English and to get qualifications. Although most pupils had attended this comprehensive school for about the same length of time, the majority of bilingual pupils did not attend primary school in Britain. Like their monolingual peers, they had to learn a new vocabulary and concepts in science, mathematics, humanities, modern languages, etc.

What language do you speak at home?

Table 5.1 shows the responses.

Table 5.1.   *What language do you speak at home?*

Group	Number	Language
Experimental bilingual	8	Sylheti-Bengali
	1	Urdu
Control bilingual	7	Sylheti-Bengali
	1	Bengali
	1	Cantonese
Experimental monolingual	9	English

Bilingual pupils in the experimental group were matched with those in the control. A mismatch occurred with the Urdu, Cantonese and Bengali speakers.

At lunch and at break times with whom do you talk?

The evidence indicates that they moved in confined social circles. Only one bilingual girl in the experimental group spoke with monolingual pupils, but not regularly. There is indirect evidence that bilingual pupils conversed in their mother tongue at break. Only one of the monolingual pupils spoke to a bilingual pupil at these times. Three bilingual pupils in the control group mentioned several names. Thus at the outset the control group led in sociability.

With whom do you travel home?

The answers show that all bilingual pupils of both groups had a tightly knit relationship. The Vietnamese boy walked home with the Bengali-speaking boy, while the Urdu speakers tended to travel together. The closest ties were with the Sylheti-Bengali speakers, who travelled in family groups which included siblings and cousins. In contrast, the monolingual pupils travelled with those they talked to at break times or with a sibling. In the main they were happy to travel with anyone going the same way. The main observations are that pupils travelled

- with those who had a similar cultural identity.
- with those having strong family ties.

Table 5.2. *Arrangement of pupils by year and subject.*

Year	Subject	No. of group	Experimental pair	Control
7	Drama/English	2	1 mono. 1 bil.	1 bil.
			1 mono. 1 bil.	1 bil.
8	English	1	1 mono. 1 bil.	1 bil.
9	Science	1	1 mono. 1 bil.	1 bil.
10	Modular technology	2	1 mono. 1 bil.	1 bil.
			1 mono. 1 bil.	1 bil.
10	Geography	1	1 mono. 1 bil.	1 bil.
10	English	1	1 mono. 1 bil.	1 bil.
11	English	1	1 mono. 1 bil.	1 bil.

Have you a friend who was born in this country?

The bilingual pupils had great difficulty in recalling someone. A few mentioned Aza, who is in the control group. The important point is that he is also bilingual and Bengali. They failed to remember a monolingual friend. Two out of 18 bilingual pupils had native English-speaking friends. Four bilingual pupils named second-generation Bengali people who were friends born in Britain.

Have you a friend who speaks two languages?

The question was addressed to native speakers of English. Seven named bilingual friends, while two could not. The relatively high friendship rate was linked with the reason they were selected as partners, i.e. they seemed reliable, of good character and sensitive to others.

Analysis of social and educational effects of peer-tutoring

This section describes the effects of peer-tutoring on educational and social achievements, ascertained through a survey of the examination marks and interviews.

The pre-study test, based on the half-term's work at the beginning of the autumn term, along with the first interview, defined the base line. Subsequent developments were assessed by mid-study and post-study examinations and interviews.

There were nine groups of monolingual and bilingual pupils, as shown in Table 5.2.

Year 7 Drama/English experimental (2 paired groups)

This was the only lesson which was not mainstream. The teacher-researcher withdrew eight pupils for intensive English. The group was cross-aged. After doing language extension work, they read plays which they concluded with their own improvisations. Subjects included 'Finding a foreigner suffering from amnesia', 'Rescuing a pot-holer', 'Shoplifting', 'Fire' and numerous others. In assessments for the teacher's own records, marks were allocated for skills in communication, imagination and projection of ideas.

Table 5.3.   *Results of Year 8 English experimental pair.*

	Pre-test	Mid-test	Post-test
Jami	25%	30%	35%
Ian	50%	60%	65%

Bilingual pupils were observed to pick up colloquial phrases such as 'I didn't quite catch your name' and 'What a terrible thing to happen'. The three sets of marks reflected improvement in skills, while the interviews indicated that relationships had matured. When Yvonne (monolingual) reported that she conversed with Hami (bilingual) at other times, this was social breakthrough. Hami expressed relief that Yvonne had desisted from yelling at her: 'I'm glad that she's changed.' Similarly, when Abul (bilingual) decided that Malcolm (monolingual) was the nicest in his class, a gulf had been bridged.

Year 7   Drama/English control (2 bilinguals)

The bilingual girl was so enthusiastic that her teacher often nominated her as group leader. She had initiative, leadership and management skills. Therefore she had good marks in her tests. However, in the interview she referred to other lessons when the teacher told the class, 'Work with someone.' She was often left out, 'So I felt a bit low.'

The bilingual boy usually worked with another boy with the same Sylheti-Bengali background. Their teacher did not separate them so that they could discuss their work in whichever language they preferred and then they could present it in English. Only if his friend was absent did he work with monolingual boys. His marks were average. In interviews he mentioned the names of a few monolingual boys with whom he worked in some other lessons. He was extremely disturbed by a racial incident which had been so violent that the police were notified.

Year 8   English experimental (1 paired group)

The pair marked each other's work in spelling tests. They read novels such as *Frankenstein's Aunt* and *The 18th Emergency*, and composed poems and stories collaboratively. In the first interview the monolingual, Ian, observed that his bilingual partner, Jami, had good ideas, and Ian corrected his written grammar. Ian commented on the fact that during Jami's first three months in the school Jami did not speak at all. Ian remarked, 'He has a nice voice. He is never nasty.' By the third interview they were friends in French, humanities and science. They played chases at break and enjoyed conversing. Their results for comprehensions and essays are shown in Table 5.3. Both made steady improvements.

Year 8   English control (1 bilingual)

The bilingual control pupil's marks were 29 per cent for the pre-study test, 33 per cent for the mid-study and 34 per cent for the post-study. In interview Bablus revealed his inability to do homework. He said he was friendly with English speakers, but he could not remember their names. He could recall the names of Bengali friends.

Year 9   Science experimental (1 paired group)

In the pre-study test on safety in the laboratory, the bilingual pupil got 35 per cent and the monolingual got 50 per cent. Thereafter they did group work on solids, liquids and gases. The monolingual usually finished his written work quickly and progressed to extension work, whereas his partner just managed to complete the basics. In the mid-study test, the monolingual got 64 per cent and the bilingual 42 per cent. They were observed explaining processes to each other. In the final test on chemical reactions, both boy's scores went up by 4 per cent. In interviews the bilingual boy was appreciative of his partner's friendship.

Year 9   Science control (1 bilingual)

There was a mismatch between the bilingual pupils in the experimental and the control group. The control pupil had resided in England for seven years. His marks were 45 per cent for the pre-study test, 58 per cent for the mid-study and 64 per cent for the post-study. He had good literacy skills and was observed interacting with monolingual pupils. In interview he was very confident, and with self-assurance said he mixed well at 'off-task' times.

Year 10   Modular technology experimental (2 paired groups)

At the time of intervention, all pupils were partnered for the practical component which involved making structures for bridges. The language of the subject was mathematical and scientific. One pair had a temporary setback when their structure broke. At the mid-study stage, marks on a written paper were as follows:

- Bilingual 6 per cent and monolingual 63 per cent.
- Bilingual 27 per cent (class average) and monolingual 30 per cent.

Language difficulties prevented the first bilingual from achieving well. The post-study test was practical. This time the bilingual pupils could show they had conceptual understanding of practical applications. Results were as followed:

- Bilingual 38 per cent and monolingual 48 per cent.
- Bilingual 42 per cent and monolingual – not applicable.

The latter monolingual pupil decided his mathematics was too weak so he gave up. As he had not completed the practical component he was not given a mark.

The interviews showed that respect had grown between the pairs. Both monolinguals gave evidence of enthusiasm for cultural pluralism. The two bilinguals were pleased they had friends in the class with whom they could converse at break times, although they did not meet out of school.

Table 5.4.   *Results of Year 10 geography experimental pair.*

	Pre-study test on relief features	Mid-study test on shopping surveys	Post-study test on national parks
Bilingual	40%	40%	52%
Monolingual	43%	45%	57%

Year 10   Modular technology control (2 bilinguals)

One bilingual gained a mid-study mark of 42 per cent on theory, which was above average. He admitted he should have done more private study. The other bilingual was interested but lacked confidence. His mark on theory was 6 per cent due to his poorer linguistic skills. The marks for practical work were 46 and 38 per cent respectively. These indicated good conceptual understanding for both, with the former being one of the highest and the latter being above average.

Interviews indicated that both preferred the company of other bilingual pupils. The Cantonese speaker pointed out with chagrin that, although he was fourth in the test, his mark for theory was low: 14/36. He thought that his peers' marks were low because they did not study at home.

Year 10   Geography experimental (1 paired group)

The key feature was the dynamic interaction in real contexts about local issues. An aim of the course was encourging the social development of pupils. As they adjusted to each other while logging in data on the computer, mature relationships grew. They printed graphs, pie charts and diagrams. In the business precinct they were observed completing surveys among shoppers. They interviewed the public, gaining confidence and language on these authentic excursions. The marks allocated to both pupils are given in Table 5.4.

Observation showed that the bilingual's attitude matured and a conscientious approach was developed. The monolingual was flexible in mixing interactively, and also encouraged another three bilingual pupils to use the computer. His bilingual partner said that he enjoyed the work, mentioning that they chose to work together in motor vehicle studies. He named several monolinguals he worked with in lessons.

Year 10   Geography control (1 bilingual)

The bilingual pupil's three marks were 44 per cent for the pre-study test, 44 per cent mid-study and 50 per cent post-study. His language and conceptual understanding improved a lot. In interviews he attributed progress to masses of work accomplished. With great pride he said that he had conducted questionnaires with eight adults. (Most monolingual pupils did less.) He was friendly mainly with bilingual boys, but by chance he met some English speakers at a local youth club, and here he sometimes played snooker or badminton with them. Usually he worked on his own in lessons.

Year 10   English experimental (1 paired group)

The bilingual had been learning English for only three years. In the pre-study test, he had 28 per cent for assignments, and his monolingual partner had 50 per cent. Initially they worked together on a comprehension. The bilingual was glad he had a partner because he could learn English idioms this way. In the mid-study test, the bilingual had 40 per cent for two assignments, i.e. Grade F. The monolingual had 55 per cent for four assignments with Grades G, F, E, and G.

In the post-study interview, the bilingual had come to realize the limitation of his partner's commitment to the study, but he still felt that Paul was the 'best' in the class; and he was pleased that Paul chatted to him out of lessons. By the end of the experimental period he had completed three assignments and got 44 per cent.

In the second interview Paul had 55 per cent for four assignments, and at the end he had 59 per cent for six assignments. Paul was pleased that his partner had introduced his twin to him. After this they would speak in the corridors. At the outset there was no communication between them.

Year 10   English control (1 bilingual)

Ahmed had lived in Britain for three years. He received much support from teachers. Creativity in English was difficult for him. When he reached saturation point he would fall asleep in class. In the pre-study test his mark was 23 per cent, and in the mid-study it was 28 per cent. By the end of the period a mark of 29 per cent indicated that he would probably not be a GCSE candidate. In the mid-study interview he recalled many English friends, but strangely in the final interview he named only bilingual friends.

Year 11   English experimental (1 paired group)

The pair did a comprehension together. They took turns in reading the passage. Then the monolingual explained the passage to his partner before they answered the questions. The pre-study assessment for the bilingual was 29 per cent for two assignments (Grade G). For mid-test each had completed another assignment. By the end the bilingual had 39 per cent for four assignments (all Grade G), and the monolingual had 55 per cent for six assignments (D, E, F, F, F and G). These boys developed a close, respectful relationship. The monolingual arranged to meet his partner out of school so that he could swap a Walkman. He also became interested in the Bengali language. Moreover, he planned to watch his partner play football at his club out of school.

Year 11   English control (1 bilingual)

After three tests Aki's marks were 30 per cent in pre-study, 33 per cent mid-study and 38 per cent post-study (all Grade G). He had a lot of teacher support in all lessons. In interview mid-study it was difficult to extract the names of English boys he liked. He was quick to name a nasty boy who had threatened him to the extent that he said he would leave the school. (The senior management dealt with the perpetrator effectively.) The victim was sensitive and nervous, preferring the company of those with similar culture. Outside of school he went to Asian Boys' Club.

Social effects on experimental group

Interview results provided evidence of the deepening of respect for partners as individuals, for their cultures, languages, religions and families.˙ This seemed to develop through stages.

Incubation period

The first stage was characterized by initial hesitations of the paired pupils. The seed of progress was germinating and they were intent on succeeding with tasks. At the same time, they were aware of each other's strengths and weaknesses. For example:

Riaz: Sometimes I ask Andrew and he doesn't know as well.

Jimmy: Muji doesn't understand the way the questions are written down so it's easy for someone to quickly explain what's meant.

Passive co-operation period

This stage was confined to co-operating within the classroom. All pupils were content · with their partner's attitude. There was an absence of racial incidents among the participants; and in contrast there were overtures of enquiries into each other's cultures and language.

Kevin: Kerchoya told me about the Bengali school. He goes to it on Saturday and Sunday. I would like to learn Bengali too.

Anamul: I like my group. All the boys are polite. Some of the others just grab things out of my hand. I think parents should train them to be polite in the home. Teachers can send a note home to tell the parents.

Active period

The third stage showed that, as knowledge of each other's character and attributes increased, they became more intimate, friendly and positive in attitude. They introduced siblings and friends to their partner. They started chatting at 'off-task' times. Kevin and Kerchoya even made an arrangement to swap a Walkman out of school. Jimmy informed us of a potential racial incident which flared up on the bus. Together he and Muji (his partner) diffused it.

Cultural differences were accepted by the pupils. In fact some even expressed their views:

Mark V.: Sometimes Shaza tries too hard to be like us. I don't think he should give up his religion or culture.

James: I enjoyed hearing about Eid-ul-Fitr and Eid-ul-Adha.

The interviews showed that pupils' hopes for the future had much in common. The Muslim pupils were strong in their faith, and valued their language. Some monolingual pupils in this study were favourably disposed to cultural pluralism.

Observations of teachers

Teacher 1: A bond of trust is developing between the paired pupils.

Teacher 2: The partners speak respectfully to each other. This controlled behaviour is affecting the group.

Teacher 3: Their concentration and serious approach to tasks has been an encouraging start.

As the study progressed into its second stage, considerable improvement in inter-ethnic relationships was observed. As well as working co-operatively in lessons, pupils were meeting at break and introducing their friends and siblings. Teachers were aware of an informality which contributed to better understanding.

Teacher 4: Their motivation is increased as they realize they have common goals.

Teacher 5: They have more consideration towards each other and to the rest of the class.

Teacher 6: The standard of language of both monolingual and bilingual pupils has been raised by increased interaction.

Near the end of the study, pupils were making progress in their subjects. During 'off-task' times they were socializing, and through conversing were deepening their understanding of each other's culture, language and religion. However, the vastly improved interpersonal and cross-racial relationship did not extend beyond the school hours (except for the pair who planned to meet out of school to swap a personal stereo). The third interview revealed that relationships with partners had developed to the extent that, when they met in different subject areas, they greeted each other as equals. Teachers' comments were as follows:

Teacher 7: When the pupils discussed their results from interviewing the public, they had learned to take other people's perspectives and also to negotiate meaning with each other.

Teacher 8: While they were forming hypotheses in science experiments, the pupils spoke in sentences as they inferred the processes. They gained linguistically, conceptually and socially from the interactions.

Teacher 9 (Head of Language Faculty): The monitoring of pupils by interviews is a method which I would like to see used more often. We can find out pupils' difficulties and help them come to terms with their studies.

These observations suggest a model capable of describing the development of interracial relationships.

A GENERAL COMMENT ON OVERALL RESULTS

The results for the experimental group are reflected in the test marks and interviews. Progress was made in the social and educational areas – in proportion to the individuals' skills and abilities. Friendships between paired pupils extended into other subject areas. The main limitation was that friendships did not extend beyond the school boundary. It is significant that the bilingual pupils who were paired with monolingual pupils perceived and appreciated the benefits of the partnership: for example, by friendly responses at off-task times.

In general, the results are similar to studies which confirmed the effectiveness of peer-tutoring in improving the performance of tutor and tutee (Levin and Meister, 1986). Moreover, pupils' liking for the subjects was promoted, which seems consistent with the findings of Cohen *et al.* (1982, pp. 241–3). The fostering of language development by the use of native speakers was effective when used by Morgan (1987, pp. 73–5) in an exercise with Russian children and Londoners in England. The usefulness of interaction as a regular practice for second language learners becomes apparent.

REFERENCES

Allport, G. (1954) *The Nature of Prejudice*. Cambridge, MA: Addison-Wesley.
Bazen, D. (1986) English – a language of its own. In B. Gillham (ed.), *The Language of School Subjects*. London: Heinemann.
Bland, M., and Harris, G. (1988) Peer tutoring as part of collaborative teaching in chemistry. *Support for Learning* **3**(4), 215–18.
Calderdale Report (1986) *Teaching English as a Second Language*. London: CRE.
Cloward, R. D. (1967) Studies in tutoring. *Journal of Experimental Education* **31**, 14–25.
Cohen, P. A., Kulik, S. A., and Kulik, C. L. C. (1982) Educational outcomes of tutoring: a meta-analysis of findings. *American Educational Research Journal* **19**(2), 237–48.
Cook, S. W. (1978) Interpersonal and attitudinal outcomes in co-operating inter-racial groups. *Journal of Research and Development in Education* **12**(1), 97.
Devin-Sheehan, L., Feldman, R. S., and Allen, V. L. (1976) Research on children tutoring children: a critical review. *Review of Educational Research* **46**(3), 355–85.
Fitz-Gibbon, C. T. (1983) Peer tutoring: a possible method for multi-ethnic education. *New Community* **10**, 160–6.
Fitz-Gibbon, C. T., and Reay, D. G. (1982) Peer tutoring: brightening up FL teaching in an urban comprehensive school. *British Journal of Language Teaching* **20**(1), 39–44.
Glynn, T. (1985) Contexts for independent learning. *Educational Psychology* **5**(1), 1–15.
Gopal, M. H. (1964) *An Introduction to Research Procedures in Social Sciences*. India: Asia Publishing House.
Gredler, G. R. (1985) An assessment of cross-age tutoring. *Journal for Remedial Education and Counselling* **1**, 226–32.
Hertz-Lazarowitz, R., Sharan, S., and Steinberg, R. (1978) Classroom learning style and cooperative behaviour of elementary school children. Unpublished manuscript, Haifa University, Israel. Quoted in Slavin (1980) p. 340.
Johnson, D. W., Johnson, R. T., and Maruyama, G. (1983) Interdependence and interpersonal attraction among heterogeneous and homogeneous individuals: a theoretical formulation and a meta-analysis of the research. *Review of Educational Research* **53**(1), 5–54.
Kennedy, G. (1969) *Quintilian*. New York: Twayne.
Levin, H. M., and Meister, G. (1986) Is CAI cost-effective? *Phi Delta Kappan* **67**, 745–9.
Lippitt, R., and Lippitt, P. (1968) Cross-age helpers today. *Education* **57**, 24–6.

Mollod, R. W. (1970) Pupil-tutoring as part of reading instruction in the elementary grades. *Dissertation Abstracts International* **31**(4b), 2260.

Morgan, G. (1987) Exploiting the natives: making use of native speakers in the classroom. *British Journal of Language Teaching* **25**(2), 73-7.

Oxley, L., and Topping, K. (1990) Peer tutored cued spelling with seven to nine year olds. *British Educational Research Journal* **16**(1), 63-78.

Sharan, S. (1980) Co-operative learning in small groups: recent methods and effects on achievement, attitudes and ethnic relations. *Review of Educational Research* **50**(2), 241-71.

Sharan, S., and Sharan, Y. (1976) *Small Group Teaching*, Englewood Cliffs, NJ: Educational Technology Publications.

Sharpley, A. M., and Sharpley, C. F. (1981) Peer tutoring: a review of the literature. *Collected Original Resources in Education (CORE)* **5**(3), 7-11 (fiche 7 and 8).

Slavin, R. E. (1980) Cooperative learning. *Review of Educational Research* **50**(2), 315-42.

Swann Report (1985) *Education for All*. London: HMSO.

Topping, K. (1987) Peer tutored paired reading: outcome from ten projects. *Educational Psychology* **7**(2), 133-45.

Topping, K. (1988) *The Peer Tutoring Handbook*. London: Croom Helm.

Wagner, L. (1990) Social and historical perspectives on peer teaching in education. In H. C. Foot, M. J. Morgan and R. H. Shute (eds), *Children Helping Children*. Chichester: Wiley.

Wise, J. (1964) *The History of Education*. New York: Sheed & Ward.

Ziegler, S. (1981) The effectiveness of co-operative learning teams for increasing cross-ethnic friendship: additional evidence. *Human Organization* **40**(3), 264-9.

Chapter 6

An Investigation into Prejudice Reduction among Young People in Youth Clubs

Peter Davies and Neil Hufton

A search for relevant United Kingdom literature on attempts at prejudice reduction in the context of youth centres has suggested that very little research has been reported. This chapter describes a research on prejudice reduction, carried out in seven youth centres in a northern local education authority (LEA), by an authority Youth Service officer, working in close collaboration with a number of youth leaders. Although the LEA officer had a research interest arising from his pursuit of study for a higher degree, the research was carried out into ongoing professional attempts to anticipate an incipient LEA policy, which predated the research concern and which continued thereafter, as part of the everyday work of those concerned.

RESEARCH IN YOUTH CENTRES: SPECIAL FEATURES

The circumstances of research posed a number of interesting challenges for research design. The researcher had, as part of his professional role, the duty to implement an innovation progressively throughout a county. It was his task to offer leadership, encouragement, support and training to youth leaders and centre leaders who ordinarily made face-to-face contact with the clients, in whom prejudice reduction was sought. Although it would have been possible for him to test some approaches directly himself with clients, the researcher had to reflect on issues to do both with maximizing his staff development function and with maintaining the momentum and dissemination of a valued development. What was chosen was a collaborative research, in which youth leaders worked with the researcher: to select and design approaches to prejudice reduction for use in youth centre contexts; to try out chosen procedures as opportunity offered; to report back to the researcher, via field notes, their experiences of trials; and to share insights and understandings, via ongoing professional meetings and a special evaluation session, held after completion of trials.

By adopting this approach, the researcher was able to maintain unbroken professional relationships with participants in the continuing policy implementation. He avoided an 'expert trainer' role, acting rather as an adviser, 'process consultant', co-ordinator of common activity and communications facilitator, to the youth leader group.

A second challenge for research design arose from the nature of youth centre work – in particular, its voluntariness, both for many staff and for all the clientele. At the start of the research, with LEA policy under review, it would not have been possible to compel staff participation. Nor was that ever desired. The perceived goal was to find workable procedures for prejudice reduction through practicable youth centre activity. Such activities needed preliminary exploration among an effectively interactive group of staff, who could exchange values and developmental experience in mutuality and trust. This seemed more likely to arise where staff were volunteers.

Voluntariness of clientele was an inevitable feature of the youth centre context. Young people attend youth centres as they feel moved and can afford to do so. Once in the centre, they are free to choose their own activities. Attendance can be sporadic. Where an activity attracts interest, it is not normally policy among youth leaders to restrict participation, except for practical reasons, such as space or group dynamic. As a result, any activity that goes on over time is likely to do so with a fluctuating client participation. This was also the case for the activities which were the focus of this research. Of course, it was then problematic to administer quantitative tests of attitude change, pre- and post-treatment, since different participants had experienced different treatments, by virtue of differential attendance. An attitude inventory, in the form of a questionnaire, was devised and administered as a pre- and post-test and it yielded some suggestive results, which are discussed below, but their main value lay in their interpretative correlation with the witness accounts provided by the participating youth leaders.

As the research evolved, it tended to become a case study of an innovation in policy and practice, but not just another instance of such case study. The research perhaps deserves wider dissemination, just because the Youth Service is potentially a major vehicle for addressing prejudice reduction. The very voluntarism, which makes conclusive research hard, creates a positive climate for the valuation of young opinion and belief by significant adults. Though it may call for real skill, in initiating and fostering valued change, youth leaders can potentially interface with the local youth culture and, both by judicious personal representation of values and by working with respected opinion-formers among young people, they may exert a much wider effect than might seem implied by their immediate efforts.

The youth leader's role is to work with others to operate centres in which young people can meet and associate, recreate themselves·sociably, lawfully and safely, and develop personally and socially (Thompson Report, 1982) towards effective and responsible adulthood. While the agenda for the youth leader probably puts the most stress on personal and social education, the young people's agenda probably mostly reverses that stress, with the main emphasis on meeting, followed by having enjoyable things to do. Youth centres have to attract young people, against the competing claims on their time and interest. Youth leaders have to work to maintain an attractive atmosphere and climate in their clubs, as well as providing attractive activities. Perhaps most demanding, youth leaders have – in no doubt multifarious ways, but at a personal level – to be able to attract young people to work with them and with each other.

Where it is thought important to foster an element of personal and social education, perhaps contrary to the prevailing norms of the youth sub-culture, such as in prejudice reduction, it is clear that (a) the attraction to work with particular youth leaders and (b) the attractiveness of any activities are likely to be important variables influencing success. The research reported here could seem to have a prime concern with the trial of activities, construed as 'treatments'. But if we refocus and recentre in the youth leaders' perceptions, we can see that the following was needed:

* An opportunistic means
* Of articulating adequately sustained discourse about, and stimulating empathy for, the experience of prejudice and discrimination
* Attractively enough to sustain young people's attention
* Sufficiently to procure effect.

In plain terms, the youth leaders involved in this research knew they would get nowhere by talking; they had to have interesting things to do. As the research progressed, it became clear that what had been designed as discrete activities was better construed as an overall package, which engaged young people with a set of interrelated concerns, rather than as a set of discrete 'treatments' each with some assignable effect.

THE RESEARCH SITUATION

As already indicated, the research grew out of an ongoing professional development. The geographical backdrop to the research was a set of large and small towns and villages. Youth centres participating in the research represented a range, from 'inner city' to virtually rural settings. The social backgrounds of the young people attending the centres varied with the character of the area served. No attempt was made to categorize social background as a variable in the research. The area as a whole had no more than a few concentrations of streets, mostly on the older margins of large town centres, housing ethnic minority communities, principally of Indian ethnic origin. These were not large communities and, though some of the young people who were involved in the research would have been acquainted with some young members of these communities at school, on the whole direct contact with and personal experience of members of ethnic minorities was probably restricted.

The researcher had been running in-service training courses for youth workers about anti-racism and youth work for three years. Several staff had been involved in all these courses and, during the evaluation of a two-day course, they expressed a desire for a review of their progress and effectiveness in their work with young people in clubs. For themselves, they identified a good level of understanding of the issues surrounding anti-racism and a clear commitment to personal action. In their clubs, where all members were white, they identified many examples of prejudice towards black people which they wished to address in a concerted way. What they felt was missing were means to reduce prejudice in their clubs – the tools, techniques, exercises or activities that might be appropriate in achieving this goal.

On their own initiative, those who had made this evaluation set up a further meeting, inviting all of their fellow course participants and the researcher. Eight people responded, with others asking to be kept informed, and the resultant meeting arrived at an agreement to develop together activities aimed at reducing prejudice in the participants' youth centres. At the same meeting, the members expressed felt needs for a better understanding of the psychology of young people, especially as it influenced prejudice and its reduction, and for a more general theoretical understanding of pertinent issues. The researcher divulged a research interest related to his higher degree and, in effect, offered to act as research assistant for the group, while expressing the hope that he might make the group's work the subject of his personal research.

This meeting set the collegial and collaborative style of both further professional development and the research, which arose from a consensus about practical needs and a commitment to meet them. Although the researcher was formally in a line management role to the other participants, they enjoyed well-established relationships, developed over some years, with each other and the researcher. Collaboration was governed by common commitments to group identity, trust, respect and shared ownership of the task (see Gustafson and Cooper, 1981; Henry, 1986) which had characterized previous dealings in training contexts. Participation was also governed by 'liking for other members; high interest in task; prestige to members' (see Back, 1952). The risks of exclusivity and élitism – in pioneering on behalf of, but with limited reference to, other youth workers – were identified (see Tesser *et al.*, 1989) and every reasonable attempt was made both to keep the group open to, and to maintain communications with, all who had expressed interest.

More practically, at this meeting, the group set themselves a programme of three-monthly meetings culminating nine months later in a 'workshop', at which they would collaborate to finalize the form of practical activities to be tried out and evaluated in their youth centres. At the first of these meetings, new attenders were brought into participation and it was also agreed that group members should share their own and the common experiences of the group with other workers in their own centres, in effect widening ownership and assisting in 'discerning the extent of prejudice' (Meeting Minutes, September 1990). Finally, the researcher was asked to prepare two papers to be considered at the next two meetings. These were to be on 'The nature of prejudice and its implications for youth work practice' and 'Anti-racist policies and the psychology of anti-racism'.

LOCATING THE INQUIRY IN THE RELEVANT LITERATURE

Exploring these two papers occupied the next two meetings. Because they had been prepared partly to fulfil academic requirements in relation to the researcher's studies, they presented some problems of accessibility, but that turned out to be advantageous, in an interesting way. In 'talking through' each paper, a rich and wide debate was initiated. Most valuably, discussion was often based on the group taking theoretical perspectives and translating them to the practical situations of which they had experience from their work with young people.

The importance of this 'translation' cannot be over-emphasized. It played a vital role in enabling the group to feel secure in what it was doing by fostering the confident exchange of common experience. Group members' insights, problems and anxieties were legitimated by the realization that these also figured in reputable theoretical debate. This furthered mutual support and cohesion in the group, and increased members' self-esteem and worth. Perhaps most potently, confident access to effective concepts and ideas for grappling with thought about prejudice and prejudice reduction gave group members a sense of empowerment – they realized they had the capacity to effect change, if they so wished.

The papers introduced youth leaders to the findings and ideas of a number of researchers in fields relevant for prejudice reduction. Pettigrew's definition of racial and ethnic prejudice as 'an antipathy accompanied by a faulty generalization. . . . Thus ethnic prejudice simultaneously violates two basic norms – the norm of rationality and the norm of human heartedness' (1982, p. 3) was taken as foundational in drawing attention to cognitive and affective aspects of prejudice, and the need for prejudice reduction to address both components. Notions of 'in-group' and 'out-group' psychology were reviewed and the relationship between self-esteem and membership of valued in-groups was explored, together with the possibility that such groups may need to be perceived as superior to others, for full valuation of membership and self. The stereotyping mechanism was explored, whereby out-groups may be generally viewed negatively, partly out of ignorance or misunderstanding of cultural practices, but also through focusing on negatively valued and untypical behaviours among their members, in order to justify in-group superiority.

The extent to which prejudice may not be shaken by disconfirming instances was reviewed, again through Pettigrew's work (1982), which noted that such instances can be treated as exceptional cases, or explained away on the basis of luck, chance occurrence or another's assistance, or ascribed to situational contexts, so denying credit to responsible individuals; or such individuals can be deemed so exceptional that, paradoxically, their achievements are, at the same time, not taken as reflecting credit on the rest of an ethnic group and yet are offered as instances of how there is no discrimination against that group.

The important distinction, pointed up by Lynch (1987), between prejudice and discrimination was considered. While prejudice is an attitude towards members of a specific group, discrimination refers to actual negative behaviour directed towards individuals one is prejudiced against. People can harbour prejudice without expressing it in discriminatory action. They can also express it by inaction, where the circumstances call for action. Equally, people can discriminate against others without feeling prejudice against them, where they carry out formal procedures which have a discriminatory effect. To Pettigrew's (1982) cognitive and affective components of prejudice reduction, Lynch (1987) adds a third, conative component – generating the will to identify and act against prejudice and discrimination.

Raab's (1965) observations about the role of law, in creating prior conditions for social change, were related to UK equal opportunities legislation and the need to develop understanding of, and consensus for, enacting that legislation in micro- and macro-behaviours in the Youth Service context. Raab's arguments for the value of 'contact' and 'working alongside as equals', in inter-ethnic attitude formation and prejudice reduction, were reviewed: 'People who behave toward blacks as full equals on every level tend to develop attitudes towards them as full equals on every level' (p. 22).

These arguments posed a challenge for the group. The demographics of their Youth Service made 'contact' and 'working alongside one another' practically difficult. To develop such approaches called for the development of a sensitive medium-term strategy for inter-ethnic relations in the community. They were also aware of Davey's (1987) doubts about 'contact' and Cohen's (1988) findings about cases where it could be strongly counterproductive.

In the interim, the group thought that it was important, as an immediate task, to combat racism and attempt prejudice reduction in the given all-white contexts of their centres. They were influenced by Raab's ideas, also exemplified by Flay (1978), of the importance of 'role-models' in enacting behaviours and expressing attitudes, which it was desired that young people should adopt and which they saw as offering a way forward in the Youth Service.

The group was also introduced to the ideas of Ijaz (1981), which support the view that reduction in racial prejudice is unlikely to arise through cognitive persuasion, but needs address through the affective and, in particular, in the absence of direct experience, through 'instructional programmes which provide majority group members with an opportunity to identify with members of the minority group through "vicarious experiences"' (p. 8).

The workshop which concluded the first phase of the development involved a great deal of discussion and practical activity by the youth leader group, to produce altogether five activities for trial back in centres. Throughout, the group had access to a substantial range of resources – books, pamphlets, articles, statistics, photographs, videos, exercises, questionnaires, handouts, quizzes, role-plays – provided by the researcher from Youth Service sources. There were also poster summaries of discussion and ideas generated in previous meetings. Most important, though, was the resource represented by the group in the form of its own previous experience of training.

Members were generally agreed that they had themselves most powerfully experienced attitude challenge and change, through practical exercises which engaged belief and feeling. They felt that developing adapted exercises of a similar kind, but for young people, could be a profitable way forward. As Walford noted: 'A large number of present users were people who have had the experience of once being in a simulation and who recognise the significance of the technique in helping their own learning' (1985, p. 21).

Thus, a number of members had experienced Gary Shirts' 'Starpower' (1965). Other members had been much affected by taking part in a multiracial quiz. A third member derived ideas from a drugs resource pack he had previously used. The group was also aware that 'the potential success of a simulation is in direct relation to the work and care invested in its invention' (Hope and Wilson, 1985, p. 86) and that 'a combination of various teaching methods is better and more efficient'. 'There is no need to stress that even the most interesting method becomes monotonous, if it is the only one used' (Soukup and Borakova, 1985, p. 40).

ACTIVITIES CHOSEN FOR PREJUDICE IDENTIFICATION AND REDUCTION

The five activities eventually chosen were as follows:

- A questionnaire for completion by young people in the centres, involving response on a Likert-type scale and seeking to establish the range and depth of race-prejudiced attitudes, for use as a pre- and post-test of change arising through centre-based work.

- A board game, 'My Opinion; Our Opinion', which, by use of a die and counters, randomized the choice of cards of two colours, on which were 33 questions bearing on racial attitudes. When players drew one colour, they had to give an individual answer to the question. When the other colour was drawn, the group had to arrive at an answer by discussion. This game was intended to generate qualitative data, in the form of young people's comments and discussion, as part of the pre-test.

- A quiz, 'Twenty Questions', involving 19 assertions with implications for inter-ethnic assumptions and attitudes, asking for a judgement of each as true or false, and one question asking what was common among a set of familiar 'English' words (actually all of Indian origin). The quiz was to be completed individually and then the answers discussed among the group. The assertions were ingeniously chosen to challenge accepted beliefs, in that there was a high likelihood of respondents making a surprisingly wrong choice.

- A workshop, 'Prejudice', which involved a preliminary brainstorm about prejudice with the group, with ideas briefly recorded; the youth leader reading an article from the *Sydney Star* called 'Scruffy, lazy poms!', without indicating the title or who the article was about, together with individual noting of ideas and impressions by group members; handing out copies of the article and clarifying that it expressed prejudicial opinions about British immigrants in Australia; and discussing feelings and implications for the group's own attitudes.

- *Either* a role-play, involving subjecting some participants to an experience of disadvantage and discrimination in the youth centre context, for a duration sufficient to evoke some strength of feeling (one hour was proposed), without provoking active aggression. This was followed by a debriefing discussion of feelings evoked and implications for those more regularly discriminated against.

    Or a video, where role-play was not thought a manageable activity in the centre context. The chosen video, *Eye of the Storm*, shows a teacher being unfair to children in a classroom context, in ways reflecting race prejudice. It, too, was followed by a debriefing discussion.

USING THE ACTIVITIES: EXPERIENCE IN THE CENTRES

Following the collaborative design of activities, the members of the youth leader group carried the activities back for trial into seven centres. It was intended that, in each centre, there would be work with a mixed group of about eight young people, with the questionnaire and the board game repeated at the beginning and end of the set of activities, to offer an element of pre- and post-test of attitudes.

In the event, three of the centres were not able to complete all activities fully, and those that did complete, often did so against some competing difficulties. These were of several kinds. In some cases, the voluntary ethos of the centres restricted, or generated fluctuating participation, for various reasons. As one leader stated:

> *Wilma*: The group started with six girls, there were two boys that were going to join in, but when they realized it was connected with attitudes to race they decided not to join in.
>
> (Evaluation transcript, p. 1)

Similar remarks were made by other leaders:

Paddy: Although we haven't got as far on with the project as we'd like . . . the problem with that has been the voluntary participation – some days one would come in, some days two of them . . .

(p. 10)

Pete: We started with eight, it was down to six, we went to four at one stage . . .

(p. 16)

There were also problems of trying to complete the exercises in competition with other activities happening in the centre, as the following excerpt shows:

Hannah: I felt I could have done more that night, but I couldn't . . . they had other things to do, they were booked on pool. We had a very limited, a very strict time limit really that we had to keep within.

(p. 12)

In one or two cases, work was disrupted by non-involved young people, often motivated by interest, but still interfering with the working atmosphere of those participating:

Sally: I used a room which was separate from the youth room . . . and other young people were actually coming along. Not wanting to join in, but just being awkward, wanting to sabotage it . . .

(p. 31)

In one centre, the leaders experienced difficulty through attracting too large a group and then finding it hard to give time to establishing working relationships between members before getting into the activities:

Paula: We didn't actually want as many as that in the group. . . . We wanted to try and keep the same group together, and we found that difficult. We started off with eleven. . . . But, what came out of it was that, it made us aware that, that we do need relationship building in the Centre.

(p. 34)

Meg: It would have been better to build up trust in the group first. . . . I think we should try to keep the same group for next term and tackle it again.

(p. 35)

Finally, and potentially more disturbing, those leaders undertaking the prejudice reduction activities sometimes found their endeavours undermined by fellow youth workers. Sometimes this seemed mostly just clumsy or insensitive, and may have reflected a lack of understanding and ownership of what was being attempted, as the excerpt below seems to indicate:

Meg: [W]e asked the staff to observe what we were doing . . . but I don't think they felt part of it. They didn't feel as strongly as us about it. They felt it was just something we wanted to do. . . . I think perhaps some other staff needed some training in anti-racism, because some had none at all, just what they had heard from us.

(p. 35)

That there was also at least unreflective racism in some youth centre staff was pointed up by one leader:

Paddy: When we broached the subject in a staff meeting about doing the project and one of the staff members . . . a volunteer who has yet to go through any training – he was overtly racist in some of the things he was saying . . .

(p. 7)

Race prejudice among youth workers is a serious matter, and will be returned to below. However, otherwise these difficulties should not be misconstrued. All work with young people in youth centres is informal and opportunistic. The skills of educative youth work lie in maximizing the value to be derived from more or less sustained encounters, some almost casual. Though these seem 'disorganized' when contrasted with more structured educational settings, there is no reason to suppose that their impact must be less. Indeed, just because the young participants are under no systematic pressure to learn and change, there is perhaps an increased likelihood that any observed change will be authentic.

The participant youth leaders were skilled and experienced in working with young people in these informal ways, and were also highly committed to anti-racism and prejudice reduction. What they were able to do, over the period of materials trial, was to draw together, from time to time and across the centres, between 30 and 50 young people for playfully managed, but fully serious discussions of race prejudice. They did this, too, without isolating themselves, or the 'experimental group', from the general life of their centres. Some were undoubtedly influential in those centres, with other leaders and a wider group of young people. The extent of this influence was not plotted in the research, but can be inferred from the post-trial evaluation:

> *Lindsay*: All the club actually has joined in. I have about thirty members on average come in and although I had six doing the main stuff, we all actually joined in, you know. Things like, 'You're not allowed to say things like "nigger" and "paki" in this club any more.' And although it is joking, they actually don't.
>
> (p. 20)

> *Sally*: [T]he whole staff team were involved in the planning of it. But were not involved in the actual doing it . . .
>
> (p. 31)

In other cases – for example, as reported above by Meg – a wider involvement was less successful. There was no doubt from the evaluation that it was important that prejudice reduction work was understood and positively supported by other centre staff, not only in terms of commitment, but at the practical level of understanding what co-workers were trying to do and the 'working conditions' they needed to do it. Some frustration arose from elementary failures of communication: one leader's co-worker refused to admit her group, because she had forgotten to ask him to admit them without payment; another leader's colleague arranged a trip on the group meeting night. Within the lively to-and-fro of centre life, these were not trivial incidents. An accidental rebuff, or loss of contact, can be a loss of personal connection, seriously undermining the sustaining of young people's interest.

These issues, of full staff involvement, of collegial practical support, of fostering and sustaining anti-racist centre climates, and of the impact of racial prejudice in staff, are important and are considered more fully below.

There is a further point about the way the youth leaders worked with their young people. They were aware, from their earlier discussions, of the risks both of generating inauthentic response and of inadvertently reinforcing prejudice by clumsiness in challenging it. Wilma drew attention to a possible problem for all her colleagues:

the group that I was working with already knew my attitudes to race. . . . They knew that I was going to be looking at them, so I think it might have affected what they were going to say.

(p. 2)

Youth leaders may be significant others for the young people with whom they work. Young people may want their liking and respect and, if they harbour views or feelings which they believe the leader would dislike, they may conceal them. This is not only a problem of bias in research into such feelings, but also a practical problem for those seeking to challenge and debate views and feelings, where these are not fully disclosed. At the same time, youth workers necessarily have an exemplar role. Divulging their own beliefs and feelings may be a key feature of their change-agency. Without sermonizing or priggery – indeed, often modestly and unconsciously – they may have to represent and stand for worthwhile values, in the hope that young people will adopt them, through coming to share commitments to the role of those values, in worthwhile forms of life.

At the same time, the leaders knew that their work could rebound in enhancing prejudice if they were unskilled or insensitive in implementation. They knew that

prejudiced people hardly ever change their initial judgements under the influence of alternative information. . . . It is a characteristic of prejudice that contradictory information as such is denied and rejected, that even the general reliability of the source of information is called into question.

(Bruin, 1985, p. 176)

They were aware of Klaas Bruin's recommendation of experiential exercises rather than cognitive methods for tackling prejudice and discrimination, but they also knew that they ran 'the risk either that negative attitudes towards foreign cultures are expressed openly (which can result in reinforcement), or even that discriminative actions occur, in a social situation that is beyond corrective influence' (Bruin, 1985, p. 177)

All in all, the youth leaders had to manage a substantial practical, social, psychological and ethical agenda in operating the chosen activities in their centres. It could be argued that this agenda should have been reduced and simplified, in the interests of more confidently supported research results, but then the research would no longer have been into attempts at prejudice reduction in the everyday context of youth centre activity. Since that was the core of the research, the results that were derived in relation to that interest necessarily arose from a less than experimentally perfect process. Despite this, there seems to be a sufficient coherence, across the whole of the data, quantitative and qualitative, to raise some issues for future research and debate on the role of youth centres in prejudice reduction.

RESEARCH FINDINGS

Results were of two kinds. There was an attempt to measure the degree of, and change in, race prejudice by means of a pre- and post-trial questionnaire. There were also qualitative data, derived from two sources: brief field notes made by each participant youth leader about expressions of prejudice among their young people, the operation

Table 6.1. *Results of the pre- and post-trial questionnaire.*

	Centre mean	Girls' mean	Boys' mean	Range
Centre 1	58:53	57:54	59:53	52/62:37/65
Centre 2	46:39	40:37	52:41	29/70:29/47
Centre 3	47:37	40:34	61:40	29/63:27/52
Centre 4	48:50	47:47	50:53	45/60:40/59
Centre 5	45	45		27/54
Centre 6	50	36	58	27/80
Centre 7	64	66	62	56/67

Notes: Scores and ranges are shown as pre-test: post-test.
Scores for Centres 5, 6 and 7, which were unable to complete a post-test, are pre-test only.
Scores of 40 or less indicate low or no prejudice; scores higher than 40 indicate prejudice.
The scale is not standardized.

of the planned activities and any discernible effects; and a substantial debriefing and evaluation meeting, which was audio-recorded and transcribed, and in which leaders elaborated on their field notes and shared experience.

The questionnaire consisted of 20 inter-mixed statements indicative of prejudice or non-prejudice, which youth leaders reported as having heard in their centres. Respondents were asked to indicate their response by ticking a four-point scale between 'strongly agree' and 'strongly disagree'. The scoring system was such that, on average, a non-prejudiced young person should have scored 40 or less, with a maximum, high-prejudice score of 80. Scores were as indicated in Table 6.1.

The table of scores can be interpreted with varying levels of confidence. Thus the results for the pre-test are probably fairly reliable in showing a tendency to prejudiced views in every centre group, more marked in Centres 1 and 7. This coincides with qualitative data (see below) reported by the leaders. Again, at both pre- and post-test, the girls appear to be generally less prejudiced than the boys, and there are qualitative data which suggest that this is a reliable finding, for all but the Centre 7 group, where there were an atypical number of prejudiced girls, and the Centre 6 group, where the girls were unprejudiced at pre-test. Where boys expressed more prejudice, this seemed, from qualitative data, to be linked to their projection of a sub-culturally defined 'hard' or 'macho' image, at least in the club context. Third, the score ranges, at both pre- and post-test, indicate both unprejudiced and highly prejudiced individuals among the respondents, and this too is supported by qualitative data (see below).

The interpretation of changes in prejudice between pre- and post-test is more uncertain. First, the data are only available from four of the seven participating centre groups. Second, and more problematic, the samples within each centre at pre- and post-test lack complete continuity of members, due to the voluntary nature of participation. In general, the post-test group is a subset of the pre-test group. Score change could thus reflect, for example, the self-removal of more prejudiced individuals from the samples. Finally, inspection of questionnaire item responses suggests a complex picture of movements in attitude so that, for example, a reduction of prejudice by reference to mean score will sometimes conceal an increase in prejudice on some items.

Prima facie, the scores seem to indicate prejudice reduction in three of the four centre groups for which data are available. The ranges also suggest a decrease of prejudice among both the least and the most prejudiced individuals. The greatest overall changes appear to be attributable more to changes in boys' attitudes than girls'. Despite some degree of overall prejudice reduction, levels of prejudice in two centre groups remained quite high. Prejudice seemed to increase or, if likely score error is taken into account, at least be unaffected in Centre 4. The evidence arising from the qualitative data supports the above conclusions. Leaders report cases of individuals where expressions of prejudice have been reduced in amount and force (see below), but individuals were not consistently qualitatively monitored, so the relation between known cases and the overall samples cannot be teased out.

Quantitative data have been reported because an attempt was made at their collection and they do seem to yield some tentative inferences. Clearly, it is desirable to explore whether, in relation to desired outcomes, particular procedures tend to produce positive, negative or nil effects. The researcher wanted some measure of attributable change, if such was to be had. The quantitative data reported above and in Table 6.1 seem to indicate some prejudice reduction, but it is not claimed that the quantitative approaches adopted could be sustained against critique. Finally, the researcher had to choose between either establishing a reliable experimental set-up or trying out some procedures in the natural setting of youth centre work. Since it was the latter that was the focus of interest, it emerged, through the experience of inquiry, that the qualitative data were more illuminating.

If concern is refocused on central characteristics of youth centre work as a practice, then there are issues arising from the qualitative data which may be of more than passing concern. On this construction, it is not the activities as such, but rather the debate and experience generated in groups undertaking the activities, which move centre-stage. The youth leader's interpersonal and social skills and the centre climate, for both staff and clientele, fill important supporting roles. Relevant knowledge-ableness and commitment of youth leaders are seen to be necessary to, but not sufficient for, success. Although these were concerns that arose from the experience of research, rather than informing its initial direction, sufficient data were available to support discussion of implications for both professional practice and future research.

First, it is clear, from the centre field notes relating to use of the questionnaire and especially the board game, that a number of the young people held a wide range of prejudiced views of the kind well enough known to those working in the field of prejudice reduction. Reported references by some of the young people to 'pakis' and 'niggers' and 'wogs', to 'curry-eating', to smells of persons and shops, to large family sizes, to the size of organs of generation, to 'jungle descent', to overwhelming immigration, to ethnic city quarters – 'Gandhi' quarters – and 'driving out' the whites, underlined by taken-for-granted assumptions of white rights and territoriality, were expressed by some young people in each centre.

As often with stereotyping, views seldom owed their origins to direct experience. Leaders reported that discussion indicated that some opinions derived from family. A typical comment, in answer to a questionnaire item asking whether whites liked blacks living in Britain, was: 'Some people don't, because of their parents' beliefs' (Field notes, p. 2.2). Other stereotypes seemed to derive from more or less overtly prejudiced treatments in the popular press, local as well as national. As one leader reported, to agreement from others during the evaluation meeting:

in the middle of all this . . . one of the lads came bursting in through the door, 'I've got a story to tell you about racism, about a black Pakistani, no, Bangladeshi family's been given a £350,000 council house, for so many years. I can't remember the full story. It was in the *Sun*, or the *Mirror*.

(Evaluation transcript, p. 24)

In other cases, it was clear to leaders observing group interaction that the prejudice of some was reinforced by the attitudes of influential peers.

At the same time, it needs to be stressed, as the pre-test figures suggest, that many of the young people were not race prejudiced and in some cases argued actively, if sometimes awkwardly, against race prejudice. As one said in the discussion over the board game: 'It doesn't matter what colour a person's skin is if you like them' (Field notes, p. 2.1). Another, defending the equal right of blacks to jobs, argued: 'It's not the black people who are lazy though, it's us, because they wouldn't be able to get a job if all the people who wanted a job in Britain worked harder' (Field notes, p. 2.6).

Others who expressed prejudice often denied that they felt or intended it. Thus, a number were unaware that it might be offensive to call someone a 'paki', or a 'nigger'. At least one boy, during the trials, asked his friend if he minded being called a 'paki' and was shocked to learn that he did. Other young people who had black friends seemed unaware that the use of some names could be felt as abusive. As one put it, 'Black people think it's just a nickname' (Field notes, p. 2.2). Partly, such young people seemed ignorant of what could cause offence; partly they seemed undiscriminating, presupposing that ethnically different others would necessarily subscribe to some set of affiliative and cultural commitments, just by virtue of ethnic origin.

For these young people, prejudice seems to reside at least in part in social ignorance or immaturity, or sometimes in an unawareness of operative principles. Thus, one young person was very unsure about receiving a transplant organ from a black person. Her reason was that she was worried if, 'years later, when you were married to a white man and you gave birth to a black baby, would they believe it was because you had had a transplant' (Field notes, p. 5.3). Of course, such a fear may have concealed, or owed its origin to, a core of prejudice, but in the case cited, the reporting youth leader thought biological ignorance was the leading feature. In these cases it seems likely that prejudice will be amenable to reduction through cognitive learning and the development of empathy.

For a small number of others, though, there was at least tentative evidence that racist views and feelings played some lesser or greater role in their psychological economy. For these, racism seemed to relate in complex ways to needs to define identity, maintain self-esteem and project ego, and this was more noticeable for boys. Thus one boy, arguing against the importance of black sporting capability, said: 'they've just come out of the jungle, so they run faster, don't they?' (Field notes, p. 1.1). Faced, in discussion with peers, with an undeniable fact, he offered a demeaning interpretation, which sustained his prejudice. In one centre, four boys 'totally disbelieved' that the proportion of the population that was black was no more than 4 per cent. They were 'stunned at the thought . . . talked of areas "totally black", i.e. Birmingham, Bradford, Leeds. Media seemed to talk of "millions and millions" in those areas' (Field notes, p. 3.3). Some recognized they had formed a false picture and 'felt that somewhere in their home life, school or media they are being misled as to what is actually going on with black people' (Field notes, p. 3.4a). But a couple continued to insist that the true figure was much higher, doubting the reliability of the figures, those who produced them and their youth leader. For a very few young people, there were expressions which can only reasonably be construed as clearly racist. One boy, having experienced anger at being himself discriminated against in the 'Scruffy, lazy poms' activity, still refused to empathize with black people: 'I don't give a shit! Fuck them all!' (Field notes, p. 4.4).

In sum, the qualitative data suggests that, although beliefs were often not grounded in experience of inter-ethnic life, the research sample represented the range of positions *vis-à-vis* race prejudice that have been reported in other studies (Cashmore, 1987; Coffield *et al.*, 1986; Mould, 1987). The youth leaders had more than an official policy to implement: they had to tackle an actual prejudice situation in their centres.

The activities had been designed to have both cognitive and affective impact and, where they ran well in practice, they seemed to achieve this for a number of young people. Of the four activities, two were generally successful, one proved fairly difficult to implement in some centres and one might have benefited from being used in an additional way to the one planned. This was the board game, which was designed to form part of the pre-test. Its purpose was to evoke oral statements indicative of prejudice or non-prejudice, from each centre's group. It certainly succeeded in that, as extracts above indicate, but in some centres, where it was solely construed as a 'test-instrument', the leaders tended to receive expressions serially as the game was played, rather than leading group discussion or challenging assertions which were in clear factual error. There was probably less scope for the non- or less prejudiced to be heard, and this exercise may have risked some reinforcement of prejudiced attitudes, by seeming group acceptance (Bruin, 1985, p. 177). This activity may need review to consider ways in which prejudice could be more directly and immediately challenged, either within the game or by youth leaders.

The 'Twenty Questions' quiz was predominantly addressed to the cognitive components of prejudice, though, in use, it surfaced a lot of feeling and discussion and sometimes fierce argument. The quiz was so designed as to challenge settled race-prejudiced assumptions in such areas as African intelligence, proportion of blacks in the British population, numbers of current immigrants, recency of immigration as a phenomenon, and preference for council housing. It also drew attention to some of the famous, who would not ordinarily be thought to be immigrants, such as the Duke of Edinburgh. The actual response in the centre groups was quite mixed. One centre reported that 'the quiz exercise was really good. . . . I got an awful lot of feedback' (Evaluation transcript, p. 11) and another that 'the quiz definitely generated a lot. . . . I couldn't believe how that really generated discussion' (p. 28).

An example of a successful outcome was the acceptance by one group that their notion of the proportion of blacks in the population was seriously wrong, and their comparison of this with observation in one of the larger towns of the area, which supported the true national picture. Another young man, described by his leader as 'my entrenched racist', was seriously challenged by the realization that Prince Philip was an immigrant – indeed, in his terms, as a Greek, 'a greasy wop'. In this case, the conflict between his feelings about the Royal Family and Prince Philip's immigrant status seems to have set up a true 'cognitive dissonance' (Festinger, 1957), with implications for prejudice in his wider attitude set.

In another case, another young man with 'loads of stories about blacks – none good'

(Field notes, p. 3.4), upon acquiring a new girlfriend whose mother was 'Asian', suggested that, 'possibly I've been a bit hasty in things that I have said and the way I've been thinking' (Evaluation transcript, p. 20).

However, in Centre 1, reaction to the quiz was the strong denial of the factuality of the answers, as reported above, in no less strong language. Here it seems likely that, for at least some members, their attitudes fulfilled an 'ego-defensive function' (Katz, 1959, 1960) in line with Thomas's observation: 'Many times the audience will resist the communication delivered by the persuader. This is a very normal occurrence as attitudes play a major role in the maintenance of self esteem and competence' (1980, p. 34). It was also in this group that there were some expressions presumptive of white superiority, and it seems likely that it was the challenge to the psychological role of such feelings for some members that led to the violence of their rejection of unwelcome facts.

In a fourth centre, factual answers were similarly rejected and the veracity of the youth leader questioned, but in this case the challenge took the form of asserting alternative sources of information, which the young person preferred. This exactly paralleled Bruin's observation about denial of information and challenge to the veracity of its source, cited above. Here the leader was in a difficulty, which she reported as: 'I don't know whether I pursued it too long. . . . I could feel myself becoming quite anxious about it. . . . I think I should have left it' (Evaluation transcript, p. 30).

The third activity, the workshop based on the *Sydney Star* article, 'Scruffy, lazy poms', was designed to give the young people a simulated experience of being discriminated against, evoking feeling which might then inform empathy for those treated with prejudice in this country. It was also hoped to bring out aspects of stereotyping, where there was identification with the group stereotyped. All leaders reported it as successful. At the point of revelation, in one group: 'There was momentary silence, then complete uproar from four of the group. Shock and disbelief. . . . The group became very excited and the abusive language increased' (Field notes, p. 1.3).

In the case of Centre 1, the leader was not able to move much beyond the group's expression of outrage during the session. Key members of that group were very offended, but did not relate their own sense of offence to how others could be similarly offended by attacks on them. Cohen's observation may apply: 'Experiential learning . . . is unlikely to have any impact on the attitudes of the hard-core racist' (1988, p. 89). In the other three centres, there was ample evidence of serious exploration of feelings of being discriminated against and offensively described, and of transfer of those feelings to ethnic minorities in this country. It really did seem as if the activity had made the young people aware of a new perspective (Ostram and Upshaw, 1968) on the feelings of those experiencing prejudice.

The final activity was either a role-play, or discussion stimulated by a video. The former involved putting some members of the group into a situation where they were unfairly discriminated against, and then debriefing their thoughts and feelings. Some leaders did not feel able to run a role-play and they were offered alternative use of a video, *Eye of the Storm*, which examines, through a dramatization, the effects of discrimination on educational opportunities. In the event, two groups used the video and two undertook role-play.

The video, which showed a teacher being unfair differentially to children on a race-prejudiced basis, was effective in eliciting expressions of sympathy for those discriminated against, in the groups that used it. Many of the expressions suggest that there was real identification, in this case with black children, and so a basis for empathy, where a context – school – could be interculturally shared and a value – fairness – was similarly held universal for the context. As one young person in Centre 3 said: 'God, what an awful thing to happen' (Field notes, p. 3.4b). This was in line with a number of findings about the efficacy of visual methods in prejudice reduction (see Cooper and Dinerman, 1951; Chivers, 1985; Wiggans, 1984; NAYC, 1984).

One leader did have reservations about the video, which was both dated and American, and sometimes provoked unwanted laughter: 'Video posed some problems because of age, dress, etc. and this made it difficult at times to maintain concentration of the young people' (Field notes, p. 2.7). However, there was no real evidence that the essential impact of the video was reduced.

The two groups which chose role-play chose to discriminate against the boys in the group, by restricting them for an hour from favoured activities, which they usually dominated to the disadvantage of the girls. In both centres, the role-play worked to the extent that the boys did experience discrimination and frustration, which they handled both by admissions of dissatisfaction and, almost more tellingly, by poses of bravado. In both groups, the connection between this limited experience of discrimination and the feeling of what it must be like to be persistently discriminated against was made. In Centre 1, this activity attracted a lot of interest and allowed the leader to explain widely what was going on and why: 'The exercise evoked an awful lot of interest and conversation. . . . I was approached for the rest of the evening and had to explain the anti-racist work we were all involved with' (Field notes, p. 1.4). In the other centre, the comment, 'It's just an hour for us, but for them [black people] it's like a lifetime, isn't it?' (Field notes, p. 4.5), expressed a widespread feeling.

Having surveyed the general responses of the young people and the youth leaders in relation to the study, we can now speculate about possible implications of the reported research for prejudice reduction in Youth Service contexts.

CONCLUSIONS

First, it is important that youth workers recognize that to condone racism and race prejudice in youth work contexts is effectively to lend them support. Both need confronting, in thoughtfully appropriate ways, as a matter of consistent practical policy. Finding appropriate ways will often be difficult and is not without risk. Youth workers taking the lead in prejudice reduction need an educated understanding of the psychological and social-psychological contexts against which their action is set, and a lively appreciation of the ways in which that action can be resisted, or prove counterproductive. The level and character of discussion in the evaluation transcripts for this research suggest that, where youth workers are accessed to such understanding, it informs their appraisal of and behaviour in practical contexts.

Indeed, in this research, youth workers were sometimes less satisfied with quite significant achievements in context, just because they had a sophisticated framework of expectation and self-judgement. This points up the need for such workers to be personally and emotionally supported while carrying out such work. Within the collaborative professional development reported here, such support was quite extensive, but there is some evidence that peer exchange during the period of trials could have reduced some anxieties and enhanced effectiveness, for one or two leaders.

Second, since it is unlikely that the wide range of people engaged in the Youth Service can be informed to the levels attempted in the research, the relationship between 'lead workers' and others needs reflective review. It would be quite inappropriate to 'professionalize', and worse still to bureaucratize, prejudice reduction work and confine it to some youth workers only. At the same time, it seems likely that maintaining appropriate centre climates is a significant feature of securing prejudice reduction. If so, it is important that all workers are sensitized to the kinds of support that this work needs, from them, in centre contexts.

Operating the practice of such climates may be expected to be an important source of understanding not only for the clientele, but also for those workers unfamiliar with theoretical issues that have a bearing on good practice. The problem of race prejudice among youth workers themselves should be associated with issues in the management of effective climates. Such climates are highly fragile and readily open to undermining, especially where it comes from those with some formal status as youth workers. The position of such workers needs review.

Third, it is important not to look to prejudice reduction activities as 'magic methods'. It is almost appropriate to construe the activities as a means of focusing and occupying young people's attention, while the 'real' attempts at prejudice reduction take the form of the skilful management and interventions of the youth worker, working with a group, within the context of a positive climate. In this research, youth leaders completed one run-through of four activities perceived to have potential. The approach was sufficiently successful to suggest that further pursuit would be valuable. At least two things now seem needed: the development of a wider repertoire of activities with potential for success in Youth Service contexts; and reflective practice of the use of a range of activities with a view to enhanced skilfulness, in both use, and opportunistic selection for use, in immediate centre contexts. In short, there are new skills to be learnt and shared here.

REFERENCES

Back, K. (1952) Influence through social communication. *Journal of Abnormal and Social Psychology* **46**, 9–23.

Bruin, K. (1985) Prejudice, discrimination and games: an analysis. *Perspectives on Simulation and Gaming* **10**. Sagset Journal.

Cashmore, E. (1987) *The Logic of Racism*. London: Allen & Unwin.

Chivers, T. (1985) Worlds apart. *Youth in Society*. London: National Youth Bureau.

Coffield, F., Borrill, C., and Marshall, S. (1986) *Growing Up at the Margins*. Wells: Open Books.

Cohen, P. (1988) The perversions of inheritance studies in the making of multi-racialist Britain. In P. Cohen (ed.), *Schooling in Multiracist Britain*. Basingstoke: Macmillan.

Cooper, E., and Dinerman, H. (1951) A study of communication. *Public Opinion Quarterly* **15**, 243–64.

Davey, A. (1987) Inter-ethnic friendship patterns in British schools over three decades. *New Community* **14**, 202–9.

Festinger, L. (1957) *A Theory of Cognitive Dissonance*. Stanford, CA: Stanford University Press.

Flay, B. K. (1978) A catastrophe theory model of attitude change. Paper presented to Annual Convention of the American Psychological Association, Toronto, Canada.

Gustafson, J. P., and Cooper, L. (1981) Co-operative and clashing interests in small groups. *Human Relations* **34**, 315–39.

Henry, J. A. (1986) *Towards an Understanding of Collaborative Research in Education*. Geelong, Victoria: Deakin University Press.

Hope, A., and Wilson, A. (1985) Simulations at Loughborough University. *Perspectives on Simulation and Gaming* **10**. Sagset Journal.

Ijaz, A. (1981) *A Study of Ethnic Attitudes of Elementary School Children towards Blacks and East Indians*, Report to Scarboro Board of Education, Ontario, Canada.

Katz, D. (1959) The functional approach to the study of attitudes. *Public Opinion Quarterly* **24**, 163–204.

Katz, D., and Stotland, E. (1960) A preliminary statement of a theory of attitude structure and change. *Psychology: A Study of Science* **3**, 423–75.

Lynch, J. (1987) *Prejudice Reduction and the Schools*. London: Cassell.

Mould, W. (1987) The Swann Report, an LEA response. *Race and Culture in Education*. Slough: NFER.

National Association of Youth Clubs (1984) Racism: breaking the web. *Youth Clubs*. London: NAYC.

Ostram, T. M., and Upshaw, H. S. (1968) Psychological perspective and attitude change. In A. G. Greenwald *et al.*, *Psychological Foundations of Attitudes*. London: Academic Press.

Pettigrew, T. (1982) *Prejudice: Dimensions of Ethnicity*. Harvard, MA: Harvard College Press.

Raab, E., and Lipsett, S. M. (1965) *Prejudice and Society*. US Department of Health, Education and Welfare, Freedom Pamphlets, Anti-Defamation League, Lexington Avenue, New York.

Shirts, G. (1964) 'Starpower', *Simile 11*, California.

Soukup, P., and Borakova, H. (1985) The position of management games in the teaching process. *Perspectives on Simulation and Gaming* **10**. Sagset Journal.

Tesser, A., Pilkington, C. J., and McIntosh, W. D. (1989) Self-evaluating maintenance and the mediational role of emotion. *Journal of Personality and Social Psychology*, **57**(3), 442–56.

Thomas, S. (1980) *Techniques of Behavior Change: Review of Theories and Research*. Final report, Florida State University, Department of Education, Tallahassee, Florida.

Thompson Report (1982) *Experience and Participation*. London: HMSO.

Walford, R. (1985) After the honeymoon – what next? *Perspectives on Simulation and Gaming* **10**. Sagset Journal.

Wiggans, A. (1984) *Making the Past Count*. London: National Youth Bureau.

Chapter 7

Women in Science: Access, Experience and Progression

Viv Shelley and Pat Whaley

This study examines the status of women in science and some of the explanations for it, the difficulties experienced by some women both in the process of 'returning to learn' and while actually studying, as well as the opportunities for progression. It outlines some of the issues surrounding the more general questions of women, education and access, and includes a quantitative case study of a successful attempt to attract mature women, who had little or no previous experience of science, on to a science course. The case study illustrates how the teacher can be the researcher, by developing the usual good practice of ongoing course evaluation to incorporate research methodology, and relating the specific outcomes to the wider context of the debate on access for women into science.

The study was motivated by a desire to find possible explanations for the dearth of women in science across the scale of age and employment levels, and also for the prevalent attitude which still exists as we approach the twenty-first century, that science is primarily a masculine subject. In addition, we are committed to exploring the development of *appropriate* courses to which women can 'return to learn', both in general and, for one of us, in science specifically.

The major outcomes are that the status of women in science has changed very little over the past two decades, that the dearth of women in science is inextricably linked to the school experience and to social stereotyping, but that women can be attracted back to science as mature learners by the provision of appropriate courses.

INTRODUCTION

The issue of women's access to science is part of the wider issue of women's access to education, training and employment, which raises a number of fundamental questions, dilemmas, perspectives and strategies. A complex web of decisions, assumptions and beliefs that define girls' and women's roles in society underpins the provision of opportunities in education and training, and the way that women are able, and *feel* able, to take advantage of these opportunities.

This study addresses some of the significant questions and issues, as well as discussing the important practical considerations and strategies, in relation to a specific initiative to attract women into science and technology. The analysis of the case study, within the context of some of the wider issues, suggests ways in which equality in, and quality of, access and progression for women in science might be achieved.

Access, women and science

Mason has suggested that 'access' was one of the educational 'buzz' words of the 1980s (1987, p. 55). He notes the important distinction between 'access' defined in its widest sense of opening up higher educational opportunities to all, and 'Access courses', which offer mature students without formal qualifications an alternative route (to A levels) into higher education (HE). Waddington also acknowledges the different meanings of the term, but highlights a related, and equally important, distinction:

> The term 'Access' has the great political virtue of meaning different things to different people. For some, it appears to be reducible to a simple issue of total quantity of students in the HE system, and as the key therefore to resources. For others, the Access issue is regarded as fundamentally about the *widening* of opportunities to under-represented and disadvantaged groups; within this perspective qualitative considerations are as important as quantitative ones.
>
> (1990, p. 18)

The present study is based on a belief that the question of access for women carries different implications to the question of access for men. That is not to suggest that women are a homogeneous group any more than men are. What is implicit in our analysis is that gender is a social construct (see Oakley, 1972, p. 158). The implications of 'gender' and the related concepts of social class and ethnicity, as well as awareness of the ages and stages of women's lives, are fundamental to any examination of the issue of women's access in general and therefore of access to science specifically.

'Science' incorporates a number of different academic disciplines and several levels of experience and expertise. Within the sciences themselves, we must acknowledge a diversity (some might even suggest a hierarchy) between the more physical sciences, which include engineering, and the more natural biological sciences. There is certainly an inhomogeneous gender mix across these areas (for example, a predominance of men in physics/engineering but of women in biological sciences), and within any one area there is a proliferation of women on the lower rungs of the promotion scales.

The problem identified: women and access

One of us worked for several years with a group of women in the Women Returners Network of the North-East, to consider the question of women's access to education and training. The resulting publication (Whaley, 1989) identified the numerous barriers to access for women. It distinguished between internal barriers, i.e. those centred in the woman herself, her anxieties, concerns, attitudes and expectations; and external barriers, i.e. those created by other individuals, institutions and structures. These barriers, and possible ways of overcoming them, were discussed in relation to five major areas: attitudes; childcare and care of dependants; curriculum; educational guidance, counselling and information; and finance.

There was shown to be a need for funding, special provision, positive action and prioritization, and the study concluded that ensuring access for women to appropriate education and training, and subsequently to employment, would be of benefit to more than the women themselves. Women will comprise more than 80 per cent of the net addition to the labour force over the next decade and it is to society's advantage to provide access to relevant, good education and training for all adults who want it.

Some of the more general barriers described above have been addressed by women-only and women-centred courses such as New Opportunities for Women (NOW) and Wider Opportunities for Women (WOW) (for a list of other such courses, see Women Returners Network (1989)). Other barriers have been addressed by the 'access movement', which has its roots in the 1970s with the innovative work of the Open College of the North-West (founded in 1975) and in the DES Circular on Access (1978). From these origins, the movement rapidly grew, and a huge number of specifically designed 'Access courses' quickly evolved, mainly in the humanities and social sciences. Mason (1987) quoted Gibson's (1986) estimate of 150 such courses, and the number has escalated as reported by the Educational Counselling and Credit Transfer Information Service (ECCTIS) report (1989) to 600 courses catering for some 10,000 students. Osborne and Woodrow's report (1989) for the Further Education Unit (FEU) on *Access to Mathematics, Science and Technology* showed that Access courses in general were not specific to any single minority group, but most were targeted towards those who had not previously benefited from the educational system for reasons of, for example, class, gender or ethnic origin. However, some (particularly in ILEA) were directed towards disadvantaged groups.

A great driving force for the access movement was the predicted decrease in the number of young people aged 16–25 in the years between 1987 and 2000 as a result of falling birth rates; this would create labour shortages. This in itself raises debate and presents dilemmas about the importance of the identified needs of women if this current trend is overturned. It is not acceptable to identify needs and raise expectations, only to reject them if they do not fit into a changed demographic and political climate. A similar criticism was levelled by Byrne, nearly 15 years ago, who attacked the idea of using women 'to clean up social and economic problems for a given period . . . and telling them, with thanks, it is no longer convenient to need them, and they are both uneconomic and redundant' (1978, p. 156).

In our view, however, Access courses, necessarily of A level standard, should not only allow entry to HE, but should stand as qualifications in their own right, demonstrating the level of competence and commitment shown by the student. This is seen to be particularly important to that group of students who do not wish to go on to HE, but who do wish to satisfy their own needs for self-fulfilment or to make a contribution to the social, economic, cultural and political life of the country by securing employment. This is particularly pertinent to the shortage of scientists and technologists, particularly at technician level, for which graduate qualifications are by no means the minimum entry requirement. Hence we will regard the subject of 'access' in the broader sense of opening up opportunities (particularly for women) for improving education, employment and/or life-style.

The problem identified: access and science

Access to science for mature students of either sex has proved to be quite difficult, as reported by Mason (1989):

> mature students have never entered the UK Higher Education system as non-standard students to take science and engineering in any great numbers, and even when they have been admitted as traditional entrants they have consistently been outperformed by their younger counterparts. Compared to the social sciences, therefore, where mature students, both standard and non-standard, have generally been more successful than the 21-year-old graduate, SETACC [second wave in science, engineering, and technology] starts from a lower base.
>
> (p. 37)

The FEU report (Osborne and Woodrow, 1989) shares Mason's concerns in its reference to the DES questioning whether the access mode, as initially conceived, is a suitable preparation at all for HE courses which demand a substantial body of specific and sequentially learnt prior knowledge and skills. It refers to an ILEA Inspectorate's view of Access courses in science which, it suggests, present an 'apparent conflict in philosophy and style, and in priorities' (p. 10) of the differing curriculum demands of such courses. Certainly, there was evidence that the 'main' topic leading to exit courses from the 30 science Access courses identified in December 1986 is studied to at least the core of A level, though the delivery and assessment methods were not necessarily influenced by A level or BTec courses. Unlike Mason's conclusions, however, the conclusions of the FEU case studies with regard to student progression and achievement suggest that those with non-standard entry fare no worse than traditional students once in the HE system. Drop-outs were most often the result of personal problems rather than academic ones and, although mathematics is seen to be a problem for mature students, it is frequently also a problem for the traditional student!

Mason (1989) asks whether there is 'some ineluctable link between the ageing process and a decline in mental performance which relates specifically to the learning of scientific concepts' and whether 'we need to take a critical look at curriculum, teaching method and assessment for mature students' (p. 38). A recent seminar organized by the Royal Society of Chemistry which focused on 'Non-traditional students and the Higher Education Curricula in Science and Mathematics' proves that Mason's latter question is being taken on board by both access providers and some HE institutions, but such changes are more likely to evolve from experiential learning by the providers of Access courses about the needs of adult learners, rather than from definitive research such as that posed by his first question.

Another problem inherent in designing science Access courses is that the majority of science and technology courses offered by HE undoubtedly require far more prerequisite knowledge and skills than can be covered in the one year that has become the normal duration of Access courses.

Pickersgill (1993) has recently described the format of a number of science Access courses.

The problem identified: women, access and science

Overall, the above constraints specific to science access present additional hurdles to mature women, and reinforce the need for positive discriminatory efforts if the full spectrum of science subjects is indeed to become accessible to this important under-represented group.

'Access' and 'New Opportunities' courses provided exclusively for women have been successfully established throughout the country for some years (for details of some of these, see Birke and Dunlop (1993), Cole (1989), FEU (1990), NIACE (1989), Replan (1989) and Whaley (1987)). This type of provision is particularly important in the areas of science and technology where, traditionally, social stereotyping has resulted in fewer women choosing, or even having the choice, to pursue studies in these areas. Returning to study in these fields or entering them for the first time requires a great deal of courage and confidence on the part of the student and a great deal of understanding, encouragement and guidance on the part of the tutor, who must also be able to present the topics in an exciting, enjoyable and relevant way (particularly for women students, whose confidence in the subjects may be very low).

However, of the 30 science Access courses discussed in the FEU report and men-tioned above, only three were targeted specifically at women (and one towards black people). Seven of these 30 courses were selected as case studies, and on average the gender breakdown was 59 per cent men and 41 per cent women, which on the face of it is quite encouraging. However, when this breakdown is considered by course, it is seen that an engineering course attracts 88 per cent men and 12 per cent women, whereas a food studies course attracts 79 per cent women and 21 per cent men. Hence the traditional stereotypes are maintained *within* specific science Access courses.

Similarly, the reports by the Royal Society of Chemistry (1989), by Parker (1991) and by Dodd (1992) show that men greatly outnumber women in the 'hard', physical/natural sciences compared with the 'soft', life/biological sciences where the reverse bias is often seen.

Overcoming the problem

The major problem does seem to be one of attracting women to science subjects across the board in the first place. However, the existence of the general barriers to access for women, compounded by the additional ones specific to access in science, presents a huge challenge to the access providers in retaining them through such courses.

Discussion about the reasons for the low numbers of women in science generally has focused on a number of key issues as described below.

Gender imbalance among teachers and sex differentiation of subject choices

Statistics from the Equal Opportunities Commission (1987) show 'that teachers' subject qualifications tend to reinforce sex stereotyping in curriculum choice, because of the absence of non-stereotypical role models' (p. 17). The marked gender bias in the subject qualifications is mirrored by the number of pupils with passes in CSE and GCE O

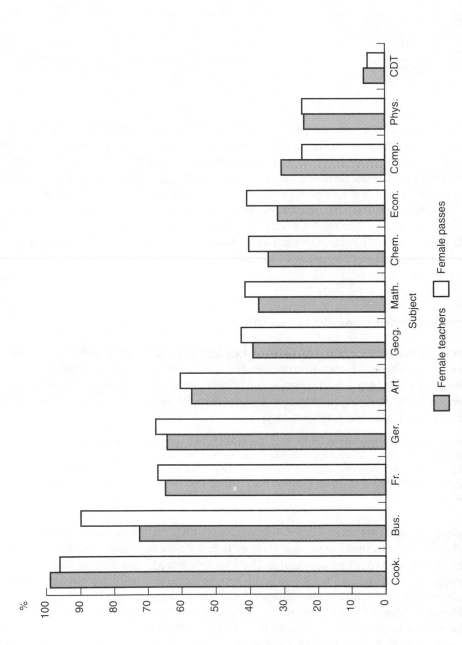

Figure 7.1 *Percentage of female passes in CSE Grade 1 and GCE O and A level exams, and secondary female teacher qualifications.*

Table 7.1. *A comparison of the percentage of girls taking A level sciences in 1983 and 1992.*

Subject	A level entries Summer 1983[a] % girls	Year 13 pupils Summer 1992[b] % girls
Biology	60	58
Chemistry	36	38
Physics	21	23

[a] Janman (1987).
[b] Sears (1992).

and A levels in selected subjects (see Figure 7.1). As Janman (1987) has pointed out, 'the sex differentiation of subject choices are more marked at A level than at O level with over twice as many boys as girls following science subjects' (p. 291). Recent research by Sears (1992) concludes that the sex ratios by subject have not changed significantly over the last five years despite huge changes in science education (such as the introduction of GCSE, the move towards balanced science courses and the implementation of the National Curriculum) during that period.

Table 7.1 compares the statistics quoted by Janman (1987) and Sears (1992) and suggests only a marginal improvement in the shift by girls towards the physical sciences over a nine-year period.

The student experience and the curriculum

According to the Association for Science Education (ASE) report (1990), it is well established that there is little difference in the background knowledge that girls and boys bring to secondary school science, but there are significant differences in their attitudes and interests, which result in a propensity of boys in the physical sciences and girls in the biological sciences:

> teachers' own attitudes to science will be transmitted to their pupils in day-to-day classroom interaction. If women and men primary teachers display differing levels of confidence and enthusiasm in teaching biological and physical science/technology themes, then early introduction of these subjects may reinforce, rather than challenge, the traditional gender bias.
>
> (p. 3)

The report suggests that more varied approaches, which recognize that boys and girls respond differently to the content and style of their science education, are needed, and emphasizes that all groups must feel that the science offered is interesting and relevant to their own lives. In secondary schools the report warns of the dichotomy presented by the introduction of 'broad and balanced science' and the choice between studying it for 20 per cent or 12.5 per cent of the curriculum time, which might lead to many more girls than boys opting for the lighter course. Of teachers, it suggests that 'we fail to recognise the symptoms of gender inequality which are present in our own classrooms. We also underestimate our power to redress the balance and so place the task low on our list of priorities' (p. 5).

Attitudes of teachers

The ASE report (1990) suggests that 'all teachers need to become aware of the values which they are transmitting through their lessons and of the attitudes which are being cultivated in every aspect of school life' (p. 1). Worrall and Tsarna (1987) have concluded that 'While science teachers in general expect relatively lower achievement from the typical girl, their self-reported responses can be interpreted as one of concern to do something about it' (p. 310). They found

> little evidence of the same-gender special relationship between teachers and pupils . . .
> although the empathy item showed no gender differentiation, science teachers as a group
> saw themselves as putting out fewer empathy signals, relative to their language teacher
> counterparts . . . this could be a contributory reason why girls do not easily model on
> science teachers – of either sex.
>
> (p. 311)

Tobin and co-workers (1990) have made an extensive study of activities in science classrooms by the in-depth observation of a male and a female teacher's interactions with their pupils. The male attitude was authoritarian, while the female was more of a mother figure who supported pupil-centred learning. However, surprisingly perhaps, neither behaved conducively with regard to attracting girls into science.

Women and careers in science

During the period from autumn 1987 to spring 1989, *AUT Woman*, a newsletter of the Association of University Teachers, published depressing statistics on the proportion of women in academic and academic-related posts in British universities. With the exception of only three subject areas (nursing studies, adult education and veterinary studies) there were less than 30 per cent women at lecturer/assistant lecturer scale. Even in subjects traditionally studied by women, the percentages were as low as 27 per cent (language and literature) and 19 per cent (business and social studies). In science subjects the figures were dramatically low, decreasing from 12.5 per cent for biological, mathematical and physical sciences to 2–4 per cent for engineering subjects. At senior lecturer level and above, women were extremely hard to find and men clearly had the monopoly on promoted posts.

In the summer of 1989 when the major findings of the survey were updated, the headline 'Progress report – no improvement, should try harder' needed little elaboration. It is true that there had been an increase in the recruitment of female full-time academic staff over the period 1965–85, but during the period 1983–5, almost 10 years after the Sex Discrimination Act was introduced, the proportion of women recruited was still only 21 per cent. If that rate of change is sustained, redressing the imbalance of male and female employees in British universities is unlikely to be achieved until well into the twenty-first century.

In 1990 attempts by one of us to glean information on 'famous women in science' proved to be less than fruitful, until all was revealed in a coveted volume which boasted (with no apology) the achievements of 9 women in a total of 426 leading contemporary scientists between 1940 and 1966 – under the title of *Modern Men of Science*! If the above describes the experience of the academics and the fate of the famous, what chance has the ordinary woman? We cannot alter the fact that few women had the opportunity to study science and technology until the latter half of the twentieth century, but it is still the case in numerous schools that stereotypical views are reinforced in many of the books, films and video tapes made by commercial organizations (ASE Education (Research) Committee, 1990).

The image of the scientist

Shortland (1991) has suggested that one of the barriers that has built up between the scientific community and the general public has been created by the belief that when a scientist enters a laboratory, 'he must hang up his emotions, temperament and feelings just as he hangs up his coat' (p. 22), and that the image of the scientist as a white-coated eccentric must be dispelled by portraying the excitement, challenges and human qualities of science. Although many scientists' feelings about the public perception of them are unjustified, they are regarded as being more secretive than others, and 'While some scientists may need to be secretive, many will be unaware of just how inaccessible they are to the public' (p. 18). The ASE report (1990) is also conscious of the need 'to influence for the better the image of science in our schools' (p. iv). 'Providing a mandatory programme in science', it suggests, 'will not in itself promote a willingness to learn science' (p. iv).

Adolescence

Janman (1987) has reviewed the educational statistics which indicate that, up to the age of 11, reading ability appears to be superior in girls, while mathematical ability shows only a few differences between girls and boys. In terms of O level achievements, girls are slightly more successful than boys (although the interests of both sexes lie within specific subject ranges). However, when it comes to A level subjects, fewer girls enter and their results, pro rata, tend to be poorer than those of boys. She has suggested that the 'Possible reasons for the girls' lower expectancies lie in the perception of school as "feminine" or "masculine" dependent upon level' (p. 298) and that

> the aspirations and attainments of girls are constrained by many factors, one of which is undoubtedly their own and their male peers' expectations for their scholastic performance, their career performance and their domestic role expectations. . . . The strong prejudices held in British society, and consequently, by its adolescent population, serve to make higher education appear both less attractive and less attainable to the females within it. It appears that, at present, the educational process does little to ameliorate this situation for girls.
>
> (p. 298)

In fact, with age, Janman suggests 'girls show an increasing tendency to aspire, and to attain, less than boys' (p. 298). Whitehead (1988) has also considered why girls appear to 'count themselves out' of higher education. She suggests that high academic achievement and a high-status job are entirely compatible with masculine stereotypes. On the other hand, only low achievement, combined with social success, is compatible with the female stereotype. 'You cannot be incompetent, irrational, illogical, dependent, unassertive, passive *and* a high achiever' (p. 2).

Having looked at the significant factors influencing the response of women to science courses, we move on to consider a case study which looks at a successful attempt to attract women, with little or no previous qualifications in science, on to a science course.

WOMEN INTO SCIENCE AND TECHNOLOGY: THE CASE STUDY

Background

James (1990) reported on the North East Regional Access to Higher Education Project, which undertook a science and technology mapping exercise. The main aims of that exercise were as follows:

- To identify the provision made by colleges in the North Region regarding science and technology access.
- To collect such data as were readily available regarding enrolment, completion and student progression to higher education.
- To collect data about curriculum, course structure, content and higher education links.

The report of the survey served to indicate that, while there were a considerable number of colleges offering such Access courses, with very few exceptions recruitment on the courses was so low that they were not able to run. This observation, however, is in line with national trends, which also indicate that recruitment on to science and technology Access courses is low.

The Open University (OU) is probably the leader in terms of access to higher education, and hundreds of adults have satisfactorily completed the science and the technology foundation courses each year. However, the OU itself recognizes that it has done little in the past for the significant numbers of students who drop out of, or fail, these courses. Recently, steps have been taken to address the problem, as illustrated by the piloting of the 'Women Make Sense of Science' course, which was offered jointly by the OU and Sunderland Polytechnic in the autumn of 1990.

This latter course illustrates the current move towards 'Access to Access' courses, particularly in the area of science and technology, where it is recognized that, in addition to the need to recap on study and communications skills, there is an important foundation to lay in the introduction of scientific method, scientific approach and the language of science.

Traditionally, science has been presented as a group of subjects which require the acquisition of a huge body of fact, often at the expense of the sense of discovery and the relevance of the theory to the real problems which an economically competitive world experiences. Recent changes in the science and technology curricula at school level will, one hopes, put these subjects in a better perspective and will convey better their excitement, relevance and importance. But these changes come too late for the adult population to whom we are currently looking in order to meet the deficiency in the supply of trained scientific staff, particularly at technician level.

In addition, the changes in the junior science curriculum mean that teachers of these age groups, traditionally a majority of women and many 'returners' to the profession after bringing up their own families, now have the responsibility of conveying these messages of science and technology to our future generations. It is through no fault of their own that many feel inadequate and lack the confidence to perform these tasks.

The Department of Adult and Continuing Education (DACE) at the University of Durham has offered a modular course leading to 'Certificates in Science' since October 1991. This course not only acts as an Access course to HE studies in science, but also stands alone with the recognition of a specified level (equivalent to A levels) of achievement. The certificates are validated by the Faculty of Science at Durham and recognized as Access courses by the Tees–Wear Access Federation. However, recruitment to the certificates has mainly been by adults who have already taken steps to secure places on HE courses in science or who work in science-related industries.

In order to attract those adults who are not as confident that they have the ability to pursue a career in science at whatever level, a 'pre-Access' course was proposed, which would familiarize students with the ideas of scientific thought, scientific reading and writing, and scientific measurement and interpretation, while surveying the scope of the four main branches of science: physics, chemistry, biology and earth science. In addition, it would put some emphasis on the development of personal and social skills, and communications skills including information technology, and would offer career and counselling advice. Visits to a selection of appropriate employers would help the students to evaluate their interest in and potential for a variety of science-related employment situations.

For the reasons outlined above, this pre-Access course was designed exclusively for women, was built around the themes 'Environment and Health' (which would be relevant to the everyday lives of all students, even if they decided at the end of the course that science was not for them) and was entitled 'Women Into Science and Technology' (WIST).

Aims and objectives of the project

- To investigate the possibility of attracting mature women, who had little or no previous experience, into science studies by devising a suitably attractive course.
- Through the course, to increase the confidence (in science and technology) of women who may have been channelled out of those subjects in their previous education.
- To use the course as a stepping-stone for women who wish to gain full-time employment by retraining or acquiring new skills, or to continue their studies through Access into HE.
- To devise methods of assessing the progress of the students using both formal and informal assessment techniques.
- Through the course, to recap on study skills, particularly communications skills.
- To arrange visits to science and technology workplaces in order to increase the awareness of the roles women play in these areas.
- To give advice about, and to monitor progression towards, employment and/or HE.

- To apply to County Durham Training and Enterprise Council for funding to develop the course, to fund 16 student places and to offer support for childcare for those who needed it.

Course structure

1. The course is designed to run over two terms of 10 weeks (excluding school half-terms) on a single day, 10.00–12.00 and 1.00–3.00 (80 hours (min.) contact time). Thus it is accessible to women with children at school.

2. One of the sessions each week focuses on the scientific aspects of the chosen themes and introduces the main branches of science (physics, chemistry, biology and earth science) through observation, experimentation, analysis and interpretation and application.

3. The second session each week focuses on self-awareness (through assessment of prior experiential learning (APEL)), communications skills (including the use of IT to produce a CV), and visits to a variety of science/technology-based employers and guidance and counselling services. These sessions ensure that students have access to sufficient information and experience in order to make informed decisions about plans for the future.

Tutors and accommodation

The course draws on the wide range of expertise of tutors (mainly but not exclusively female), full time and part time, both from within the Department of Adult and Continuing Education (DACE) and from other University departments.

A *course co-ordinator* has the responsibility of managing the course and ensuring that the teaching programme is cohesive and well co-ordinated.

The course is delivered in an informal and interactive way and draws on the experiences and expertise of the students where appropriate.

It is delivered at DACE in the centre of Durham, which is easily accessible by public transport. Teaching rooms are comfortably furnished and well suited to the informal delivery methods employed in the world of adult education. There is a strong departmental library, well equipped with up-to-date books on the above-mentioned themes. In addition there is a small but well-equipped laboratory for practical sessions.

Course progression

This course is seen as ideal preparation for the Department's Certificate in Science (mentioned earlier), from which the students might progress to employment or to higher education.

Marketing and publicity

It is recognized that this course will be seen as a challenge to many women, even daunting to some, and therefore there is a need to focus on that challenge, but also to offset it with an understanding of the starting point and possible apprehension of the target group. The course leaflet and the advertisement were devised to do both by asking such questions as:

Are you:
- looking for a new career direction?
- keen to learn word-processing skills?
- interested in health and environment?
- keen to support your children in science?

But:
- feel apprehensive about science study?
- need to brush up on study skills?

One advertisement was placed in a regional evening newspaper in the July preceding the autumn start, and it also appeared in three local free newspapers. Course leaflets were placed in local libraries and job centres. This first round of advertising resulted in 74 inquiries, mostly from the newspaper advertisements. The course leaflet and application forms were sent to all inquirers. Twenty-five firm applications were received as a result of this first round of publicity, of whom 23 were interviewed (2 withdrew before the interview because of change of circumstances). Of those interviewed, 16 (the maximum possible) were offered places, 3 transferred their applications to the Science Certificate course and 4 were placed on a waiting list (though these four had expressed interest in other courses or part-time employment).

Eight further applications were received as a result of the Departmental Course Brochure (but by that time, unusually for a science course, it was fully recruited). Though extremely disappointed that the course was over-subscribed, these women were also placed on the waiting list for the second run the following January, which took off with 16 more recruitments. Only 2 students required funding for nursery care for pre-school children. The majority of the remainder had school-aged children (or even older).

A request to the TEC for 'top-up' funding for the second group was rejected, but it was agreed that the remainder of the funding in the 'publicity' and 'childcare' categories could be used to subsidize the course fees for the second group, and each student paid a contribution of £20.

Selection of students

A conscious decision was made that there should be no formal prerequisites for embarking on the course. There was a wish to offer the course as a 'fresh start' and a new opportunity to enter into an area of study which would be unfamiliar to most of the group. All applicants were offered an informal interview, however, to ensure that they were fully aware of the scope, content and demands of the course. In

Table 7.2. *Age and background of applicants and course members of two WIST groups.*

Age group	No. of applicants	No. of course members
20–29	7 (14.0%)	5 (15.6%)
30–39	19 (38.0%)	13 (40.6%)
40–49	13 (26.0%)	9 (28.1%)
50–59	8 (16.0%)	3 (9.4%)
60+	3 (6.0%)	2 (6.3%)
Total	50 (100.0%)	32 (100.0%)

addition, since the first run of the course attracted external funding, which meant that student fees were paid, it was felt prudent to ensure that all course members would be prepared to commit themselves, in so far as was reasonable, to full participation, particularly if the course was over-subscribed.

Most of the students were more enthusiastic about the course after the informal interview, which also served to describe the course in more depth than the publicity material was able to do. The application form did ask for details of previous qualifications and age band, but only as data for the final evaluation of the suitability of the course for the specific groups recruited.

For practical reasons, places were limited to 16 and in the first year of the course two groups of 16 were recruited.

Age and background of applicants and course members

There was a wide spread of ages, as indicated in Table 7.2, which gives the spread for applicants and course members of two groups. The wide spread was felt to be particularly desirable, since it would give a measure of the applicability of the course to women of all ages (post-18).

There was also a very wide spread of qualifications and background experience, from CSE/O levels to degrees, and from secretaries to a midwife and occupational therapist. During the interviews, 24 (75 per cent) of those accepted expressed the significance of it being a 'women's' course.

Reasons for applying for the course

Table 7.3 gives the student responses at interview and on application forms (in order of popularity of response).

Assessment

Informal assessment took the form of a comparison and evaluation of pre- and post-course questionnaires. The pre-course questionnaire was designed to give a self-assessment by the students of their existing knowledge and understanding of topics to be taught on the course, and to explore previous experience of word processing. One might expect that members of the general public would have a reasonable 'general

Table 7.3. *Reasons for applying for the course.*

Reason for applying	No. of responses
• Interest in health and environment	8
• To learn how to use a word processor	7
• To improve chances of an interesting/different career	5
• To broaden experience/qualifications to find suitable employment	4
• Opportunity to return to study in an adult environment	3
• Opportunity to study science not available at school	3
• Primary teachers needing to update now that science is in National Curriculum	3
• Interest in science and technology	2
• To obtain a better understanding of science	1
• To obtain confidence to go on to further study	1
• Need to brush up on study skills	1
• To help children with science education	1

knowledge' of many of the topics to be covered, gathered incidentally, but that their understanding of the fundamental concepts might be limited. A similarly worded end-of-course questionnaire to self-assess as above would give a measure of the students' development of knowledge and understanding in the areas covered. The results of these questionnaires are given in Figures 7.2–7.6.

The pre-course questionnaire also asked how the participants felt about joining the WIST group, their worries and fears, how they felt about discussion, and how they viewed the social aspects. By focusing on these issues from the outset, it was hoped that the group would discuss them freely, identify similar concerns, and hence begin to dispel anxieties.

Formal assessment was used for the word-processing module. The package covered was the one adopted by the University of Durham, and offered to all undergraduates as one of three modules required for the Certificate in Computer Literacy. Each module carries with it a Statement of Proficiency, and the opportunity to offer this qualification to the WIST group was seized. The students were required to submit two assignments during the course, and to sit an end-test of one hour's duration.

Student progression

A follow-up questionnaire was sent out to all students who embarked on the first two runs of the course, six to nine months after the course ended, in an attempt to monitor their progression into either HE or the workplace.

RESULTS

Introduction

Two separate courses ran during 1991–2, overlapping in the Epiphany term (January–April), and they were most successful. The response to the course was tremendous, as was the enthusiasm of tutors and students alike. Attendance overall was excellent

Table 7.4. *Student responses to general statements.*

	Statement	Responses
1	I'm afraid I won't have anything to say	4
1	I didn't have anything to say	0
2	I'm afraid I'll talk too much	3
2	I'm afraid I talked too much	1
3	I'm worried I'll make a fool of myself	3
3	I felt that I made a fool of myself	1
4	I'll be too embarrassed to join in	6
4	I was too embarrassed to join in	1
5	I'm afraid I may be bored	0
5	I'm afraid I was bored on occasion	3
6	1 want to share my experiences with others	7
6	1 was happy to share my experiences with others	14
7	I enjoy putting my point of view across to others	10
7	I enjoyed putting my point of view across to others	9
8	I'll enjoy listening to the others	18
8	I enjoyed listening to the others	19
9	I'm afraid I might find it difficult	10
9	I'm afraid I found the course difficult	1
10	I'll enjoy the chance of a chat	8
10	I enjoyed the chance of a chat	15
11	I'll enjoy meeting people	20
11	I enjoyed meeting people	18
12	I'll enjoy getting out of the house	8
12	I enjoyed getting out of the house	12
13	Any other feelings? *Will I get hold of the technology bit? I am hoping to find renewed energy I might find it physically tiring (ME sufferer) Very keen to be able to use a computer*	
13	Any other feelings? *The course was very stimulating I looked forward to Thursdays and the WIST course*	

and 15 of the 16 who started the first course (9 out of 16 on the second) completed. (In a more recent run of the course on Teesside, 12 out of 15 students completed.)

Analysis of the questionnaire responses

Of the 32 students who were recruited for two courses, 20 completed both pre- and post-course questionnaires.

General questions

The students were asked to tick the statements that came closest to how they felt about joining the WIST group. They were asked to tick as many or as few as they wished.

Table 7.5.   *Pre- and post-course scores for assessment of study skills.*

Skill	Pre-course score	Post-course score
1 Reading effectively	50	60
2 Note-taking	48	54
3 Writing	54	54
4 Communicating	44	55

Table 7.6.   *Health topics.*

Topic	Pre-course score K	Post-course score K	% increase K	Pre-course score U	Post-course score U	% increase U
1 The links between health and science	36	57	58	38	59	55
2 Simple genetics	33	53	61	33	55	67
3 The links between genetics and disease	34	53	56	34	54	59
4 The way diseases develop	39	55	41	40	58	45
5 The way diseases are transmitted	41	56	37	39	58	49
6 Issues of current concern:						
(a) AIDS	49	56	14	46	59	28
(b) Chemicals as pollutants and health risks	39	52	33	37	56	51
(c) Cancers	40	54	35	38	56	47
(d) Drug and alcohol use	44	58	32	42	59	40
7 New treatments for disease	37	49	32	35	52	49
8 Nutrition	55	59	7	53	58	9
9 Ways of achieving good health	54	58	7	53	58	9

The statements and student responses are shown in Table 7.4, where the pre-course question is followed by the post-course question for comparison.

Study skills, health and environment

The students were asked to assess their study skills and their knowledge and understanding in a range of health and environment-related topics under the headings:

Excellent = E   Good = G   Fair = F   Poor = P

In scoring the questionnaires, a point scale was used where:

E = 4   G = 3   F = 2   F = 1

Tables 7.5 to 7.7 give the total scores of the 20 respondents calculated on this basis.

The students were asked to assess their *study skills* in the areas of reading effectively, note-taking, writing and communicating. The total scores are listed in Table 7.5.

These scores are illustrated in Figure 7.2, which shows that overall the students assessed their study skills to have increased marginally in the areas indicated. The significance of the scores is discussed below.

Table 7.7. *Environment topics.*

Topic	Pre-course score K	Post-course score K	% increase K	Pre-course score U	Post-course score U	% increase U
1 Different types of energy	42	50	19	41	54	32
2 Sources of energy	44	52	18	40	53	33
3 Relationship between different types of energy	30	47	57	32	48	50
4 Methods of waste disposal	32	51	59	31	53	71
5 Waste-derived energy	27	51	89	28	54	93
6 Recycled products	39	51	31	37	54	46
7 Water purification	29	50	72	30	54	80
8 Sewage treatment	29	49	69	30	53	77
9 Types of water-borne pollution	29	49	69	29	53	83

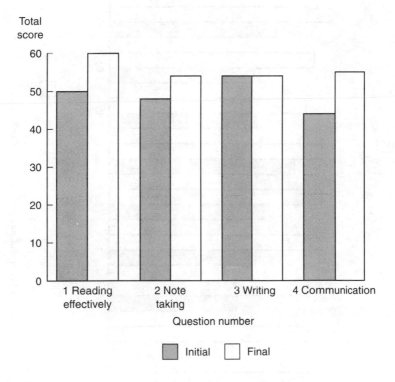

Figure 7.2 *Responses from WIST initial and final questionnaires: study skills.*

Knowledge (K) and *understanding* (U) of the health and environment topics listed in Tables 7.6 and 7.7, which were to be taught on the course, were self-assessed by the students both before and after the course. Their responses were scored as described above from the pre- and post-course questionnaires, and the total scores are also listed in Tables 7.6 and 7.7. The percentage increases in the scores (relative to the initial scores) are also listed.

The initial and final (total) scores for health topics are plotted in Figure 7.3 for

154

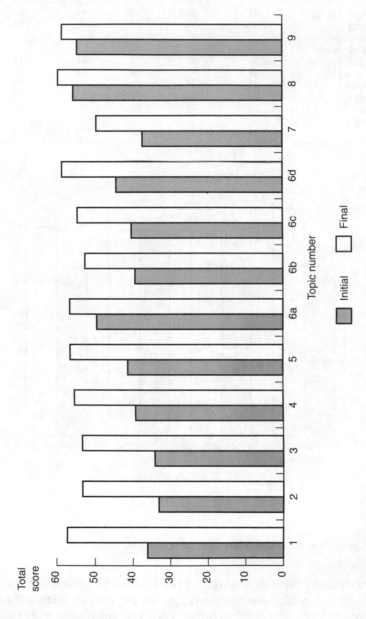

Figure 7.3 Responses from WIST initial and final questionnaires: health – knowledge.

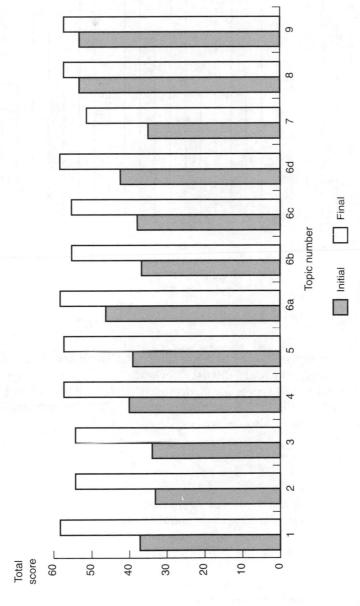

Figure 7.4 *Responses from WIST initial and final questionnaires: health – understanding.*

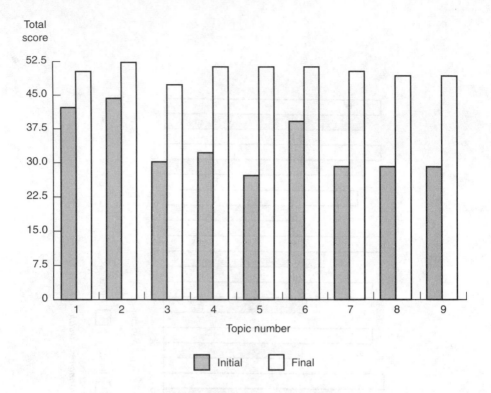

Figure 7.5   *Responses from WIST initial and final questionnaires: environment – knowledge.*

knowledge (K) and in Figure 7.4 for understanding (U). There are clearly significant increases in these scores, which are discussed below.

The initial and final (total) scores for environment topics are plotted in Figure 7.5 for knowledge (K) and in Figure 7.6 for understanding (U). There are clearly significant increases in these scores also, which are discussed below.

Word processing

The students did not need any typing or computing experience for this module, but we felt that it would help in planning the sessions to know what experience they had. They were therefore asked a number of questions relating to their use of computers, those shown in Table 7.8 being the most significant.

Discussion of questionnaire responses

General questions

Statements 7, 8 and 11, which related to putting over points of view, listening to others and meeting people, did not differ significantly from pre- to post-course questionnaire.

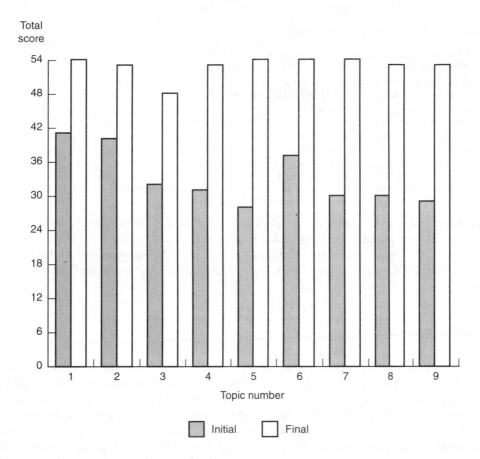

Figure 7.6 *Responses from WIST initial and final questionnaires: environment – understanding.*

The latter two statements had been ticked by almost all students, and clearly their expectations had been closely met. Only half of the students apparently expected to enjoy and did enjoy putting forward their point of view, probably reflecting a reluctance to appear dominating. On the other hand, 70 per cent had enjoyed sharing their experiences with others (statement 6), despite only half that number expecting that they would.

The remaining negative statements (1, 2 and 3) had only a few responses each, but in most cases the fears proved to be unfounded. Six women feared that they might be too embarrassed to join in, but only for one had this been true. Similarly, 10 had thought that they would find the course difficult, but only one felt, at the end, that it had been so. Eight students had admitted initially to looking forward to the chance of a chat and enjoying getting out of the house, but in reality 15 (75 per cent) and 12 (60 per cent) respectively acknowledged in retrospect that this had been true. Whether there was an initial reluctance on the part of the students to acknowledge these reasons initially is not evident from the questionnaires. The only disappointing response was statement 5, which indicated that three people had been bored on

Table 7.8.   *Responses to questions about word processing.*

1.   *Have you used a computer at school/college/work?*
     Responses: School = 0 College = 3 Work = 6 Not used = 11

2.   *Have you any qualifications in computing or IT?*
     Responses: 17 had none; 3 had (BTec, RSA1, View W/P)

3.   *Is there a computer in your home?*
     Responses: No = 13 Yes = 7

4.   *If YES to 3, do you use it?*
     Responses: No = 3 Yes = 1 Sometimes = 3

5.   *Can you touch type: well/a bit/not at all?*
     Responses: well = 5 a bit = 9 not at all = 6

occasion, but one of these was a qualified nurse, and understandably some of the health sessions would have been low key to her.

Overall, the responses in this section were found to be encouraging and indicated that the positive expectations had been met, while the fears had largely been unfounded.

Study skills

Figure 7.2 shows that the responses in self-assessed study skills increased only marginally, by a maximum of 25 per cent for communicating skills, and not at all for writing. However, they are interesting because they reflect only marginal (less than 10 per cent) input in terms of contact time on the course. Since there was no formal assessment using the skills covered by the 'study skills' section of the course, no great emphasis was placed on them. However, interestingly, the two areas where the students had to focus most, effective reading (skill 1) to produce their health project, and (oral) communication (skill 4), for the 10-minute delivery of a synopsis of the project to the group, showed the greatest increases in skill levels (20 and 25 per cent respectively). Undoubtedly, the thought of giving an oral presentation raised the anxiety levels, but the students were encouraged to use the overhead projector to summarize points, or as an *aide-mémoire*, and the outcome was excellent. Although it had been impressed on the students that no one would be pressurized to give a talk, no one in fact refused, and the majority admitted that, despite the nerves, it had been a valuable experience.

Health topics

Comparison of the total scores for initial and final responses indicate very little difference between assessed knowledge and understanding. This probably reflects the difficulty the students have in differentiating between what they think they 'know' and what they think they 'understand'. It is likely that they have not been asked to make such judgements before, and it might be worth the course co-ordinator focusing briefly on this issue prior to the filling in of such questionnaires in the future. Nevertheless, the percentage increase in the scores of understanding is greater in almost all cases than the percentage increase in knowledge. This is not unexpected, since the topics covered are likely to have been discussed superficially (or even sensationally) by the media or in magazines without giving fundamental explanations for the phenomena discussed.

However, the differences between pre- and post-course responses are much more significant, as Table 7.6 and Figures 7.3 and 7.4 show. The percentage increase in the scores varies from 7 per cent for knowledge of nutrition (topic 8) and ways of achieving good health (topic 9) to 67 per cent for understanding of simple genetics (topic 2). The majority of the students assessed their knowledge and their understanding, initially, as 'fair/poor' in the areas of links between health and science, genetics, disease, chemicals as pollutants, cancers, drug and alcohol abuse, and new treatments for disease, but as 'good/fair' in their knowledge of AIDS and in their knowledge and understanding of nutrition and ways of achieving health. Clearly, as Table 7.6 shows, the lower the level of knowledge initially, the greater the percentage increase at the end of the course. For example, the minimum initial score of 33 for the understanding of genetics increases by the maximum 67 per cent, whereas the maximum initial score of 55 for knowledge of nutrition increases by the minimum 7 per cent. This very small increase in the assessed level of knowledge and understanding in the areas of nutrition and ways of achieving good health is revealing. For these are the areas in which the students felt that they already had a good understanding and the depth of coverage of these topics was clearly too small. In the future, tutors should be encouraged to note these initial responses and set the level of tuition accordingly in order to stretch the students in all areas.

Environment

Virtually all the students assessed their knowledge and understanding of all the topics listed as 'fair/poor'. The percentage increases in scores were more significant in this section and, as Table 7.7 shows, there was a greater difference between increased knowledge and increased understanding. For example, in the area of waste-derived energy, knowledge increased by 89 per cent and understanding by 93 per cent, and knowledge of water-borne pollution increased by 69 per cent compared with an increase of 83 per cent in understanding. Clearly there has been a very worthwhile learning experience here.

Word processing

The answers to the questions in this section (Table 7.8) show that only 45 per cent of the students had used a computer previously and only three (15 per cent) had a qualification in computing. While seven (35 per cent) had a computer at home, only one of these used it regularly.

Hence with very little foundation on which to build, the majority of the students found the word-processing component of the course quite a struggle. However, the anticipation of assessment and examination of the module undoubtedly introduced fears and anxieties which the rest of the course did not, and it is likely that this in itself made adverse contributions to the learning process. Nevertheless, 13 out of 14 students who took the assessment achieved a Statement of Proficiency in Word

Table 7.9.   *Progression of WIST students.*

Going on to further study:	
(i) in science	3
(ii) other	6
Continuing in the same (part-time) employment	5
Finding new employment:	
(i) in a science-related field	3
(ii) other	0
Looking for a further course	6
Looking for employment	3

Processing, several with credit, awarded by the University of Durham. Of these, eight continued on to a further course in the Easter term, to complete two more modules and thereby gain the full Certificate in Computer Literacy.

Progression

As discussed above, one of the objectives of this course was to lay the foundations for further study or to enable mature women to go back into the labour market. It may be regarded as a 'pre-Access' course, and it had been envisaged that a significant number of WIST students would progress on to the Department's Certificate in Science course, which is a validated Access course. In the event, only three did, one of the most important reasons being that it was run as an *evening* course. Considerable care had been taken in planning the WIST course to make it accessible to women with families. The follow-up that was in place expected them to study in the evenings, and there were few who were able to, or even wished to, at the time when their family commitments had to take priority.

Twenty-one follow-up questionnaires (66 per cent) were returned from the 32 mailed, nine with letters or personal messages accompanying them. Table 7.9 summarizes the progression.

The three 'new jobs' in science-related areas were in a pathology laboratory, as a school science technician and as a primary teacher, and all three felt that the WIST experience had helped them to secure the job. Of the six who are still looking for a course, it is likely that a significant number would have continued with science study if a suitable course in the same department had been in place.

As a result of similar enthusiasm from another WIST group who are just completing their studies at Teesside, a new Access to the Environment course is being planned on to which the WIST students can progress. It will run on a similar format to the WIST course but on two days per week over 30 weeks – a progression to 120 sessions from 40. This course will be seen as ideal preparation for the numerous environment-based undergraduate courses which run at HE establishments in the north-east of England. The content of this new follow-on course will include the following subjects:

Basic chemistry.
Environmental chemistry.
Organic chemistry – from crude oil to artificial fibres.
Ecology and environment.

Diversity of life.
Physiology of plants and animals.
Experimental measurement and interpretation.
Energy.
Basic maths/statistics.
Study skills.
Environmental issues.

These topics will be taught from scratch or will build on the foundations laid in the WIST course, and will be taught on a topic-centred basis.

This follow-on course will be designed to meet the specific needs of the target group and to sustain the momentum and enthusiasm of science study. It marks the progression of both the students and the providers.

CONCLUSION

Overall the study reported here shows that, in spite of there having been an equal opportunities policy for 20 years or more, and despite the dramatic changes which have taken place in the secondary science curriculum over the last 10 years or so, the status of women in science has changed little. It is evident that within the science disciplines themselves, whether in school, on Access courses or in employment, there is also a huge disparity in the spread of women, which has changed little over two decades, despite numerous initiatives which have attempted to redress the balance both in Britain (e.g. projects such as Girls Into Science and Technology (GIST), Women Into Science and Engineering (WISE), Girls And Technology Education (GATE) and Women into Information Technology (WIT)) and elsewhere (e.g. Parker (1991), University of Adelaide; Berry (1993), Canada).

The fundamental reasons for the low numbers of women in science have been linked, to a significant extent, to their experiences in school and to the stereotypical images of science and scientists and of women in society.

However, the case study described above indicates that, even if those experiences have precluded women from science by adulthood, it is possible not only to *offer* them a second chance to study science, but actually to *recruit and retain* them if the curriculum has been designed appropriately in order to meet their specific needs. Support for this latter point has recently been shown by Klein (1991), Nash (1991), Mant and Winner (1991), Access News (1990), and by Birke and Dunlop (1993), who focus on two important issues that need to be addressed in making science courses for women attractive:

> courses should be focussed around issues of relevance to women rather than determined by vocational outcomes – rooted in their experience, in time-honoured adult education fashion. The second is that however relevant the course, women do have fears and anxieties around science.
>
> (p. 182)

In addition, this work shows how, with sufficient forethought, it is possible to assess informally and in a non-threatening way the objectives of a course, in order to give organizers valuable feedback in the absence of the more traditional examination system. However, it also illustrates that bringing mature women into science carries with it huge demands and responsibilities on the part of the organizers, not only to ensure a supportive and exciting learning experience over the duration of the course, but also to ensure that progression to the next stage is actually possible given the numerous barriers to study which many mature women experience.

Undoubtedly, there is enormous merit in making the curriculum relevant to the lives of the students, so that even if they do not continue to work or study in science, they will not feel as if they have 'wasted' time. In making the curriculum relevant, however, there is a danger that the stereotypical role of women may be perpetuated if teachers go along with the suggestion made that they

> balance topics to counteract the tendency for science, design and technology to appear predominantly masculine by including investigations of things with which the girls are more familiar. For example a study of 'wheels' can include a look at push-chairs or shopping trolleys as well as trucks.
>
> *(Times Educational Supplement*, 1991)

Are such suggestions really contributing to 'Pushing gender out of science' as the article is entitled? The report was referring to the Engineering Council (Brown, 1990) booklet for staff in primary schools, which suggests that stereotypical feminine interests like babies and shopping be used to encourage girls into non-stereotyped thinking!

As women in education generally, and women in science more specifically, we have a continuing part to play in the struggle for equality of access for women. While acknowledging that considerable initiatives regarding women in science are taking place, many of which have been cited throughout this chapter, we are concerned that the problem is appreciated in its entirety: that is, the access to, the experience of and the progression within. But with the 'blue-stocking' image of females in science, and the problem of the dual identity, described by Thomas (1990) as 'trying to be a scientist on the one hand – which means proving that one is "as good as a man" – and being a woman on the other – which, in its social definition, entails being uncompetitive' (p. 138), in addition to all the barriers previously discussed, we may be surprised that any females choose science at all!

REFERENCES

Access News (November 1990) *Women into Science and Technology* 3.

ASE Education (Research) Committee (1990) *Gender Issues in Science Education*. Hatfield, Herts: ASE.

AUT Woman (1987–1989) **12–17**.

Berry, J. (ed.) (1993) Women in science and engineering. Association of Commonwealth Universities, *Bulletin of Current Documentation* **107**, 23.

Birke, L., and Dunlop, C. (1993) Bringing women into science? *Adults Learning* **4**(7), 181.

Brown, C. (1990) *Engineering Equals*. London: Engineering Council.

Byrne, E. (1978) *Women in Education*. London: Tavistock.

Cole, S. (1989) *Women Educating Women*. Cambridge: NEC Trust and Open University.

DES (1978) Circular on Access. London: HMSO.

Dodd, J. (1992) *Linking Learning in Science-Based Industry and Higher Education*. Leeds: University of Leeds.

Educational Counselling and Credit Transfer Information Service (1989) *Access to Higher Education Courses Directory*. Milton Keynes: ECCTIS.

Equal Opportunities Commission (1987) *Women and Men in Britain: A Statistical Profile*. London: HMSO.

Further Education Unit (1990) *Curriculum Design and Methodology in Women-Only Classes*. London: FEU.

Gibson, A. (1986) Providing for the learning needs of adult students in higher education. *Journal of Access Studies* 1(2), 38.

Greene, J. E. (ed.) (1966) *Modern Men of Science*. New York: McGraw-Hill.

James, A. (1990) *North East Regional Access to Higher Education Project Report*. Newcastle upon Tyne: Northern Council for Further Education.

Janman, K. (1987) A-level expectancies and university aspirations of males and females. *British Journal of Educational Psychology* 57, 289.

Klein, R. (1991) Girl-friendly. *Times Educational Supplement*, 8 March.

Mant, J., and Winner, A. (1991) A second chance to learn science. *Adults Learning* 2(6), 178.

Mason, R. (1987) The logic of non-standard entry: mature students and higher education. *Journal of Further and Higher Education* 11(3), 51–9.

Mason, R. (1989) Adults and science: new prospects and perennial problems. *Adults Learning* 1(2), 37.

Nash, I. (1991) Queuing up to conquer male domain. *Times Educational Supplement*, 8 March.

National Institute of Adult Continuing Education (1989) *Adults Learning*, Special Issue on Women's Education 1(4).

Oakley, A. (1972) *Gender and Society*. London: Temple Smith.

Osborne, M., and Woodrow, M. (1989) *Access to Mathematics, Science and Technology*. London: FEU.

Parker, S. (1991) *Report of Phase II of the Women-in-Engineering Project*. Adelaide: University of Adelaide.

Pickersgill, D. (1993) Access courses: what are they? *School Science Review* 74(268), 130.

Replan (1989) Women-only provision. *Issue Sheet* 7. Bedford: Replan.

Royal Society of Chemistry (1989) *Education, Employment and Attitudes of Men and Women Members*. London: Royal Society of Chemistry.

Royal Society of Chemistry (1993) Non-traditional students and the higher education curricula in science and mathematics. Seminar, London. London: Royal Society of Chemistry.

Sears, J. (1992) Uptake of science A levels: an ICI and BP sponsored project for ASE. *Education in Science* 149, 30.

Shortland, M., and Gregory, J. (1991) *Communicating Science*. Harlow: Longman.

Thomas, K. (1990) *Gender and Subject in Higher Education*. Milton Keynes: SRHE/Open University Press.

Times Educational Supplement (1991) Pushing gender out of science. 25 January.

Tobin, K., *et al.* (1990) *Windows into Science Classrooms*. Lewes: Falmer.

Waddington, P. (1990) Does you does or does you don't give access? *NATFHE Journal* 18, May/June.

Whaley, P. (1987) New opportunities for women. In *At the Works*, Tyne-Tees Television.

Whaley, P. (1989) *Breakthrough: Charter for Access*. Newcastle upon Tyne: Northern Council for Further Education.

Whitehead, J. (1988) Why so few? *AUT Woman* 14, 2.

Women Returners Network (1989) *Returning to Work: A Directory of Education and Training for Women*. Harlow: Longman.

Worrall, N., and Tsarna, H. (1987) Teachers' reported practices towards girls and boys in science and languages. *British Journal of Educational Psychology* 57, 300.

Name Index

UNIVERSITY OF WOLVERHAMPTON
LEARNING RESOURCES

Aboud, F. 42, 57
Adelman, C. 80, 81
Allen, T. N. 78, 82, 84, 85, 89
Allen, V. L. 3, (Devin-Sheehan
  et al.) 101
Allport, G. W. 1, 5, 78, 87, 95, 100
Altrichter, H. 44, 93
Angelou, Maya 62
Aristotle 100
Aronson, E. 4, 42, 57

Back, K. 121
Bagley, C. 85
Balch, P. 42, 57
Baldwin, J. 43
Banks, J. 76, 78, 89
Banks McGee, C. 78
Batters, J. D. 35
Bazen, D. 104
Beddis, R. 78
Berry, J. 161
Birke, L. 140, 161
Bland, M. 102
Blaney, N. T. 4
Boal, A. 13, 62, 65–8, 73
Boardman, B. 78, 86
Bols, R. 81, 86
Bolton, G. 64–5
Borakova, H. 123
Boud, D. 93
Bourne, J. 22
Brandes, D. 80, 91
Brandt, G. 77, 78, 92
Braun, D. 44
Brazier, C. 62
Brewer, J. 8
Brigham, J. C. 4
Brook, P. 63–4
Brown, C. 162
Bruin, K. 127, 131, 132
Bruner, J. 53, 56, 63–4
Bryan, T. H. 2
Burgess, R. 6, 7, 8
Butt, G. 80
Button, E. 43
Byrne, E. 138

Carnie, J. 84, 87
Carr, M. 88
Carrington, B. 40, 42, 57
Cashmore, E. 131
Cater, J. 77
Catling, S. 78
Chivers, T. 133
Cloward, R. D. 101
Coffield, F. 63–4, 131
Cohen, E. G. 5, 11
Cohen, L. 6–7, 44
Cohen, P. A. 90, 116, 122, 132
Cole, S. 140
Comenius, J. A. 100
Cook, S.W. 1, 2, 42, 55, 57, 79, 100
Cooper, E. 133
Cooper, L. 121
Corbishley, P. (Davies et al.) 9

Davey, A. 122
Davies, B. 8, 9
De Vries, D. L. 42, 55, 57
Deutsch, M. 1
Devin-Sheehan, L. 101
Dinerman, H. 133
Donaldson, M. (Bruner et al.) 63
Dunlop, C. 140, 161

Edwards, V. 19, 23
Eisenstadt, N. 44
Eisner, E. 71–2
Elliott, J. 7–8, 9, 25, 80, 81
Epstein, J. L. 2
Evans, J. (Davies et al.) 9
Evans, R. 44

Feldman, R. S. (Devin-Sheehan
  et al.) 101
Festinger, L. 56, 131
Finemann, S. 9
Fischer, W. F. 2
Fitz-Gibbon, C. T. 4, 101, 102, 107
Fitzpatrick, F. 21
Flay, B. K. 123
Freire, P. 13, 65–6, 73
Fry, R. 93

Garrett, P. 21–2, 40
Gibbs, G. 80
Gibson, A. 138
Gill, D. 79, 89
Ginnis, P. 80, 91
Glaser, B. 80
Glock, C. 78
Glynn, T. 101
Goodlad, S. 80
Gopal, M. H. 103
Graves, N. 79
Gredler, G. R. 4, 101
Gregory, A. 23
Grey, P. 95
Gustafson, J. P. 121

Hackett, G. 78, 79
Hammersley, M. 80, 96
Harris, G. 102
Harvey, O. J. (Sherif et al.) 2
Hawkins, E. 19
Heathcote, D. 61, 64–5
Henerson, M. E. 47
Henry, J. A. 121
Hertz-Lazarowitz, R. 101
Hicks, D. 76, 78, 79, 89, 92
Hilton, K. 79
Hirst, B. 80
Hirst, P. 1
Holly, P. (Reid et al.) 81
Hood, W. (Sherif et al.) 2
Hope, A. 123
Hopkins, D. 37, 81
Hopson, B. 43
Houlton, D. 19, 23, 24, 27, 28
Howes, P. W. 2
Hunter, A. 8

Ijaz, A. 123

Jackson, T. 71, 72
James, A. 145
James, C. 21–2, 40
Janman, K. 142, 144
Johnson, D. W. 3, 4, 57, 100
Johnson, R. T. 3, 4, 57, 100
Jones, T. 77

Katz, D. 132
Katz, J. 77
Katz, P. 42, 55
Kemmis, S. 80, 93
Kennedy, G. 100
Kenrick, C. (Davies et al.) 9
Kent, A. 79
Keogh, R. (Boud et al.) 93
Kidron, M. 96
Klein, G. 78, 79, 86, 90
Klein, R. 161
Knapp, B. 79, 88
Kohlberg, L. 94
Kolb, D. 93

Lambert, D. (Graves et al.) 79
Lawlor, Sheila 79
Lee, Harper 62
Leicester, M. 44, 78
Leslie, J. W. 42
Leslie, L. L. 42
Levin, H. M. 116
Lippitt, P. 101
Lippitt, R. 101
Lynch, J. 57, 78, 91, 92, 94, 96, 122
Lyons Morris, L. (Henerson et al.)
  47

McCall, C. J. 8, 9, 80, 81
McFee, G. 8
McIntosh, W. D. (Tesser et al.) 121
MacKenzie, R. F. 96
McPhail, P. 43
McRae, D. (Knapp et al.) 88
McTaggart, R. 80, 93
Malpas, R. S. 4
Manion, L. 6–7, 44
Mant, J. 161
Marks, G. 4
Marshall, L. D. 76, 89, 90
Maruyama, G. (Johnson et al.) 3,
  100, (Marks et al., Warring et al.)
  4
Mason, R. 137, 138, 139
Meister, G. 116
Merchant, G. 19
Miller, N. (Marks et al.) 4
Mollod, R. W. 101
Morgan, G. 116
Morrison, Toni 62

Naish, M. 79
Nash, I. 161
Nixon, J. 6, 63, 64–5, 78 (Stenhouse
  et al.), 96

Oakley, A. 137
Oppenheim, A. N. 47
Osborne, M. 138, 139
Osherow, N. 42, 57
Ostram, T. M. 132
Oxley, L. 102

Papert, S. (Bruner *et al.*) 63
Parker, S. 140, 161
Partington, D. 25
Paulsen, K. 42, 57
Penfield, D. A. (Leslie *et al.*) 42
Pettigrew, T. 122
Pickersgill, D. 139
Pilkington, C. J. (Tesser *et al.*) 121
Posch, P. 44, 93
Powell, L. 47

Quintilian 100

Raab, E. 122, 123
Reay, D. G. 102
Reid, K. 81
Richardson, R. 76, 92
Rogers, C. 90, 95–6
Roper, S. 5
Rosenfield, D. (Blaney *et al.*) 4
Ross, S. (Knapp *et al.*) 88
Rudduck, J. 9, 10, 96

Sayo, J. N. 80
Scally, M. 43
Schlesinger, A. 83–4, 87, 89, 91, 92,
    93, 95
Schwartz, C. G. 25, 81
Schwartz, S. M. 25, 81
Scrivens, M. 72

Sears, J. 142
Segal, R. 96
Shachar, H. 4
Shallice, J. 78
Sharan, S. 1, 4, 5, 42, 57, 100, 101
Sharan, Y. 101
Sharpley, A. M. 4, 101–2, 107
Sharpley, C. F. 4, 101–2, 107
Sherif, C. W. 2, 42
Sherif, M. 2, 3, 42, 55
Shirts, G. 123
Short, G. 42, 57
Shortland, M. 144
Sikes, J. (Blaney *et al.*) 4
Simmons, J. L. 8, 9, 80, 81
Singh, B. 78
Slater, F. 79
Slavin, R. E. 1, 3, 4, 42, 55, 57, 101
Soukup, P. 123
Starkey, A. 96
Steinberg, R. (Hertz-Lazarowitz
    et al.) 101
Stenhouse, L. 25, 78, 80, 94
Stephan, C. W. 3
Stephan, W. G. 3
Stephen, C. (Blaney *et al.*) 4
Strauss, A. L. 80, 81, 93

Tansley, P. 21, 26
Taylor-Fitzgibbon, C. (Henerson
    et al.) 47
Tesser, A. 121
Thomas, O. 44
Thomas, S. 55, 56, 132, 162
Topping, K. 4, 80, 100, 101, 102
Troyna, B. 40
Tsarna, H. 143
Tyler, R. 71

Upshaw, H. S. 132

Verma, L. G. 78 (Stenhouse *et al.*),
    85

Waddington, P. 137
Wagner, L. 100
Wakeman, B. 43
Walbeck, N. 2
Walford, R. 89, 123
Walker, D. (Boud *et al.*) 93
Walker, R. 81, 93
Wandor, M. 64
Ward, D. 77
Warring, D. 4
Waterhouse, P. 77, 96
Waugh, D. 79
Weigel, R. H. 2
Weiner, G. 9
Wells, H. 43
Whaley, P. 137, 140
White, J. (Sherif *et al.*) 2
Whitehead, J. 144
Wiggans, A. 133
Wild, R. (Stenhouse *et al.*) 78
Wilder, D. A. 3
Willey, R. 23
Wilson, A. 123
Winner, A. 161
Wise, J. 100
Woodrow, M. 138, 139
Woods, P. 46
Woollard, N. 23
Worrall, N. 143

Zalk, S. R. 42, 55
Ziegler, S. 100

Subject Index

Access
- barriers to 137–8
- definition 137
- to higher education 145
- to mathematics, science and technology 137–8
- for men 137
- to science for mature students 138–9
- for women 137–40
- women and science 137
- for women into science 136

Access courses 137–9
- to HE studies in science 145–6
- in science 139

Acquaintance potential 3–4
Action research 6, 9, 12, 13, 19, 25, 44, 95–6
Affective learning methods 42, 57
Aid, international 89, 91, 94
Anti-racism 43, 68, 103
Anti-racist organizations 103
Anti-racist policy 26, 78
Anti-racist teaching 63–4
Assessment, of students taking the WIST course 150–1
Assessment of prior experiential learning (APEL) 147
Association for Science Education (ASE) Report 142–4
Attitudes 43–4, 47–8, 54–6
- measuring of 47–51, 54–6

'Bilingual', definition of 21, 100
Bilingual friends 99, 113
Bilingual pupils 12, 14, 19, 99–116
Bilingual support 25–6, 99–100
Bilingual tutors 22, 99
Bilingualism 19, 23

Careers in science 146
Centre for Policy Studies 79
Change of attitude 77–80, 82–8, 93–4
Children's Languages Project 24
Cognitive benefits of peer-tutoring 102
Cognitive learning methods 19–20, 42, 56–7
Collaboration between colleagues 106
Collaborative group work 76, 86–7, 92
Collaborative investigation 10–11, 12–13, 14–15, 58
Collaborative learning 99
Collaborative research 118–19, 120–1
Collaborative teaching method 25
Colonialism 87
Common goals 2, 100–1
Community languages 19–23
- definition of 21
Contact theory 100–1
Co-operation, promoting of 101–2
Co-operative group inquiry 101
Co-operative learning 3–6, 100–1, 102, 107
Co-operative methods 48, 57, 101
Co-operative structure 100–1
Co-operative tasks 76, 84–6
Cross-cultural relationships 99–100
Cross-ethnic friendship 99, 105, 107
Cross-ethnic relationship 102, 115
Cross-ethnic tutoring 99–100
Curriculum material 77–8, 96

DES circular on Access 138
Developing countries 76, 86–8, 90, 94

Dialect 20, 23, 24, 100
Disadvantaged groups 138
Discrimination 44, 54
Discriminatory behaviour 77, 86
Drama 60, 61–2, 66–7, 72–4
- as a learning experience 64
- as a method for reducing prejudice 13
Dual-language books 23–4
Durham, University of 146, 147

Education Reform Act 11, 43
Educational Counselling and Credit Transfer Information Service (ECCTIS) Report (1989) 138
Engineering course, attracting mainly men 140
English as a second language (ESL) 99–100
Equal Opportunities Commission 140
Equal opportunities policies 78
Equal opportunity 42–3
Equal status 100–1, 105
Equal-status contact 5
Equality 42–3, 77–8, 82
Equality of access for women 162
Ethnicity 137
Ethnocentric perspective 78
Ethnocentricity 47
Evaluation 45, 46, 53, 56–7, 60, 72
- formative 72
- reflexive 72–4
- summative 72
Expectation states theory 5
Expectation training 5
Experiencing temporary disadvantage 60, 61–2, 64, 66–7, 70, 72–3
- evaluation and discussion 71–4
- result of project 68–71
- see also Role play in prejudice reduction
Experiential learning methods 61
Expressive objectives 72

Female stereotype 144–5
Films, use of 85, 87–92
Food studies course, attracting mainly women 140
Ford Teaching Project 25, 81
Forum Theatre 13, 60, 65–8, 70–1, 72–4
Friendship between pupils 99, 100
Further Education Unit (FEU) 13, 80, 138
- case studies 139
- report 140

Gender bias 142
Geography 76–96
- approaches to the teaching of 78–9
- syllabus 77, 78, 95
Girls
- lower expectancies held by 144
- percentage taking A level science 142
Global perspective 77–88, 95

Home language 21
Human geography 76

Image, of scientists 143
Inequality 78
Interdependence 101
Inter-ethnic relations 100, 115

Intervention 42, 45, 54–5, 57
Interviews 26, 45, 46, 81, 102–16

Joint goals 100–1
Justice 1

Language awareness 19–25, 40
Language awareness project 26–8
    methods 27–31
    results 32–41
Language support teachers 103–4
Languages, definition of 21
Law, role of in prejudice reduction 122
Likert scale 47, 49, 123
Linguistic diversity 22–3
Linguistic Diversity in the Primary School (LDIP)
    Project 22
Luzac storytellers 24

Male attitude 143
Masculine stereotypes 144
Matching of pupils 105–6
Mature learners 136–7, 140
MC College Project 77–96
Media 52–3, 56–7
Method of inquiry 26–32, 45–8, 66–8, 77–84, 103–7,
    119–27, 145–50; *see also* Research methods
Modification of behaviour 42, 54, 57
Module, PSE 42–3, 45–8, 53–4, 57
'Monolingual', definition of 21
Monolingual pupils 14, 99, 104–5, 107–8, 112–16
Monolingual teachers 11–12, 19, 23
Monolingual tutors 99, 100
Mother tongue 21, 22, 108
Multicultural classroom 23
Multicultural education 23–4, 42–4, 60–6, 78
Multilingual classroom 23–4
Muslim pupils 114–15
    importance of religion to 103

National Curriculum 43, 77, 142
National Writing Project 24
Negative images 80, 88–90, 93–4
New Commonwealth, children from the 99
New Opportunities for Women 138
NIACE Report 140
Non-standard entry 139
Normative support 2
North East Regional Access to Higher Education
    Project 145

Open University 145
Oppression 66–8
Osborne and Woodrow's report 138

Pairing of pupils 103–6
Participant observation 25, 67–8, 80–1
Participation 13, 64, 72
Pastoral system 43
Pattern analysis 81, 93
Pedagogy of the Oppressed (Freire) 66
Peer pressure 2–3
Peer-tutoring 4, 14, 76, 101–2, 107, 116
Percentage of girls taking A-level science 142
Performance of tutor and tutee, improvement by
    peer-tutoring 116
Personal and social education 12, 42–8, 49, 57
    project 45–50
    result 51–8
Positive discrimination 140
Positive images 89–90, 93–5
Pre-Access course 146

Prejudice 47–57, 82, 86–94
    reduction of 1–5, 11, 12, 24, 42, 44, 55–8, 64, 68,
    74, 76–8, 84–5, 87–92
    reduction of, in youth work contexts 123–7
Professional collaboration 20, 26, 100, 103–4
Professional development 9–10
Projects
    Language Awareness Project 29–41
    Peer-tutoring Project 107–16
    Personal and Social Education Project 49–58
    Strategies for Reducing Prejudice in Youth Centres
        Project 127–34
    Teaching of Geography Project 82–96
    Use of Drama for Prejudice Reduction Project
        68–74
    Women Into Science and Technology 150–62
PSE, *see* Personal and social education

Racial attitude measure 5–10, 15, 20, 45, 47–58
    Thomas Allen Racial Attitude Test (TARAT) 82,
        86–92, 94
Racial Harassment Project 62–3
Racism 42, 44, 53–7, 62–5
    behaviour 63
    economic reasons for 63
    institutional 63–4
    as power and control 62–3
Racist attitudes 54
Racist incidents 42–3
    record of 43, 103
Research methods 6–15, 44, 45–8, 49, 56; *see also*
    Method of inquiry
Resistance to prejudice reduction 122
Resources for teaching geography 78–80
Results of projects, *see* Projects
Role play in prejudice reduction 124, 132–3; *see also*
    Experiencing temporary disadvantage

Science, difficulty of attracting women to 140
Science foundation courses (Open University) 145
Science teachers 143
Scientific community 143–4
Self-esteem 3, 12, 20, 24, 36–7, 38, 101, 132
Sex differentiation of subject choices 140–2
Simulation exercises for prejudice reduction 123, 132
Status characteristics 5
Stereotyping 42–8, 52–3, 56–7, 100–1, 107, 129–33,
    136–7, 140, 162
Sunderland Polytechnic 145
Swann Report 22, 78, 100

TARAT, *see* Thomas Allen Racial Attitude Tests
Teachers as researchers 6, 25, 44, 93–4, 102, 104–5,
    109–10
Teaching, approaches to
    collaborative 80, 90–2, 94
    direct 13–15, 77–92, 95, 104
    neutral 78, 88–90
    peer group tutoring 80, 83–5, 89, 90–1, 95
    thematic 79, 88
Technology foundation courses (Open University) 145
Thomas Allen Racial Attitude Tests (TARAT) 82, 83,
    86–92, 94
Thompson Report 119
Tolerance 42–3, 56
'Triad' method 81, 85
'Triangulation' 8, 14, 81

Unconscious expression of prejudice 130

Validity 8
Video, use of in prejudice reduction 132–3

Wider Opportunities for Women (WOW) 138

Women
    careers in science 143
    problem of attracting to science 140
Women-centred courses 138
Women Into Science and Engineering (WISE) 161
Women Into Science and Technology case study
    aims and objectives 146–7
    background 145–6
    course structure 147
    marketing of 148

results 150–61
students 148–9
Women Returners Network of the North East 137–8
Women scientists, famous 143–4

Young people, racism in 130–1
Youth centres, ethos 119
Youth leader
    role 119–20, 126–7, 129, 133–4
    training and development of 120–1